NOBODY UNPREPARED

2nd Edition 2021

First published in 2002 by

Woodfield Publishing Ltd
www.woodfieldpublishing.co.uk

ISBN 978-1-903953-15-0

Printed in England

Typesetting & page design: Nic Pastorius
Cover design: Klaus Schaffer

Source document
Nemo Non Paratus (2021) final-2.ppp

NOBODY UNPREPARED

Nemo Non Paratus

*The Achievements of 78 Squadron
4 Group, RAF Bomber Command
during World War Two*

VERNON HOLLAND

woodfieldpublishing.co.uk
Publishing Ltd
WOODFIELD
independent book publishers

Woodfield Publishing Ltd
Bognor Regis ~ West Sussex ~ England ~ PO21 5EL
tel 01243 821234 ~ **e/m** info@woodfieldpublishing.co.uk

Interesting and informative books on a variety of subjects

For full details of all our published titles, visit our website at
www.woodfieldpublishing.co.uk

This book is dedicated to
the memory of
all those who served
in 78 Squadron RAF
during World War Two 1939-45

"I have nothing to offer but blood, toil, tears and sweat'... Victory at all costs, victory in spite of all terror, victory however long and hard the road may be; for without victory there is no survival."

Winston Churchill, *first speech as Prime Minister, House of Commons, 13 May 1940*

"The Nazis entered this war under the rather childish delusion that they were going to bomb everyone else, and nobody was going to bomb them. At Rotterdam, London, Warsaw, and half a hundred other places, they put their rather naive theory into operation. They sowed the wind, and now they are going to reap the whirlwind."

Air Marshal Sir Arthur Harris Commander-in-Chief, RAF Bomber Command *in 1942, at the start of the bombing campaign against Germany.*

Contents

*A twin-engine Armstrong Whitworth Whitley
similar to those flown by 78 Squadron from 1939 to 1942.*

*A four-engine Handley Page Halifax III
similar to those flown by 78 Squadron from 1942 onwards.*

~ CHAPTER 1 ~

The Origins of 78 Squadron

WORLD WAR I STARTED IN August 1914 and at that time the nation's air force, such as it was, consisted of just seven squadrons. Within a very short time, orders were issued for five of them to be moved to France, to operate with the British Expeditionary Force. They crossed the Channel from a small landing ground near Dover, which at that time was under the control of the Royal Naval Air Service. It soon became obvious that more aerodromes would be required and in 1916 the Government transferred the Home Defence commitment from the Admiralty. This meant completely overhauling the organisation, which was when the Royal Flying Corps came into existence. Soon after, extra aircraft were based at Dover and 15 Squadron was formed. Later in the year, the Home Defence Squadrons were split into three flights and sent to the most suitable landing grounds, these became known as Class 1 landing grounds.

50 Squadron used landing grounds at Detling, Throwley and Bekesbourne, their headquarters being a large house at Harrietsham, which did not have an airfield. In early 1916 patrols were extended westward and 78 Squadron was formed, with its headquarters situated at Hove in Sussex. Its Commanding Officer was Major H.A. Ryneveld.

78 Squadron's first aircraft were BE2C and E, and these were followed by BE12 and 12A. The task that followed was a formidable one, that of forming new squadrons from the large numbers of men being enrolled to crew the aircraft being sent to France in increasing numbers. Following a period of active service in France, pilots were withdrawn and given a short break, before going to bases in England to become instructors to newly-recruited air crews.

Germany's introduction of the Gotha twin-engine bomber was a major development in aircraft design. They were a great deal faster than any planes used by the RNAS (Royal Navy Air Service) and the RFC. However, their first raid on London was foiled by bad weather and they bombed Lympne and Folkestone instead, killing 95 people and injuring another 200. The RNAS and RFC fighters took off immediately, but the new faster bombers got away, although one was shot down by a RFC fighter stationed at Dunkirk.

On 27th April 1917 Major J.C. Halahan took command of 'B' Flight of 78 Squadron at Telscombe Cliffs (Newhaven). It was then equipped with Sopwith 2-seaters.

Another raid was carried out on London by the Gothas on 30th June, when 72 bombs were dropped, killing 162 people and injuring a further 400. Once again, the RNAS and RFC fighters took off in pursuit but again were left far behind by the speedy bombers.

With loud calls for action starting to come from the public, 56 Squadron was recalled from the Western Front, but it did not prove to be of any use, for in the two weeks that the squadron was based at Bekesbourne, no raids took place. On their return to France, the Gothas struck again, which caused riots among the public. This meant proposals for a new defence system had to be implemented. By the end of July, the London Defence System had been put into operation, having the responsibility for the whole of the south-east from Harwich to Portsmouth. More aircraft were quickly made available and 61 and 62 Squadrons were formed, giving support to 50 and 78 Squadrons. During this time, Major G. Allen had taken command of 'C' Flight of 78 Squadron at Chaddington Causeway (Tonbridge). They were now flying the Sopwith Camel.

On 12th August 1918, Major Truran took command of 'B' and 'C' Flights, and in September, Sutton's Farm (Hornchurch) became the Headquarters of 'A', 'B' and 'C' Flights. This was to be for a very short period, for in September 1919, 78 Squadron was disbanded at Sutton's Farm. When they were at Hornchurch, the landing ground at Orsett in Essex had also been used to carry out the Home Defence duties with which it had been charged. This airfield was situated to the south east of the village after which it was named and was two miles from Stanton-Le-Hope railway station.

The site covered an area of 80 acres and was in open surroundings. No permanent buildings had been erected and all accommodation was under canvas. Orsett was under 49 Wing, South East area, and the landing ground operated from 1917 to 1919. After the war it reverted to its former use as prime agricultural land.

CHAPTER 2

World War II Begins

IT WAS TO BE A further seventeen years before 78 Squadron was reformed, at Boscombe Down in Wiltshire on 1st November 1936. It consisted of one flight. The Commanding Officer was Wing Commander M.B. Frew. DSO, MC, AFC. This flight was formerly 'B' Flight, No. 10 Squadron, equipped with Heyford Mk III aircraft with Kestrel engines. These were large twin-engine biplanes with a top speed of 142 mph which became obsolete with the introduction of the new Armstrong Whitworth Whitley.

On 1st March 1937, 78 Squadron moved to Dishforth to join 10 Squadron, who had moved up there from Boscombe Down a month earlier, with their Heyfords, as part of the expansion in 1934. Known as Scheme 'A', the intention was to increase the number of squadrons from 50 to 84 by 1939. It was meant to be a deterrent to the Germans. However, it did not have the effect the government hoped for, the German air force was already well equipped, with a strength equal to the Royal Air Force, and getting stronger as each day passed.

On 2nd March 1937 Wing Commander R. Harrison DFC, AFC was posted supernumerary, pending taking over command of the Squadron. He finally assumed Command on 8th March.

On 2nd March 1937 Wing Commander Frew was posted to RAF Station Hornchurch (formerly Sutton's Farm).

The second Flight was formed at Dishforth on 1st April 1937 under the Command of Flying Officer M. Hallam. Their Equipment consisted of aircraft that had been immediate reserve when the first Flight that was formed.

Officers and airmen pilots posted to 78 Squadron on its being reformed were: Flight Lieutenant R.G.B. Catt, Flying Officer E.A. Verdon-Roe, Pilot Officer E.F. Curry, Pilot Officer H.A.R. Holford, Pilot Officer D. Nolan-Neyland, Pilot Officer F.W. Thomas, Acting P/O F. Aikens, Acting P/O F.C. Rivers, Sergeant C.A. Deakin, Sergeant C.R. Heayes, Sergeant W.S. Hillary, Sergeant J.R. Denny and Sergeant H. Cornish.

RAF Dishforth had been opened on the 26th November 1935 and established as a base for two bomber squadrons as per No BC/329 Home

Defence. Each squadron was provided with its own headquarters, with four officers and 33 men, and two flights that consisted of 12 officers and 109 men.

It was one of several early bomber stations planned under the pre-war RAF expansion schemes and was located to the south of Dishforth village, from which it took its name. The station had been provided with substantial brick-built accommodation and had an arc of five 'C' type hangars facing the airfield. It had three runways, complete with 'frying pan' type hard-standings that gave plenty of room for the two squadrons planned to be stationed there.

On 2nd June 1937 78 Squadron moved to Aldergrove, County Antrim, Northern Ireland, for their Annual Practice Camp and returned to Dishforth on 25th June. On 1st July 1937 Dishforth was transferred to 4 Group, with the Group Headquarters being based at Linton-on-Ouse.

On 1st July 1937 the squadron began re-arming with the new Armstrong Whitworth Whitley heavy bombers, fitted with twin Tiger IX engines. From then until December 1937 they carried out flying exercises, logging a total of 1,782 daylight flying hours and 125 night flying hours. Training continued during 1938, with the squadron taking part in mass Empire Day formation flights over the North of England.

On 2nd June 1939 the Squadron was re-equipped with Whitley Mk IVa and V bombers fitted with Merlin engines and 10th June saw them move to Catfoss, Yorkshire for their Annual Practice Camp, returning to Dishforth on 2nd July.

A mobilisation order was issued on 1st September 1939 and the Squadron came under the control of 4 Group, with 10 serviceable aircraft at Dishforth. The rest were at Tern Hill, re-arming with Mk IV and V Whitleys.

With the outbreak of war on 3rd September 1939, 78 Squadron, whose code was previously 'YY' was now given the code 'EY'. By the 21st September re-arming had been completed, and all the aircraft were at Dishforth, under the Command of Wing Commander R. Harrison DFC, AFC. The Unit was nominated as a 4 Group Reserve Squadron and was to remain under the command of the Operational Group Commander and to be used as a supplement to the Group Pool, as a reservoir between first line squadrons and Group Pool Stations. It had a force of just 16 aircraft. Any surplus aircraft were to go to 77 Squadron and Storage Units.

During September several of the crews were posted to operational squadrons, as it had now become the 4 Group Pool, with trained air crews ready to replace crews lost in action by other squadrons.

Orders were received on 14th October for 78 Squadron to move to Linton-on-Ouse at 23.30 hours, but they were unable to take off until 05.00 hours the following day, due to Linton-on-Ouse aerodrome being unfit to land on, except in daylight.

On 15th October 1939 the flying log book for RAF Linton-on-Ouse reads:

> "Eight aircraft landed soon after dawn and were dispersed. They were the No.78 Squadron Whitleys from Dishforth, and they were stopping at Linton-on-Ouse as part of the Group pool scheme. They were joined within an hour of landing, by their maintenance staff, who had travelled by road."

TRAINING OF THE CREWS in the ZZ system of approach began with the regional control station on the aerodrome. On 22nd October one of the 78 Squadron Whitleys returning from a flight to RAF St Athan in South Wales ran into bad visibility and was diverted to Grantham. This aircraft was 'homed' and brought onto the aerodrome at Linton-on-Ouse in very low visibility by wireless direction using the ZZ system.

During the rest of October 1939 extensive work was carried out at Linton-on-Ouse, laying concrete runways, which interrupted the flying training; aircraft had to use Dishforth landing ground for their day and night dual training.

HM King George visited Linton-on-Ouse on 1st November. During his tour of the station he visited the squadron headquarters and inspected a parade of servicing flight personnel, after which he was invited to inspect one of the Whitley Mk V aircraft belonging to 78 Squadron.

On 22nd November 1939 the Chester Herald Inspector of Air Force badges informed the headquarters of 78 Squadron that the design for a squadron badge had been approved. This news was acknowledged gratefully.

Throughout November flying training proceeded, with most the work being in connection with conversion courses on Merlin-powered Whitleys for pilots from 97 and 166 Squadrons who were preparing to join operational squadrons.

Because of ongoing work still being carried out at Linton-on-Ouse and the soft state of the surface, the aircraft were maintained at Linton-on-Ouse but nearly all the flying was carried out at Dishforth.

Whilst landing after a training flight on the night of 29th/30th November, a 78 Squadron Whitley V K9054 overshot the runway, causing slight damage to the aircraft. The pilot Sergeant R.N. Peace and his crew were unhurt. Two weeks later, on 14th December, a further incident took place when another 78 Squadron Whitley was involved in a night landing accident but again good fortune was on their side, for the pilot P/O J.A. Piddington and his crew were unhurt.

On 1st December 1939 orders were issued from No 4 Group Headquarters, that 51 Squadron, which was also at Linton-on-Ouse, was to move to Dishforth, allowing 78 Squadron to take over the vacant accommodation and hangar. 78 Squadron came under the Command of the Officer Commanding RAF Station Linton-on-Ouse from that date and the officers vacated the wooden hutments to occupy quarters in the permanent mess buildings on 11th December.

Personnel were granted Christmas leave on 19th December and proceeded on four days leave, in four batches.

Wing Commander R. Harrison DFC, AFC was promoted to temporary Group Captain on 1st January 1940 and Wing Commander M. Wiblin arrived from Cranwell to take over Command. Group Captain Harrison left on posting to Command RAF Station Honington in Suffolk on 16th January.

Bad weather had made the airfield too wet for use by the heavy Whitleys and by the end of December the squadron had completed only 237 flying hours. This state of affairs was to continue throughout January 1940. Flying continued to be badly restricted, with severe frosts making it impossible to level the ground. As a result, safe landing areas were restricted, but despite using due care, tail wheel fittings were damaged.

Heavy snowfalls in the middle of the month made the aerodrome unsafe for use and almost continual bad visibility seriously hampered flying training. Immediately the airfield was declared fit for use, Group Captain Harrison issued orders for the resumption of intensive training at Linton-on-Ouse, which continued by night and day. With 78 Squadron being due to become operational within the next few months, the crews were constantly kept on their toes.

Squadron Leader J.A.P. Harrison was posted to No.4 Group Headquarters on 5th February, with Squadron Leader C.S. Byram, who had recently joined the squadron for a refresher course, being appointed to take his place as OC 'B' Flight with effect from 10th February 1940.

Flying was still considerably curtailed by snow and frost, followed by fog and rain, which persisted during the first half of February. Due to the poor state of the aerodrome it was decided to send a detachment of aircraft to a satellite landing ground at Brackley, near Upper Heyford, in order that pilots could continue their training. Accordingly, six aircraft were flown there between 21st and 23rd February, having been preceded by a road party on the 20th.

On a busy training station, the occasional accident will happen, as on 15th March, when Whitley N1350 was damaged while taxiing. Fortunately, the pilot, F/O F. Aiken and his crew were safe. On 25th April another Whitley, K9050, burst a tyre while taking off from Brackley landing ground. The pilot, Sergeant D.A. Rix, and his crew were unhurt.

Meanwhile at Linton-on-Ouse it was intended to continue with the air training of wireless operators, air gunners and observers, but this too was very limited by bad weather and aircraft becoming unserviceable due to lack of spares.

On 22nd February 1940, Whitley V N1416 was collected from RAF Brize Norton and flown directly to Brackley. This brought the aircraft strength of the squadron to seven Mk IV and seven Mk V Whitleys, a total of 14 aircraft.

As the build-up continued, it became obvious that 4 Group Headquarters needed more space and on 6th April 1940 the HQ moved to Heslington Hall, York, thus allowing Linton-on-Ouse to concentrate on becoming a fully operational bomber base.

Air Marshal Lord Portal CB, DSO, MC, AOC Bomber Command, visited Linton-on-Ouse and other stations in 4 Group on 22nd April, in a Whitley V belonging to 78 Squadron, flown by Flying Officer A.P.G. Hyde. The visit took place in poor weather conditions.

This was followed by a visit on 11th May by the Air Officer Commanding No.4 Group, Air Marshal A. Coningham DSO, MC, DFC, AFC. During his visit to the station he outlined a change of policy for 78 Squadron. Orders were given to recall the Brackley detachment and they began returning the following day. This was completed by 13th May 1940, with the exception of two aircraft that remained, with a maintenance and guard party.

Following a visit to the station by Sir Archibald Sinclair, the Secretary of State for Air on 23rd June 1940, 78 Squadron became fully operational.

In the middle of June 1940 it was decided to move 78 Squadron to Leeming in Yorkshire, where it was to assume a new status. The latter part of the month was taken up in organising the move to Leeming, which had just opened but was still only partially complete. By 29th June the squadron stores and equipment had been sent to Leeming and were being distributed by an advance party. The main party was standing by to proceed on the morning of 30th June and crews were detailed to fly the aircraft to York at the same time.

However, in the evening a telephone message was received from 4 Group Headquarters saying that the move was cancelled and that the squadron was to move to Dishforth instead, there to take the place of 10 Squadron, which was to move to Leeming.

A few days later 78 Squadron moved back to Dishforth, from where they flew their first mission. This took place on 19th July, when four of their Whitleys attacked marshalling yards in the Ruhr. 'A' Flight Commander, Squadron Leader Wildey, bombed the primary target, the railway yards at Recklinghausen, while the remainder of the aircraft attacked alternative targets: Sergeant Monkhouse tackled the Munster railway yards; Pilot Officer Eno bombed the Gelsenkirchen-Buer oil plant and Pilot Officer Denny attacked a marshalling yard some forty miles north of the primary target. All four aircraft returned safely to base.

The squadron was again in action the following night, the 20th July. This time, the aircraft assembly plants at Wenzendorf and Wizmar were their targets. Squadron Leader Whitworth in Whitley P5001 joined aircraft from other squadrons in 4 Group in the attack on the Wenzendorf plant. Believing he had bombed the target, he returned to base but found the bombs still in their racks. A blown fuse in the electrical system of the Whitley had cut the current from the bomb release gear. They had no idea that anything was wrong until after the aircraft had landed.

The following night of 21st July, 78 Squadron took part in an attack on Soest and Hamm, when five of their Whitleys bombed the important railway marshalling yards. Whitley V N1487 EY- was shot down, killing all on board. They were buried at Reichswald Forest War Cemetery.

Pilot Sgt V.C. Monkhouse | **Nav** Sgt N.H. Burton | **Obs** Sgt C.G. Hill
W/Op Sgt L. McCrurie | **A/G** Sgt J. Sulter

THE 23RD JULY 1940 saw an attack carried out on Osnabruck. The attack commenced at 00.25 hours from a height of 8,000 feet. Aiming was poor and the nearest a stick of bombs fell to the left of the target across a railway line. Flak was light to medium and no night fighters were seen.

The oil plants at Sterkrade became the primary target for 78 Squadron on the night of 25th July. It was bombed at 01.05 hours, with extensive fires being started. Large columns of smoke were seen rising from two oil tanks that had been hit. A self-illuminated target was bombed at 00.35 hours from a height of 9,000 feet, with large explosions being observed. Extensive searchlight activity was encountered, but the flak was light. The weather was 7/10 cloud at 6,000 feet with considerable haze and rain in patches. Bursts of red tracer were seen coming from above, which indicated the possibility of night fighters being in the vicinity. Over the target area searchlights were seen converging in bunches of 15-20, each moving in unison, so that they kept converged. A form of flare was also seen coming up from the ground, to remain stationary in the air for a long period. One wireless operator reported seeing an aircraft, believed to be a Whitley, go down and crash in flames, at 03.00 hours.

Following a raid on Dusseldorf on the night of 3rd/4th August 1940, 78 Squadron Whitley V P4941 EY- force-landed near Pickering in North Yorkshire. Though the aircraft was severely damaged, the crew members were unhurt.

Pilot F/O D.A. Robertson | **Nav** P/O M.L. Stedman | **Obs** Sgt R.V. Collenge
W/Op Sgt F.A. Barton | **A/G** F/Lt N.W. Mcleod

SEVERAL MORE OF THE squadron's Whitleys sustained flak damage in raids that took place over enemy territory during the nights that followed but they all returned safely and their crews were unhurt, one of them being Whitley V N1490 which crash-landed at Linton-on-Ouse following a raid over Germany. P/O Robson and his crew emerged from the wreckage unharmed but four nights later this same crew's luck was to run out. At 05.00hrs on the night of 14th/15th September, 78 Squadron Whitley V N1478 EY- took off from Dishforth to take part in a raid on Vlissingen and was lost without trace. The names of the crew are listed on the RAF Memorial at Runnymede.

Pilot F/O C.S. Robson | **Nav** Sgt L.J. Furze | **Obs** Sgt R.M. Heyworth
W/Op Sgt J. Kelly | **A/G** Sgt J.C. Grieg

DURING AN ATTACK ON Antwerp on the night of 17th/18th September, one 78 Squadron Whitley was badly damaged by flak and the rear gunner, Sergeant R. Graham, badly wounded, but the pilot brought the aircraft back to Dishforth with the rest of the crew safe and well.

78 Squadron may have been a little late getting into action but they were certainly making amends for that now. On the night of 1st/2nd October, 78 Squadron aircraft took off at 19.06 hours from Dishforth to carry out an attack on synthetic oil installations in the Holten district of Sterkrade. At 01.30 hours Whitley V P4964 EY- crashed on land owned by a Mr Demnink of Hesseweg, Humelo (Gelderland) about 21 km east of Arnhem in Holland. It is believed to have been shot down by a night fighter working in conjunction with radar guided searchlights. The crew were all killed:

Pilot P/O N.H. Andrew | **Nav** P/O H.W. Morgan | **Obs** Sgt G.E. Matson
W/Op Sgt P.H. Richmond | **A/G** Sgt A. Roscoe

Berlin became the target for the 4 Group aircraft during the night of 7th/8th October when 78 Squadron's primary target was the BMW works. The attack was carried out in favourable conditions and all the squadron's aircraft returned to base safely.

A series of attacks were carried out on oil refineries and synthetic oil plants during the latter part of October, without incurring any losses of aircraft or crews. On 5th November 78 Squadron were ordered to join 77 Squadron in a raid on the Fiat motor works in Turin, but this proved to be an unsuccessful mission for 78 Squadron, whose bombs fell short of the target. The next night, they were sent to attack the synthetic oil plant at Hamburg and this raid was a success, with all the squadron's aircraft returning safely to base.

During the night of 19th/20th November 78 Squadron's aircraft took off at 17.30 hours to carry out an attack on a synthetic oil plant at Ruhland. During this raid Whitley V T4156 EY- was shot down. The crew escaped safely but were subsequently captured and became prisoners of war. They were:

> **Pilot** P/O R.E.H. George | POW Stalag Luft 3 Sagan
> **Nav** Sgt J.W. Knight | POW Stalag 357 Kopernikus
> **Obs** P/O R.C. Mordaunt | POW Stalag Luft 3 Sagan
> **W/Op** Sgt S. Cawkswell | POW Stalag 357 Kopernikus
> **A/G** Sgt J. Wilkinson | POW Stalag 357 Kopernikus

NINE DAYS LATER, ON 28th/29th November, 78 Squadron were called upon to take part in a raid on Stettin. The raid was a success but one of the Dishforth aircraft was shot down. All the crew baled out safely but were quickly captured by German soldiers and made prisoners of war. The aircraft was Whitley V P5026 EY-

> **Pilot** P/O J.R. Denny, POW Stalag Luft 3 Sagan
> **Nav** P/O B.V. Kerwin, POW Stalag Luft 3 Sagan
> **Obs** P/O G.C. Brown, POW Stalag Luft 3 Sagan
> **W/Op** Sgt J.E. Everson, POW Stalag 357 Kopernikus
> **A/G** Sgt J.W. Massie, POW Stalag 357 Kopernikus

As WHITLEY V P4958 EY- was taking off at 16.15 hours on the afternoon of 2nd December 1940, to carry out a raid on Lorient, it crashed before it could gain height. The only member of the crew to be named in the squadron ORB is that of the pilot, Sergeant C.A. Smith, though it would appear that every member of the crew was injured in the crash.

78 Squadron was briefed to take part in an attack on Kiel during the night of 13th/14th December. The aircraft took off at 16.36 hours from Dishforth, crossing the coast just south of Hull to rendezvous with aircraft from other 4 Group squadrons heading for the Dutch coast. Their outward journey was uneventful but they found Kiel a mass of flak and searchlights. After Whitley V N1485 EY- had dropped its bombs the Captain, Pilot Officer M.L. Stedman, asked the crew if there were any casualties, but although the aircraft was badly damaged no injuries were reported. Unfortunately, as the aircraft crossed the Dutch coast on the homeward run it was attacked by a night fighter and cannon fire caused one engine to burst into flames and it had to be feathered. The Whitley continued to lose height until it was over the Wash on the Lincolnshire coast, where the crew were forced to bale out. Sadly, three of them were drowned.

Pilot P/O M.L. Stedman | Drowned after ditching
Nav Sgt D. Angell | Drowned after ditching
Obs Sgt F. Waldren | Rescued by ASR Launch
W/Op Sgt F.T. Allcock | Drowned after ditching
A/G Sgt E.A. Grunsell | Rescued by ASR Launch

ON THE MORNING OF 28th/29th December, 78 Squadron were briefed to take part in a raid on Lorient. One of the Whitleys, piloted by Sergeant John Mott, was hit and it caught fire. He ordered the crew to bale out and when they had done so he followed them. He landed to the north-west of Lanvollon, where he quickly found a hiding place. After landing safely, three members of his crew were soon captured and made prisoners of war. A fourth member managed to avoid capture for some time but was eventually caught by German soldiers and he too became a POW.

Sgt Mott managed to evade capture and, after making his way to Lanvollon, received assistance from a series of helpers. On 6th January 1941 a Monsieur Hevin took him to the home of Mme Delavigne in Nantes, Brittany. He stayed there until 26th September. Monsieur Hevin was later arrested by the Germans and shot on 22nd October. Mott stayed in Nantes and changed safe house five times, whilst his helpers sought a means of escape for him. In August he was briefly reunited with his rear gunner, Sergeant McMillan, who had also managed to evade capture. He was taken to stay with a Mme Flavet but unfortunately on 22nd September the Germans raided the Flavet home and arrested the family and Sgt McMillan. Mme Delavigne later recalled.

"Claude Lamirault was the local leader of our organisation and was to ensure the escape of both the airmen, but with the arrest of the Flavet family, no one knew where he lived. We decided to do all we could to save Mott. A Pole (who in reality was a Hungarian Jew) with whom we had become slightly acquainted in connection with the passing of letters in the occupied zone, was contacted. At first he refused to help but changed his mind when the financial side had been discussed. During the night of 26th September, with Sgt Mott riding a bicycle which had been given to him by my nephew, they travelled to Bordeaux, to the home of another Pole called Selk, and this man got the pilot across the line of demarcation."

On 4th October, Mott reached Toulouse. He recalls:

"On 12th October I crossed the Frontier of Spain. Once I got there I on kept walking and eventually got to the British Consul, who passed me to the British Embassy in Madrid. On 14th November 1941 I arrived in Gibraltar. I left there in a Sunderland flying boat on 13th December, arriving in Pembroke Dock on 14th December 1941, thankful to be home once more."

The members of Sergeant Mott's crew were:

Pilot Sergeant John Mott | evaded and returned to UK
Nav F/Lt J.B.T. Loudon | POW Stalag Luft 3 Sagan
Obs F/Lt J.V. Saunders | POW Stalag Luft 3 Sagan
W/Op Sgt L. Abeckett | POW Stalag 357 Kopernikus
A/G Sgt W.O. McMilland | POW Stalag 357 Kopernikus

~ CHAPTER 3 ~

Tragino ~ an Italian Misadventure

I N 1940, AFTER A GREAT deal of prompting by Prime Minister Winston
Churchill, plans were prepared to form an experimental British
paratroop force. Should it prove a success it could lead to the formation
of an airborne capability for the British Army, which would prove useful
if the envisaged invasion of Europe were to take place.

The formation and training of this new force, to be known as 'X' Troop
No. 11 SAS Battalion, was to lead to one of the most unusual operations
carried out by 4 Group Bomber Command. By January 1941 'X' Troop was
ready and eager for action, though at this time a target to try out the
experimental force had yet to be decided. This was very much an untried
force and a great deal of consideration went into choosing where the first
operation would take place.

Possible targets in Italy were examined, with a view to future bombing.
One suggestion was that the huge aqueduct spanning the River Tragino
in the province of Campagna might warrant some attention. This aqueduct
was part of an elaborate system built during the 1930s and carried the
main water supply for the province of Apulia and the towns of Brindisi,
Bari and Foggia, where there were dockyards and factories. Bombing the
aqueduct had been ruled out, as the mountainous terrain was too
dangerous, but this could be an ideal target for a small commando strike.
In January 1941, preparations for the raid were set in motion and it was
given the codename 'Colossus'.

Bomber Command was asked to supply the aircraft and crews needed
for the operation. The Whitley could be adapted for mass parachute
dropping, since the floor of the fuselage was already framed and stressed
for the 'dustbin' lower gun turret, which could be removed to create a
circular hatch that could be fitted with doors to make a suitable exit for
paratroopers.

The operation would be carried out by eight crews selected – four each
from 51 and 78 squadrons – under the command of Wing Commander
'Willie' Tait. The plan was to drop all the parachutists on the north side
of the aqueduct, whereupon sappers would place explosive charges against
one of the pillars. Meanwhile, two Whitleys would carry out a diversionary

raid on nearby marshalling yards at Foggia. When the operation was completed, the commandos were to make their way to the west coast, a distance of 50 miles, where the submarine HMS *Triumph* would rendezvous with them for evacuation at the mouth of the River Sele. Eight Whitleys were to be used for this operation, which was planned to be launched from Malta on 10th February, weather permitting. Squadron Leader Wally Lashbrook was one of the crew members selected from 51 Squadron. He recalls:

> "The operation was being carried out by four crews from each of the two Whitley squadrons stationed at Dishforth, Nos 51 and 78. I was privileged to be selected as Captain of one of the crews involved. Each Captain was allotted crewmembers and attached to Ringway on 15th January 1941 to undergo a course in parachute dropping.
>
> The dropping practice was carried out in Whitley Mk II aircraft. Drops were made from 300 feet and I flew Whitley Mk II K7220 under dropping instructions, until becoming proficient enough to practice in the aircraft I was to fly on the operation. This was Whitley Mk V T4165.
>
> The dropping load for the operation was to comprise of six paratroops and six containers of explosives or stores to each aircraft. Each container had a different coloured parachute, making its contents quickly recognised. The Whitleys were also fitted with autopilots and auxiliary tanks mounted in the bomb bays."

On 3rd February 1941, Wing Commander Tait flew to RAF Mildenhall with his Whitley force. The 39 members of 'X' Troop arrived that same day by road, under conditions of absolute secrecy. Warrant Officer Albon, a wireless operator with one of the 78 Squadron crews (that of Pilot Officer Wotherspoon in Whitley V T4167) recalls the welcoming reception he and his crew received at RAF Mildenhall:

> "On the day we arrived at Mildenhall from Ringway the locals were awaiting the imminent arrival of an enemy raider that had been making regular attacks on the station. When we broke cloud above the airfield, we were met with anti-aircraft fire from the defences. The mistake was quickly rectified and no damage was done, but the operation had not got off to the best of starts."

Neither the parachutists nor the bomber crews were told in advance of the target for their mission, as complete secrecy was the order of the day. All participating air crew were issued with service revolvers and told to wear them at all times, because their destination, Malta, was under threat of invasion at that time. This led to some awkward questions being asked by inquisitive personnel at Mildenhall and, as a result, relations between the air crews in the mess were strained.

On 7th February Admiral Sir Roger Keyes, Chief of Combined Operations and the man who was responsible for Commando training, arrived to give the men an official send off. 'X' Troop and the Whitley crews were assembled in one of the hangars.

Wally Lashbrook recalls the occasion:

> "The Admiral shook hands with each man, stopping to chat briefly, but it soon became obvious to those present that his face was extremely grave. When he came to me, the Admiral seemed rather puzzled to have a sergeant (which I was at that time) introduced as the captain of an aircraft, when most of the remainder of the crew were officers."

THAT NIGHT THE EIGHT Whitleys took off for Malta. The aircraft were routed over France, down the Rhone Valley and over the Mediterranean. Flying west of the coast of Corsica and Sardinia to a point on the northern coast of Tunisia, they passed south to a position inland from Sfax, before heading due east to a DR point south of Malta, then north to the island.

At dawn on 8th February 1941 they arrived at RAF Luqa and were immediately told they couldn't land until bomb craters from the previous night's bombing raid had been filled in. However, after almost eleven hours in the air, the Whitley pilots opted to risk landing between the craters, which was accomplished without any mishaps.

Operation 'Colossus' could not begin at once, as bad weather prevented any photographic reconnaissance over the target area. In the meantime, crews were briefed and the aircraft prepared for the expected take-off date of 10th February.

On the evening of the 10th the members of 'X' Troop were gathered together by the Commanding Officer, Major T.A.G. Pritchard, who revealed the object of their mission. The party of 35 parachutists allocated to the six carrier aircraft included three Italian interpreters. Wally Lashbrook recalls:

> "The weather conditions that night were perfect, a cold, dry night with plenty of moonlight. We carried out a 30-minute air test before take-off; this had been scheduled for dusk. Finally airborne, we formed up into two loose formations, led by Wing Commander Tait, and were soon flying at 10,000 feet over Mount Etna, bound for the Italian coast of Salerno.
>
> In addition to our load of commandos and all their equipment, we also carried two 250lb bombs, an extra present for the Italians. The two Whitleys

detailed to bomb the marshalling yards at Foggia, some thirty miles from the aqueduct, left us to make their own way to the target.

The flight to within a few miles of the target was carried out at 9,000 feet, with Wing Commander Tait leading the first formation, while I maintained beam position. It was a beautiful moonlit night and we were at our dropping height of 300 feet just before we reached the valley, more or less in line astern. I saw the leader overshoot the turning point to the dropping zone and turning in before him, we reduced our flying speed to just over 100 knots and lowered the flaps.

The rear gunner, F/Lt Williams, reported over the intercom that we were on target and the troops and containers were on the way down. During this time we were heading directly towards Mount Vulture. I can recall opening up the throttle while carrying out a climbing turn to port and we just managed to scrape over the side of the valley.

Our next task was to select a suitable target for our 250-pounders. After circling over the town of Calitri I decided that there was no justification in bombing such a sleepy looking town, so I followed a railway line to a junction and dropped our bombs on a station. We returned to Luqa after seven hours in the air, to learn that all but one aircraft had returned safely."

The missing aircraft, Whitley V T4167 piloted by P/O Wotherspoon, was one of the two aircraft detailed to carry out the diversionary raid on Foggia. W/O Albon recalls what happened:

"We were forced to abandon our aircraft due to some engine troubles. After baling out south of Naples, I landed inside an Army Barracks and was captured at once. The rest of the crew were captured within a few hours".

P/O Wotherspoon and crew were unaware at that time that their capture was to result in the cancellation of the rendezvous of 'X' Troop with the submarine HMS *Triumph* because their Whitley had come down near the area designated for the departure of the parachutists to rendezvous with the submarine. Fears that a search for the Whitley crew could compromise the pick-up, led to the cancellation of the submarine's sailing orders.

Meanwhile, at the aqueduct, 'X' Troop had run into a problem. Five Whitleys had dropped the parachutes bang on target, but the sixth aircraft spent forty-five minutes circling around, apparently lost, before dropping its cargo into the next valley. Included in this party were some of the sappers and their explosives. In addition, icing had caused the bomb racks on one of the Whitleys to jam, robbing the force of yet more of their explosives. Consequently, there were not enough explosives to destroy the aqueduct. Nevertheless, the commandos did succeed in placing the available charges at one end of the aqueduct and the resulting explosion caused considerable damage.

Unaware that there would be no submarine to pick them up, the members of 'X' Troop then made their way to the rendezvous point where, the following day, the whole party was captured, after which they were conveyed in triumph by their captors to the prison in Naples, where they were joined by the remaining members of the downed Whitley crew.

They would all spend the rest of the war as POWs.

*Members of No.2 Commando (No.11 Special Air Service Battalion)
who participated in Operation 'Colossus' aka 'The Tragino Raid',
the first airborne commando operation of World War II.*

Whitley MkV Z6640 which as 'R-Robert' completed 29 operations with 78 Squadron.
Its final raid before 'retirement' was against Emden on the night of 1st January 1942,
skippered by Sgt Stevens. Shown here whilst serving with No.1484 Target Towing Flight,
based at Driffield, North Yorks. [CHRIS BLANCHETT]

**Instrument panel
of a Whitley Mk V**
Clearly shown in
this photo is the
open door to the
bomb aiming
position in the
nose. [D. WEBB]

CHAPTER 4

Back to More Familiar Targets

D URING THE TIME THE FOUR Whitleys had been away, engaged on Operation 'Colossus' the rest of the squadron were kept busy carrying out various bombing raids.

After taking off at 18.50 hours from RAF Dishforth on the night of 11th/12th February 1942, Whitley V N1491 EY- along with other aircraft of 78 Squadron, carried out an attack on Bremen. On returning from the raid, it crash-landed at Hill House farm, Newmilns, 7 miles east of Kilmarnock, Aryshire. Fortunately, the entire crew escaped uninjured. They were:

Pilot Sgt J.W. Quincey | **Nav** Sgt P.F.G. Alcock | **Obs** Sgt H. Clark
W/Op Sgt R. Bradbury | **A/G** Sgt J.F. Hollingworth

TWO WEEKS LATER, ON the night of 26th/27th February 78 Squadron were to suffer the loss of another aircraft over the hills of Scotland. This time it was a Whitley V P4996 EY- which had taken off at 18.45 hours to take part in the bombing of oil refineries situated at Koln in West Germany. Straying from the track on its return journey, it crashed into a mountainside three miles east of Craig, Ross & Cromarty, Scotland, killing the entire crew.

Pilot Wg/Cdr G.T. Toland | **Nav** Sgt G.A. Forsyth | **Obs** P/O D.H. Gates
W/Op Sgt G.R. Armstrong | **A/G** Sgt N.L. Lane

ON THE NIGHT OF 1st/2nd March 1941 Bomber Command lost 13 bombers – 1 Wellington; 6 Whitleys and 6 Hampdens – with more than 40 air crew either killed or badly injured. Although these losses were light compared to those that were to follow during the next four years, at that time they were unprecedented, and tragic for the squadrons to whom they belonged.

That night 78 Squadron had taken off at 19.01 hours from Dishforth and after joining other 4 Group squadrons they carried out an attack on Koln. After the bombing, a W/T message was received from one of the Whitleys to say the attack had been successful, but nothing further was heard from them. The aircraft was Whitley V N1525 EY-E and its crew disappeared without trace. Their names are recorded on the Runnymede Memorial.

Pilot Sgt J.W. Quincey | **Nav** P/O M.J. David | **Obs** Sgt R. Clark
W/Op Sgt R. Bradbury | **A/G** Sgt J.G. Earley

THOUGH MANY NEW AIRCRAFT were being built, losses were rising. In the first ten weeks of 1941, Bomber Command lost 123 aircraft and this would escalate in the coming months. Fatigue was starting to show in the faces of the air crews, who could not be expected to continue flying night after night into intense flak and searchlights without showing the strain.

On the morning of 27th March, orders were received from 4 Group Headquarters for 78 Squadron to join other Group squadrons in an operation to attack Dusseldorf. They took off at 19.00 hrs and, following a successful attack on the heavily-defended target, turned for home.

On the return journey Whitley Z6470 EY- was attacked over the Netherlands by a night fighter (Ofw Herzog 3./NJG1) and crashed at 23.05 hours at Helenaveen near Venlo (a Luftwaffe night-fighter station). The crew were all killed and buried at Jonkerbos War Cemetery.

Pilot P/O K.F. Seager | **Nav** Sgt A.K. Mills | **Obs** Sqdn/Ldr P.J. Hoad RN
W/Op Sgt E.A.F. Grunsell MiD | **A/G** Sgt J. Mitchell

IN MID-APRIL 78 SQUADRON moved to RAF Middleton-St-George, with 16 Whitley Mk Vs, under the command of Wing Commander B.V. Robinson, DFC. They found themselves immediately in action. During the remainder of that month raids were made on enemy shipping and on Berlin.

The night of 3rd/4th May saw a further attack mounted on Koln by 78 Squadron aircraft. They took off at 20.45 hours from Middleton-St-George. Arriving over the target they saw fires started by aircraft from other squadrons who had arrived earlier, now burning furiously. After conducting a concentrated attack on the oil refineries, they turned for home. On the return journey one of the Whitleys developed a wireless failure and shortly afterwards the crew discovered they were short of fuel. With no wireless to aid them, the aircraft went off track and eventually crashed near Leominster, Herefordshire. Fortunately the crew escaped uninjured.

Pilot Sgt L. Hatcher,[1] **Nav** Sgt R. Chandos, **Obs** Sgt H.B. Buttell,
W/Op Sgt T.K. Moodie and **A/G** Sgt T. Hall

THE BOMBING REACHED A new height of intensity on the night of 8th/9th May, when 364 aircraft attacked Hamburg and Bremen, the largest number yet despatched by Bomber Command in a single night. 78 Squadron was

---

[1] Sgt Hatcher was commissioned and rose to the rank of Squadron Leader, winning the DFC and AFM in the process. Regretfully, he lost his life in December 1944 and is buried at Woolwich. Thanks to W.R. Chorley for permission to use this information from *Royal Air Force Bomber Command Losses of the Second World War*. Vol II.

one of ten squadrons from 4 Group taking part. The raid caused heavy damage and casualties to the city, with 1,399 people being made homeless. Eleven RAF aircraft were lost in the raid, one of which was a 78 Squadron Whitley Mk V that crashed in Heisfielde in the outskirts of Leer in Germany. It was Whitley V T4147 EY-D. The crew all lost their lives.

Pilot Sgt L. Thorpe | **Nav** P/O R.W. Wallis-Stolze | **Obs** Sgt P.J. Lewis
W/Op Sgt H.E. Bailey | **A/G** Sgt P.W.R. Emmett
5 killed near Leer, Germany

ON THE NIGHT OF 16th/17th May 1941, 78 Squadron's designated target was the oil refineries at Koln once again. The squadron lost one aircraft during this operation when Whitley V Z6493 EY-V was shot down by a night fighter (Uffz Pross, 3./NJG) and crashed between Helenaveen (Noord Brabant) and Maasbree (Limburg) in the Netherlands, killing all the crew, who were buried in Jonkerbos War Cemetery, Nijmegen, Holland.

Pilot P/O J.T.A. Garrould | **Nav** Sgt R.S.L. Keymer | **Obs** F/Sgt R.J. Garlish
W/Op Sgt E. Oakes | **A/G** F/Sgt A.P. Smith

DURING THE NEXT TEN days 78 Squadron carried out several raids without incurring any losses, but on the night of 28th/29th May, twelve aircraft took off at 23.55 hours from RAF Middleton-St-George to mount an attack on Kiel. Little flak was encountered on the outward flight, and on approaching the target area they could see it lit up by large fires that had been started by incendiary bombs dropped by the first wave of bombers earlier that night. They carried out a concentrated attack, helping to stoke the fires already burning. During the bombing Whitley V Z6484 EY- was shot down. The crew were all killed and buried at Becklingen War Cemetery in Germany.

Pilot Sgt A.T. Copley | **Nav** Sgt W.B. Smith | **Obs** Sgt A. Cooke
W/Op Sgt A. Gregory | **A/G** Sgt D.R. Strickland

A BOUT OF UNSETTLED weather at the end of May 1941 prevented a sustained effort being mounted by 4 Group. However, Cologne, Kiel and Dusseldorf were attacked during this period with moderate results. 37 Whitleys took part in the attack on Dortmund on the night of 8th/9th June, but haze prevented accurate bombing. Low clouds over the Yorkshire moors caused two Whitleys to crash as they searched vainly for their airfields. One was a 51 Squadron aircraft that crashed in a quarry in the Cleveland hills, killing the crew. The second was a 78 Squadron aircraft, Whitley V Z6571 EY- which crashed while descending through cloud and burst into flames in a small valley near Ellingstring, four miles west of Masham in Yorkshire. The crew all died in the crash.

Pilot Sgt D.R. Simm | **Nav** Sgt J.S. Tomkinson | **Obs** P/O A.V. Snelling
W/Op Sgt J.B. Stevens | **A/G** F/Sgt G. Billing

THE SYNTHETIC OIL PLANTS at Koln received a further visit from 4 Group's bombers on the night of 16th/17th June. Weather conditions on the outward route and over the target area were good, with thin to medium cloud at around 18,000 feet. As they approached the target, the crews could see fires already burning. Once again heavy damage was inflicted to the oil refineries, though at the cost of five aircraft, one of them from 78 Squadron. Whitley V Z6492 EY-K had taken off at 22.32 hours from RAF Middleton-St-George and was lost without trace. The names of the crew are commemorated on the Runnymede Memorial.

Pilot P/O D.S.W. Lake | **Nav** Sgt H.T. Ivory | **Obs** Sgt R.C. Rae | **W/Op** Sgt H. Bailey

No record of a fifth member of the crew can be found in the Squadron ORBs. One must assume that either the Wireless Operator or the Observer doubled as an air gunner on this mission.

During the night of 18th/19th June, aircraft of 78 Squadron took part in an attack on the heavily-defended port of Bremen. They took off at 23.00 hours from Middleton-St-George to rendezvous with other 4 Group aircraft before setting course for the German port. On arrival in the target area, the bombers found a large number of night fighters waiting for them. Although the German aircraft did not carry airborne interception radar this early in the war, their Freya equipment gave early warning of the approach of a bomber and then two Wurzburg radars would plot the target and the selected night fighter, enabling the ground controllers to vector the hunter to within 400 yards of its victim, a distance at which the fighter pilot could see the glow of the bomber's exhaust stubs.

The raid was deemed successful but Bomber Command lost six aircraft in the process, three Whitleys and three Wellingtons. Two of the Whitleys belonged to 78 Squadron and were shot down by night fighters after attacking the target. Once again, the Squadron ORB shows only four crew members in each of these two Whitleys.

The crew of Whitley V Z6560 EY- were lost without trace and their names recorded on the Runnymede Memorial.

Pilot F/Sgt V.H. Marks | **Nav** Sgt J.G. Woolley | **Obs** Sgt W.P. Herman
W/Op Sgt J.H. Harris

The second aircraft, Whitley V Z6661 EY-, was shot down while on its way to the target. It crashed at Lorup in Schleswig-Holstein, killing all the crew, who were buried at the Reichswald Forest War Cemetery.

Pilot P/O T.C. Richards | **Nav** F/Sgt H.R. George | **Obs** Sgt C.F. Cook
W/Op F/Sgt R.C. Berwick

TOWARDS THE END OF June 1941 operations continued to concentrate on the Ruhr Valley and, on the night of 27th/28th June, 4 Group Headquarters ordered 80 aircraft to attack Bremen. On arrival over the target they met with heavy flak accompanied by many searchlights. Night fighters were attacking from all angles. This was to prove Bomber Command's worst night of the war to date with regard to losses. Fourteen aircraft failed to return, eleven of them Whitleys, along with three Wellingtons from 5 Group. 78 Squadron were fortunate on this occasion, for all their aircraft returned safely to base. However, two nights later, during a further raid on Bremen, 78 Squadron Whitley V Z6664 EY- faile to return, presumed to have ditched into the North Sea. No trace of it was found. The names of the crew are commemorated on the Runnymede Memorial.

Pilot Sgt R.S. Green | **Nav** Sgt E.R. Ingram | **Obs** Sgt K.I. Jones
W/Op Sgt A.W. Adams | **A/G** F/Sgt L. Bird

AIRCRAFT FROM 4 GROUP played a major role in bombing operations over Bremen, Duisburg and Koln during the night of 2nd/3rd July 1941. These areas included rail centres, inland waterways and steelworks vital to the German war effort. A directive was issued, emphasising the effect these bombing raids were having on the morale of German industrial workers in the area. During this raid 4 Group lost four bombers, one of them being 78 Squadron Whitley V Z6558 EY- which had taken off at 23.34 hours from Middleton-St-George to bomb a synthetic oil plant at Koln. After carrying out the bomb run it was intercepted by a night fighter (Lt Reinhold Knacke 11/NJG) and crashed at 0103 hrs at Itteren (Limburg) 5km N of Maastricht, killing all the crew, who were buried at Jonkerbos War Cemetery.

Pilot Sgt A. Jepson | **Nav** P/O G.M. Kennedy | **Obs** Sgt G.A. Avory
W/Op Sgt J.F. Hollingworth

DURING THE NEXT FEW nights, the squadron carried out normal operations without any losses being incurred, but their fortunes were to change on the night of 8th/9th July. They took off at 22.45 hours, to join aircraft from 4, 5 and 8 Groups to raid the marshalling yards at Hamm. This was a major target, well protected by flak, searchlights and night fighters. In spite of

A Typical Day on Operations
for a Bomber Command Squadron

WHEN AIR CREWS OF 78 Squadron saw their names posted on the 'Ops Tonight' board they would follow a routine repeated throughout Bomber Command. After their aircraft had been air tested by the pilot and crew to ensure that all was in full working order, the next thing was a visit to the crew room to check their personal equipment before going to the mess for lunch. Later they were called to the briefing room and after they were all assembled, a roll-call of pilots/captains was made.

Everyone rose to attention when the Station Commander entered the room, followed by his senior officers. An RAF policeman stood outside on guard, to prevent anyone entering the room while the briefing took place. The curtain covering the map of Europe was then drawn back to reveal the target for that night. The route to be taken was marked in red tape. Also displayed on the map were all the known flak and searchlight positions, with various coloured pins giving further essential information. Of most interest to all those assembled was location of their target that night.

The first man to speak was the Senior Intelligence Officer, he explained the nature of the target, its importance, plus any special information that was necessary for the operation. A succession of other officers then gave details of signals, bombing and navigation. The 'Met' Officer displayed charts giving wind speeds and cloud heights, probable weather to be expected over the target area, and the forecast of what the weather would be like on return to base. Lastly, the Wing Commander added his views about the operation. When he finished there was complete silence in the room. After wishing them good luck, the Senior Officer dismissed them. The pilots and navigators collected their maps while the wireless operators obtained their 'flimsies' (sheets of rice paper that could easily be disposed of) on which were printed the radio frequencies to be used and the 'colours of the day' (the combination of coloured flares that could be released in emergency circumstances to identify the aircraft to other aircraft, shipping or anti-aircraft batteries as 'friend' rather than 'foe').

Some men sat down to write letters home before going to the parachute section to draw their parachutes and 'Mae Wests'[1] and then it was on to the crew room to empty their pockets of any personal possessions that could prove of any value to the Germans in the event of being shot down and captured.

Checking to ensure their escape kits were safe, they went out to the crew bus that awaited them. A few minutes later, they stopped by their aircraft. After having a last cigarette, they got aboard and carried out the pre-flight checks, then the pilot gave the thumbs up signal to the ground crew on the battery cart to tell them he was ready to start the engines.[2]

A puff of smoke came from each engine as the pilot pressed the starter button, then the engines coughed and a moment later they roared into life. A check on oil pressures and magneto drops was carried out by the flight engineer, as the pilot tested each engine, before signing the Form 700, afterwards handing it back to the Flight Sergeant in charge of the plane's ground crew.

After checking the intercom to each member of the crew, the pilot waved away the chocks and the Whitley trundled onto the perimeter track, joining the other bombers waiting to get on the runway. When their turn came, they turned onto the runway and waited for the signal to go. A green Aldis lamp[3] flashed and with the brakes held on, the throttles were pushed forward by the pilot with the engineer following through with his hands, to lock them fully open. The brakes were released and, very slowly, the heavily-laden bomber began to move forward, slowly gaining speed, until the tail came up, then it accelerated down the runway and finally became airborne.

❖ ❖ ❖

[1] Pneumatic buoyancy vests jokingly named after the well-known busty Hollywood star of the era.

[2] Starting the aircraft engines required an external electrical power source and this was provided by a 'trolley accumulator', a handcart loaded with an array of lead acid batteries capable of delivering sufficient power to fire up the engines, even when cold.

[3] Named after British inventor Arthur C.W. Aldis, this was a handheld signalling lamp used by the RAF in World War II for air traffic control, which could show one of three colours; red, white or green.

the flak barrage, the bomber force pressed home the attack, causing a great deal of damage, before turning for home. One 78 Squadron aircraft, Whitley V T4209 EY-W, piloted by Sergeant W.M. McQuitty RAAF, suffered serious damage over the target. With only one functioning engine, he set course for home. When crossing the Dutch coast, the bomber was attacked by a German night fighter.

After a duel that lasted several minutes, the fighter was seen to dive away. The Whitley rapidly lost height but McQuitty continued in trying to reach the English coast. Just nine miles from safety, the remaining engine cut out and the Whitley ditched into the sea. While getting into the dinghy, the crew found it had been damaged in the crash. Being a strong swimmer, Sgt J.F. Hafferden offered to swim ashore to get help for his colleagues. On reaching land he walked about four miles before finding anyone who could help. In spite of a thorough search of the area, no trace was found of the aircraft or the rest of the crew. Their names are recorded on the Runnymede Memorial.

Pilot Sgt W.M. McQuitty RAAF | **Nav** P/O E.A. Scott
W/Op Sgt D.J. Clow | **A/G** Sgt W. Forster (*all lost at sea*)
A/G Sgt J.F. Hafferden (*survived*)

The second aircraft that failed to return that night was also lost without trace in the North Sea. It was Whitley V Z6555 EY-. There were no survivors. The names of the crew are recorded on the Runnymede Memorial.

Pilot Sgt O.W. McClean RAAF | **Nav** Sgt Mack Martin RCAF
Obs P/O H.H. Mountain | **W/Op** Sgt L. Byrne | **A/G** Sgt K. Noddle

The third aircraft lost that on that operation was Whitley V Z6625 EY-L, which crashed into a haystack at Shernborne, near Bircham Newton in Norfolk while making an emergency landing following failure of the port engine. The crew all escaped uninjured.

Pilot P/O Wright | **Nav** Sgt Jones | **Obs** F/Sgt R. Jopling
W/Op Sgt R. Boucher | **A/G** Sgt A.D. White

The loss of ten aircraft in this operation brought the total losses suffered by Bomber Command since 22nd June to 130 aircraft lost, 449 aircrew killed, 16 injured and 109 made prisoners of war.

The arrival of trained personnel from Canada and Australia, as well as Polish squadrons now becoming operational was encouraging but nevertheless Bomber Command was finding it hard to replace aircraft and crews at the same rate as they were being lost.

It was now three weeks since 78 Squadron had suffered the loss of three of its aircraft, but with three new Whitleys to replace them, along with three new crews settled in their billets, the Squadron was once again at full strength with ground crews making certain the new aircraft were on top line. There was an incident when Whitley V Z6838 piloted by Sergeant Turnbull RCAF crashed immediately after take-off on a training flight from Middleton-St-George on 29th July. Fortunately, no one was injured; the crash was put down to jammed ailerons.

On 25th July 1941 Air Vice-Marshal Arthur Coningham, after completing two years' service in command of 4 Group, moved on to take command of the Desert Air Force. His successor was Air Vice-Marshal C.R. Carr, a New Zealander, who proved to be a worthy successor. In 1939 he was in France with the advance striking force. He quickly moved on to become AOC RAF Northern Ireland in 1940, a post he held until he was appointed AOC No.4 Group in 1941.

The personnel of 78 Squadron were fortunate in not having suffered any casualties in recent weeks, but knew it was only a matter of time before another of their aircraft became a statistic on the list of missing bombers. Fortunately, when it did happen, there was a happy ending for the crew.

On the night of 6th/7th August, along with aircraft from other 4 Group squadrons, 78 Squadron attacked Frankfurt. Whitley V T4158 EY- was badly shot up in the raid but managed to make it back to the English Channel, where it ditched 12km north of Dunkerque. The crew was picked up by RAF High Speed Launch HSL145, out from Dover, in the face of heavy gunfire from coastal batteries. The crew were all rescued safely.

Pilot P/O Atchison | **Nav** Sgt Harwood | **Obs** Sgt McMullan
W/Op Sgt Elliot | **A/G** Sgt J. Bell

ON THE NIGHT OF 8th/9th August 1941, eight squadrons from 4 and 5 Groups took part in another raid on Kiel, a heavily-defended area due to its importance in the movement of vital war materials by ship, barge and rail. The aircraft of 78 Squadron took off at 22.19 hours from Middleton-St-George and in spite of the heavy flak pressed home their attack. Several aircraft were badly damaged over the target and on the return leg Whitley V Z6655 EY- failed to reach the English coast after the pilot was forced to ditch some eighty miles northeast of Blyth, Northumberland. The crew, who were all rescued, little the worse for their ordeal, were:

Pilot Sgt L.W. Bell | **Nav** Sgt Pindon | **Obs** Sgt Buttell
W/Op Sgt R. Boucher | **A/G** Sgt Porter

A LARGE FORCE OF bombers from 1, 4 and 5 Groups took part in an operation on the heavily-defended areas of Koln, Duisburg and Dusseldorf on the night of 16th/17th August 1941. Heavy damage was inflicted in the target areas but the price paid was also very high, with 16 aircraft failing to return to their bases. Total aircrew casualties for this raid amounted to 50 killed, 5 injured and 33 made prisoners of war. Two men evaded capture.

This was the first time in two months that 78 Squadron had suffered any losses and it brought home to everyone that their good luck could not be counted upon. The squadron's Whitleys had taken off at 23.00 hrs and, after reaching their rendezvous point with the rest of the force, set course for Koln, a target they were familiar with, having attacked it on several previous occasions, so they were keenly aware that they would be met by hundreds of searchlights and heavy flak, backed up by night fighters. This, however, did not deter the crews from carrying out a concentrated attack on the target. 78 Squadron was to lose three aircraft before the raid was over, the first was Whitley V Z6577 EY-F, which crashed at Ohe en Lak (Limburg) on the west bank of the Juliana Kanaal, 14 km SW of Roermond, Netherlands. The crew were all killed and buried at Jonkerbos War Cemetery.

Pilot Sgt T.A. Sherman RCAF | **Nav** Sgt G. Olsen RCAF | **Obs** F/Sgt R. Jopling
W/Op Sgt D.A. Wilson | **A/G** Sgt D.F. Hawkes

The second aircraft was Whitley V Z6754 EY- which crashed at Buggenum (Limburg), 5km NNW of Roermond, killing all the crew, who were interred at Jonkerbos War Cemetery.

Pilot Sgt J.H. Malet-Warden | **Nav** Sgt J.C. Beardmore
Obs Sgt A.J.R. Millard-Tucker
W/Op Sgt G.H.P. Buchanan RCAF | **A/G** Sgt A. Brown

The third bomber lost was Whitley V Z6823 EY-B, which crashed at Velddriel (Gelderland), 6km SE of Zaltbommel, Netherlands. Two of the crew were killed and the rest taken prisoner.

Pilot F/Lt J.A. Cant | POW Stalag Luft 3 Sagan
Nav P/O J.L. Asprey RAAF | Killed, Jonkerbos War Cemetery
Obs Sgt W.E. Kerr | POW Stalag 357 Kopernikus
W/Op Sgt A.D. Willis | Killed, Wounsell Cemetery, Eindhoven
A/G Sgt J. Geary | POW Stalag Luft 6 Heydekrug

IN JULY 1941, A report was received by Lord Cherwell, Chief Scientific Adviser to the Prime Minister, stating that the bombing campaign was not producing the desired results, going by photographs taken during night raids in June and July. He immediately ordered Mr D.M. Butt, a Senior Civil Servant working in the War Cabinet Secretariat, to carry out a detailed analysis on the bombing. Butt received his brief in early August and his report was in Cherwell's hands by the 18th. His findings were rather disturbing. Even in good weather, bombing results were adjudged to be poor, with only a small percentage of bombs falling anywhere near their targets. When the report was circulated among the Air Council, grave doubts were expressed as to the accuracy of Butt's findings. It was, however, accepted that the present bombing results were certainly not satisfactory, and agreed that improvements needed to be sought, urgently.

As a result of the Butt Report, steps were immediately implemented to hasten the development of electronic aids to improve bombing accuracy. Meanwhile, Bomber Command, despite its present failings, was to be expanded by the beginning of September 1941, with further plans already prepared for it to be brought up to a first line strength of 4,000 aircraft.

In the meantime, bombers continued to attack Bremen, Kiel, Duisberg and Dusseldorf, in addition to other targets.

On the night of 24th/25th August, 78 Squadron joined aircraft from 4 and 5 Groups to carry out another raid on Dusseldorf. They took off at 20.00 hrs from RAF Middleton-St-George, ready for the 400-mile trek into the heart of Germany. On crossing the Dutch coast they encountered heavy flak and searchlights, as usual, and on arriving over Dusseldorf they found clouds of smoke from decoy fires covering the target. This prevented them finding their designated targets and forced them to look for alternatives. Several aircraft were damaged in this operation and among them were two 78 Squadron Whitleys, one of which crashed near Wavre (Brabent), 27km SE of Brussels. The crew were all killed and laid to rest in Wavre Communal Cemetery. This was Whitley V Z6466 EY-A.

Pilot Sgt W.G. Roberts | **Nav** Sgt E.C. Findon | **Obs** Sgt J. Hadfield
W/Op Sgt W.D. Edge | **A/G** Sgt B. Douglas

The second aircraft lost was Whitley V Z6742 EY-, which managed to make it back to England but had to be abandoned in mid-air after catching fire. The aircraft crashed at 02.27 near Mistley, Essex on the banks of the River Stour. The crew all baled out and landed safely, with the exception of the navigator, whose body was later found in the wreckage.

Pilot P/O Fransden | **Obs** Sgt Becker | **W/Op** Sgt Young
and **A/G** Sgt Gales, *all landed safely*
Nav Sgt D.A. Sinclair RCAF, killed, *interred at Ipswich Cemetery*

MANNHEIM WAS THE TARGET for the 15 Whitleys of 78 Squadron which took off at 01.35 hours from Middleton-St-George on the night of 27th/28th August. On reaching the target they pressed home their attack but were badly mauled by heavy flak on the return journey. Whitley V Z6508 EY- crashed into the sea off the French port of Dunkerque with the loss of all on board. Their names are recorded on the Runnymede Memorial.

Pilot P/O K.W. Davies | **Nav** Sgt S.E. Rowed RCAF | **Obs** Sgt G.T. Harper
W/Op Sgt J.W. Bills | **A/G** Sgt P. Gennon RNZAF

A second aircraft, Whitley V Z6872 EY-, which had taken off at 02.02 hours, failed to reach its target, bombing Bruges as an alternative. On return to base it crashed and burst into flames. All the crew were injured but safe. Once again, a four-man crew instead of the normal five.

Pilot Sgt H.A. Woodhatch | **Nav** Sgt Childs | **Obs** Sgt Olley | **W/Op** Sgt Davidson

DURING RAIDS CARRIED OUT during the next ten days, 78 Squadron did not suffer any casualties, but this run of good luck came to an end on the night of 6th/7th September, when aircraft from 4 Group attacked Huls, in the heavily-defended Ruhr. Eleven aircraft were lost in the operation, two of which belonged to 78 Squadron. The first was Whitley V Z6864 EY-, which crash-landed at 03.15 hours, a few hundred yards SE of Markington Church, 4 miles SSW of Ripon in Yorkshire, after being attacked by an intruder. The crew all escaped without injury:

Pilot Sgt Jones RAAF | **Nav** Sgt Jones | **Obs** Sgt Miller,
W/Op Sgt Vere | **A/G** Sgt Rouse

The second aircraft reported missing that night was Whitley V Z6881 EY-, which had taken off from Middleton-St-George at 20.37 hours but was shot down by a night fighter (Oblt Helmut Lunt 4./NJG1) and crashed at 01.25 hours at Bergum (Friesland) in the Netherlands. The crew were all killed and interred at Bergum Protestant Churchyard.

Pilot P/O F.B. Thorpe | **Nav** Sgt C.V. Matheson | **Obs** Sgt D.V. Logan RAAF
W/Op Sgt G. Carman RNZAF | **A/G** Sgt C.J. Storer

WITH THE LONG DARK nights of autumn now approaching, Bomber Command aircraft were able to intrude further into Germany, with Berlin, Frankfurt, Stettin and the city of Turin in Northern Italy coming in for attack during September. Though these targets were among the most heavily defended by flak, radar controlled searchlights and night fighters, good bombing results were claimed by the crews taking part in the raids.

During one such operation by the bombers of 4 Group, which took place on the night of 29th/30th September, eleven aircraft were lost. That number included 78 Squadron Whitley V Z9126 EY-, which had taken off at 21.39 hours from Middleton-St-George. Its crew was heard on W/T while homeward bound, calling for help. A bearing taken at the time indicated the bomber was near Sylt, but nothing further was heard. No trace of the plane or its crew was ever found. They are commemorated on the Runnymede Memorial:

Pilot Sgt R.W. Bird | **Nav** Sgt I. McCarthy | **Obs** Sgt H. Buttell
W/Op Sgt R. Ward | **A/G** Sgt R.R. Vosper

FOLLOWING AN ATTACK ON Essen on the night of 10th/11th October, all the aircraft returned safely to Middleton-St-George but, on landing, two Whitleys collided on the flarepath. One member of the crew in each aircraft was injured. The first aircraft involved was Whitley V Z6825 EY-

Pilot P/O Fransden | **Nav** Sgt Dennis | **Obs** Sgt Bowden
W/Op Sgt Young, all escaped uninjured
A/G Sgt Taylor, injured but safe

The second aircraft was Whitley V Z9127 EY-

Pilot P/O Leyland | **Obs** P/O Geddes
W/Op Sgt Donaldson | **A/G** Sgt Vere, all escaped uninjured
Nav Sgt Dench, injured but safe

RETURNING FROM AN OPERATION over Nurnberg, during the night of 14th/15th October, one of 78 Squadron's aircraft was abandoned due to being low on fuel. It crashed at 06.15 hours near Hythe, Kent. It was Whitley V Z9213 EY- The crew all landed safely by parachute.

Pilot P/O D.S.King RCAF | **Nav** P/O Pruden | **Obs** Sgt Jupp
W/Op Sgt Lyndon | **A/G** Sgt Campbell

ON 16TH OCTOBER A 78 Squadron Whitley took off from Middleton-St-George on a training flight to a new airfield known officially as Croft, though it was still known to all the local inhabitants as Neasden. RAF Croft opened in 1941 as a satellite for Middleton-St-George, a few miles to the north-west. Both these airfields were in 4 Group, Bomber Command. On 16th October Whitley V Z6646 EY-, piloted by Pilot Officer B.O. Smith, crashed at 20.10 hrs in the circuit of Croft airfield, injuring four members of the crew, though there is no record of their names in the squadron ORBs. The accident was attributed to engine failure.

On 20ᵗʰ October 1941, 78 Squadron moved to RAF Croft and became the first squadron to be based there. On the night of 1ˢᵗ/2ⁿᵈ November, they took part in an operation over Kiel, losing one of their aircraft during the operation. It was last heard on W/T at 01.16 hours at Linton-on-Ouse, at which time, the crew were in touch with Bircham Newton. Nothing further was heard and the aircraft was presumed lost over the North Sea. It was Whitley V Z9152 EY-. The names of the crew are recorded on the Runnymede Memorial.

Pilot Sqdn/Ldr J. Mercer | **Nav** Sgt R.F. Duggan | **Obs** Fl/Lt J.R. Campbell
W/Op Sgt T.P. Woodhouse | **A/G** F/Sgt V.G. Wright

ON 7TH NOVEMBER AIR Marshal Peirse, Commander in Chief at High Wycombe, gave orders for an attack to be carried out on Berlin by over 200 aircraft. Weather conditions were less than favourable, with strong winds and icing forecast in large areas of northern Europe that lay directly in the path of the bombers, and 5 Group protested at the folly of risking their Hampdens in such conditions, warning that Berlin was a high-risk target even when the weather was at its best. After a long discussion, Bomber Command HQ at High Wycombe agreed to the removal of 5 Group from the operation; they would instead become part of a force of 55 aircraft to attack Mannheim, thus reducing the Berlin force to 169 aircraft. From the time this operation began it was obvious to everyone that it was doomed to failure. Less than half the bombers managed to reach the target area and the route was littered with the wreckage of aircraft shot down by flak or night fighters.

The result was 21 bombers lost, 91 aircrew killed and 36 made prisoners of war. Of the 55 aircraft that attacked Mannheim, 13 were shot down, 27 aircrew were killed and 36 were made POWs. A further six men managed to evade capture. Another four aircraft were lost that night whilst engaged in 'gardening' (mine-laying) raids near Oslo, Norway, resulting in eight aircrew killed and four becoming POWs. It had been a black night all round for RAF Bomber Command.

78 Squadron lost two aircraft during that Berlin raid. Whitley V Z6948 EY-F had taken off from Croft at 22.31 hours. It was shot down by a night fighter (Oblt Ludwig Becker. 4./NJG). It crashed at 06.30hrs between Oudemirdum and Nijemirdum (Friesland), killing all the crew.

Pilot Sgt J.W. Bell | interred Lemmer General Cemetery
Nav P/O G.M. McCombe | **Obs** Sgt G.T. Webb | **W/Op** Sgt D. Cameron
A/G Sgt R. Boucher, all interred Nijemirdum Cemetery.

Whitley V Z9151 EY- became a victim of the heavy flak while over the target area. The pilot was killed and his remains lie at rest in the Berlin 1939-45 War Cemetery. The rest of the crew were made prisoners of war.

Pilot Sgt E.J. Sargent, interred Berlin 1939-45 War Cemetery
Nav P/O J.V. Saunders RCAF – POW Stalag Luft 3 Sagan
2nd **Pilot** Sgt E.W. Penn | **Obs** Sgt T. Hall | **W/Op** Sgt T. Paterson
A/G Sgt E.G.S.H. Freeman, all POWs Stalag 357 Kopernikus

WITH THE LOSS OF 38 aircraft, 126 aircrew killed and 76 made prisoners of war, though six successfully evaded capture, the night's operations proved very costly and reaction was swift in coming. A meeting of the War Cabinet was swiftly convened and after some deliberation it was decided that the bombing should be strictly limited, at least for the immediate future, while present policies were given a thorough review.

This decision was signalled via the Air Ministry to High Wycombe. It meant Bomber Command's operations being under strict control during the remainder of the winter period. In his preliminary report to the Air Staff, Sir Richard Pierse, C-in-C Bomber Command, stated that much of the blame for the high losses was due to weather conditions prevailing at the time of the raid. At first this was accepted, but murmurings of disquiet persisted and by early December, several amendments had been added to his original findings. However, none of these amendments fully satisfied the Air Staff, or the very astute Secretary of State for Air, Sir Archibald Sinclair. He insisted on the Prime Minister being apprised forthwith. What followed is now history. Sir Richard cleared his desk on 8th January 1942 from the office he had held for only 14 months.

In spite of suffering the worst losses sustained in the war so far, Bomber Command returned to Germany the following night, 8th/9th November. This time it was a much smaller force but again they suffered heavy losses.

During the night of 17th/18th December 78 Squadron attacked the port of Le Havre. Following the attack, the starboard engine of Whitley V Z9129 EY- caught fire. Prompt action by the crew put the fire out and the bomber made it back to the English coast. It crashed into the sea off Spithead with no injuries to the crew being reported. The crew was:

Pilot P/O Bedford | **Nav** Sgt Howell | **Obs** P/O Ponds
W/Op Sgt Oliver | **A/G** Sgt Parks

WITH OPERATIONS OVER GERMANY being restricted, 78 Squadron mounted an attack on Brest during the afternoon of 18th December. This port was vital to the Germans, because its deep-water facilities were capable of handling the heavy cruisers *Scharnhorst* and *Gneisenau*, as well as being vital to U-boats returning from the Atlantic after long patrols. Two aircraft were lost as a result of this operation.

With thick cloud preventing them from finding their airfield and unable to obtain any response to constant W/T calls for assistance, the pilot of Whitley V Z9277 EY- broke through cloud and crashed on high ground, 17 miles from Harrogate, in Yorkshire. Fortunately, the crew survived.

Pilot P/O J.F. Beadle | 2nd **Pilot** P/O Franklyn | **Nav** Sgt White | **Obs** Sgt Cox
W/Op Sgt Gale | **A/G** Sgt Kendall

The second aircraft was Whitley V Z9308 EY-, which took off at 16.07 hours and crash-landed at 16.30 hours at Keanley Sides farm near Harwood, Durham after losing power in the starboard engine. All crew members escaped uninjured.

Pilot Sgt J.A. Attwell RCAF | **Nav** Sgt Turpin | **Obs** Sgt Martin
W/Op Sgt Howitson | **A/G** Sgt Johnston

78 SQUADRON'S LAST OPERATION of 1941 took place on the night of 27th/28th December and the target was Dusseldorf, which every crew member knew was heavily defended, though no one would think of shirking their duty. One of the bombers destined not to take part that night was Whitley V Z9276 EY-. Due to severe icing, the aircraft failed to gain height and eventually collided with high tension cables and crashed at Foxholes, ten miles North of Driffield in Yorkshire. The impact started a fire that injured three of the crew. Squadron ORBs do not show who they were.

Pilot P/O Shattock | **Nav** Sgt Wado | **Obs** Sgt Lee
W/Op Sgt Newman | **A/G** Sgt Lyndon

SQUADRON ORBS SHOW THAT 78 Squadron lost 42 aircraft on operations during 1941 and that a further two were lost in ground incidents.

1942 STARTED BADLY FOR the squadron when a raid on the French port of St Nazaire resulted in the loss of one of their aircraft. Whitley V Z6656 EY- took off from RAF Croft at 16.22 hours on the afternoon of 2nd January along with the rest of the squadron to carry out an attack on the port, little knowing that within the next three months, this target would become one of the most famous names of World War Two, for during the night of 27th March 1942 the port was attacked by Royal Marine Commandos, and HMS *Campbeltown*, an elderly destroyer that had been loaded with explosives, rammed and blew up the lock gates. This was a serious blow to the Germans, for it denied them the use of the only port on the western seaboard with a dry dock that could accommodate the battle cruiser *Tirpitz*.

The bombing raid was carried out successfully and when 78 Squadron turned for home, the port had suffered a great deal of damage. Returning to Croft, they found it blanketed with cloud. Z6656 EY, piloted by Sgt A.J. Attwell, descending through cloud, crashed on high ground 15,000 feet above sea level at Woogill Moor, Widderdale, 14 miles from Ripon, Yorkshire, completely destroying the aircraft and badly injuring the crew.

Pilot Sgt A.J. Attwell RCAF | **Nav** Sgt J.D. Johnson RCAF | **Obs** Sgt E.C. Smith
W/Op F/O K. Blyth | **A/G** Sgt V.E. Shirley

DURING THE REST OF January 78 Squadron, in company with other squadrons, repeatedly attacked targets in northern France and Holland. Following an attack on Rotterdam during the night of 28th/29th January, one of the Whitleys was approaching Harwich when it was shot down into the sea by armed trawlers. All the crew were killed. Two bodies were recovered from the sea but F/Sgt D.R. Campbell's remains were later committed back to the sea. The names of the crew are recorded on the Runnymede Memorial. The aircraft was Whitley V Z9305 EY-A:

Pilot Sgt A.N. Williams RAAF | **Nav** P/O D.L. Williams
Obs F/Sgt D.R. Campbell RCAF
W/Op Sgt D. Curnick | **A/G** Sgt R.W. Dobson

ALL THE SQUADRONS IN 4 Group were ordered to take part in an operation on the night of 14th/15th February. The target was Mannheim. At 17.35 hours 78 Squadron took off from RAF Croft and, after reaching the rendezvous point, were soon making their way to what they knew would be a cauldron of flak and searchlights. As they approached the target area they could see the city lit up by hundreds of fires raging below. The flak was very heavy at first, then it eased a little, and this gave the night fighters a chance to get at the bombers. At this time Gee was just starting to be fitted to RAF bombers but at its extreme range of 400 miles it was susceptible to jamming by the enemy. Added to this was a feeling by some of the crews that although Gee was invaluable as a guide to their target, German night fighters could use the signal to zero in on any bomber using the equipment.

As a result of this operation, 78 Squadron lost one aircraft whilst it was returning to base from the attack. Due to their w/t equipment being u/s, they strayed off the track, crashing into the sea at around 02.20 hours, twenty miles off the Hampshire resort of Bournemouth. Fortunately, all the crew were rescued and taken to the Royal Naval Hospital Haslar at Portsmouth for treatment. The lost aircraft was Whitley V Z9320 EY-

Pilot Sgt J.C. Steven | **Nav** F/Sgt Rogers | **Obs** P/O Atkinson
W/Op Sgt R. Shipley | **A/G** P/O Turner

AROUND 20TH FEBRUARY AIR Marshal Arthur Harris arrived at High Wycombe to take up take up his duties as C-in-C Bomber Command. It was to be some time before any changes occurred to alter the way of life on the bomber stations. However, changes did occur and, when they came about, many people were affected.

During a raid on Boulogne on the night of 13th/14th March, 78 Squadron lost two aircraft. They were the last Whitleys to be lost by this squadron. Since commencing operations in mid-July 1940, the squadron had lost 55 aircraft of this type on operational duties and a further two in training accidents. Two aircraft were lost on the present operation. The first was Whitley V Z9214 EY, which took off at 18.08 hours from Croft and was lost without trace. The names of the crew are recorded on the Runnymede Memorial.

Pilot Sgt H.D. McColl | **Nav** Sgt P.W. Bland | **Obs** P/O D.R. Hockaday
W/Op Sgt R.A. Ash | **A/G** Sgt A. McCleod

THE SECOND AIRCRAFT RETURNED to base but crashed at 04.00 hours while making a fifth attempt to land, killing all but one of the crew. It was Whitley V Z9389 EY-

Pilot P/O C. Ferris | **Nav** Sgt J.I.E. Davies, died later in hospital | **Obs** Sgt R.C. Bell
W/Op Sgt N.T. Gander (all killed) | **A/G** Sgt M.M. Henshall (badly injured)

CHAPTER 5

Conversion to the Halifax

D URING THE MONTHS OF MARCH and April 1942, 78 Squadron was re-equipped with a new breed of heavy bomber in the form of the Halifax Mk II. Crews carried out many training flights to ensure they were fully conversant with their new aircraft, although accidents could, and did, still occur. Pilot Officer H.E. Bedford was instructed to ferry a Halifax II R9427 EY- to 405 Squadron at Pocklington on 23rd April. It crashed while trying to land in a strong crosswind. Fortunately, no injuries were reported.

78 Squadron's first casualties after converting to Halifaxes came on the night of 29th/30th April 1942 during an attack on the Belgian port of Ostend. The crew of Halifax II W7663 EY- were all killed and buried in the Dunkerque town cemetery. They were:

> **Pilot** F/O R.M. Shattock | **Nav** Sgt T.J. Naish | **B/A** P/O J.B.F. Brown RCAF
> **W/Op** Sgt R.W. Watson | **F/E** Sgt T.J. Naish | **A/G** Sgt C.R. Campbell
> **A/G** Sgt S.K. Springham

During an operation to Hamburg on 3rd/4th May 1942, the list of missing aircraft and crews increased when two more Halifaxes were lost, these were Halifax II R9391 EY-, which crashed into the North Sea, killing every member of the crew. They were:

> **Pilot** Sqdn/Ldr A.J.D. Snow | **Nav** Sgt F.R. Mills
> **B/A** P/O E.C.L. Hebblethwaite | **A/G** Sgt T.P.W. Davies *all Kiel War Cemetery*
> **W/Op** P/O J.R. Kennedy RCAF | **F/E** Sgt E.C. Smith *both Sage War Cemetery*
> **A/G** Sgt G.M. Edwards, Runnymede Memorial

Halifax Mk II W7662 EY- crashed on Luneburg Heath while returning from Hamburg. Only one crew member survived and was taken prisoner. The rest were interred at Hamburg Cemetery, Ohlsdorf.

> **Pilot** P/O A.W. Hedge RAAF | **Nav** Sgt F.R. Hipwell | **B/A** Sgt J. Hewitson
> **W/Op** Sgt J.A. Lloyd | **FE** Sgt D.W. Drew | **A/G** P/O G.W. Copeland RAAF
> all killed and buried at Hamburg Cemetery, Ohlsdorf
> **A/G** P/O J.E. Hanna, POW Stalag Luft 3 Sagan

Bomber Command carried out four attacks on Rostock during the four nights from 23rd to 26th April and Warnemunde was attacked on the night of 8th/9th May. Rostock was the location of a cluster of aircraft factories forming part of the Heinkel group. During the first attack the concentration was heavy, with all the bombs falling within an hour. From 02.00 hours onwards fires raged in the harbour and the Heinkel works, with smoke rising to a height of 8,000 feet. One of the crews arriving towards the end of the raid said the fire was 'too good to be true' and was probably a dummy fire, but closer investigation showed it to be in the midst of the Heinkel works. Damage to the factory was considerable; the walls of the largest assembly shed fell in and destroyed all the partially finished aircraft within. Two engineering sheds were burnt out and in the docks area five warehouses were destroyed by fire and seven cranes fell into the dock. All the station buildings of the Friedrich Franz Station were gutted and the Navigation School and the town's gasworks were destroyed. Photographs taken later showed swarms of black dots near the main entrance to the station and thick upon two of its platforms. These were civilians seeking trains to take them away from the devastated city. This raid resulted in the loss of 20 bombers, 100 aircrew killed and 16 made prisoners of war. On this occasion 78 Squadron were fortunate; all their aircraft returned safely to base with no injuries to their crews being reported.

At 11.05 hours on 20th May, Squadron Leader G.D. Leyland took off from Croft to carry out an air test on Halifax II W1103 EY-. It crashed at Spa Farm, roughly two miles north of Croft airfield, while on finals. One member of the crew was slightly injured. In a second air-test incident on 27th May, Sergeant W.G. Dench took off in Halifax II W1090 EY- and crashed with another Halifax, DG220. This aircraft was later repaired. Fortunately, there were no injuries among the crews of either aircraft.

Following an attack on Cologne on the night of 29th/30th May, Halifax II V9991 EY was returning from the target when it began to ice up at 12,000 feet and the instruments became unserviceable. Ordering the crew to bale out at 04.30 hours from a height of 1,600 feet, the pilot made a belly landing at Wittering airfield. All the crew survived with the exception of the mid-upper gunner. The crew was:

> **Pilot** Wg/Cdr Seymour-Lucas | **Nav** Sgt D.W. Griffiths | **B/A** Sgt Tait
> **W/Op** P/O A. Markland | **F/E** Sgt Morgan – all escaped uninjured.
> **A/G** Sgt E.T. Webb was badly injured and died on the way to hospital
> Sgt **Ernest Thomas Webb** 1260304 RAF(VR) W/Op/AG, age 21. Died of injuries.
> Grave 1213. SB. Battersea (Morden) Cemetery, Surrey UK.4171

PILOT OFFICER ALAN MARKLAND eventually became the CO of 78 Squadron while it was at Breighton. He was unique in being the only Wireless Operator to rise to this distinction in Bomber Command. It is also worthy of note that the navigator of this aircraft, Sergeant D.W. Griffiths, went on to complete 93 operations and rose to the rank of Squadron Leader.

A report in December 1943 states Halifax II V9991 force-landed at Spaulding. Cat 'B'. The Halifax was repaired and later issued to 1658 HCU and eventually SOC 27/9/45. (The correct date being 27/1/45)

The night of 30th/31st May 1942 saw the first of the '1000 bomber raids'. This attack was the culmination of months of training, weeks of planning and days of organisation; but it was only the beginning of an intensified effort which, in the words of Air Marshal Sir Arthur Harris, AOC Bomber Command, "will cause the Germans to look back to the days of Lubeck, Rostock and Cologne as men lost in a raging typhoon and remember the gentle days of a past summer."

Records show that Harris had the plan for these raids firmly in mind from the time he had been chosen for the post of C-in-C Bomber Command. During this time his Senior Air Officer, Air Vice-Marshal R.H.M.S Saundby, had been sounding out all the squadrons to find out how many aircraft and crews could be made available in readiness for the heavy raids that he knew would be taking place in the near future.

When the plan was put before the CAS, Sir Charles Portal, his response was immediate. He apprised the Prime Minister of Sir Arthur's intentions and on 20th May official approval to proceed reached Bomber Command Headquarters in High Wycombe direct from the Air Ministry.

The Admiralty expressed their disapproval on hearing Coastal Command aircraft would be used to make up the bomber force to the number required for the raid, but they eventually consented. Though AVM Saundby still had a shortfall, he succeeded in meeting the target of 1000 aircraft. Though this operation had been Sir Arthur Harris's idea from the start, it was only made possible by the devotion to duty shown by Air Vice-Marshal Saundby.

The days leading up to the raid were full and strenuous. Ground staff worked as never before and it is appropriate at this point to give some explanation of their labours, for without the expert and unremitting toil of the electricians, fitters, riggers and armourers, and the repair parties provided by the firms that build the aircraft, no bomber would be able to take to the air each day, until a thorough inspection of engines and airframe, was carried out by the ground crew directly responsible for it.

Each ground crew consisted of a fitter for each engine and two fitters or 'riggers' who attended to the airframe. All the ancillary equipment, such as the instruments, electrical gear, guns and so forth, would be checked by specialists in each trade. When all this had been carried out and inspected, the aircraft was certified as being airworthy on the appropriate form, this being a log containing the details of each daily inspection and every 'tradesman' initialled the column in which his part of the inspection had been recorded. The aircraft was not allowed to leave the ground until every item on the form had been initialled. Its crew, who would be flying it on operations that night, then took it over, to carry out a night-flying test, during which all the work of the ground crew was put to the test in the air. On landing, any complaints were entered in a book and immediately put right by the waiting ground crew.

During the remainder of the day, before the aircraft took off for its target, fitters, riggers and other tradesmen prepared it for its special task. The riggers applied de-icing paste to the leading edge of the wings and of the tail-plane and to the propellers. The paste applied to the propellers spread as the blades revolved, to form a thin film. The electricians tested all the electrical equipment and the condition of the storage batteries. The armourer checked the hydraulic turret system for leaks, while the air gunner himself sighted the guns.

On the night of 30th/31st May 1942, a force of 1,047 bombers took off from their bases all over Britain and set course for the German city of Cologne. Only 678 aircraft were from the main bomber squadrons, the rest came from bomber HCUs, OTUs and Training units. Many were crewed by instructors who had already completed tours of operations and their trainees who were in final stages of their training. Of the 1,047 aircraft that set out, at least 900 bombed the target, dropping close to 1,500 tons of high explosive bombs and incendiaries, completely devastating the city. Over two hundred factories engaged in the manufacture of chemicals, rubber and iron were destroyed, also an oil storage plant and blast furnaces. Added to this, many public buildings were totally destroyed; these included hospitals, schools, four universities and several department stores. All power supplies to the city were put out of action and gas and water supplies were badly disrupted. German records showed nearly 500 people were killed, over 5,000 injured and more than 59,000 made homeless.

A devastating blow had been dealt to Germany by that attack but the cost to Bomber Command was also very high, with the loss of 53 aircraft, 194 aircrew killed, 82 made prisoners of war and eight seriously injured.

Six men managed to evade capture and returned to the UK in due course, thanks to the underground movements in Holland, Belgium and France. A further 24 air crew survived their badly-damaged aircraft crashing on return to the UK.

78 Squadron lost only one aircraft during the operation, when a Halifax collided in the air with a 14 OTU Hampden P-5321 and crashed at 04.05hrs at Whitmore, Huntingdonshire. It was Halifax II W1013 EY- The crew was:

Pilot P/O G.C. Foers | **Nav** Sgt A.H. Warner and
W/Op F/Sgt A.W.H. Gamble – all injured but safe.
B/A Sgt H. Bolton and **A/G** Sgt A. Caie – killed
F/E Sgt Curtiss escaped uninjured.

No record of a seventh crew member was found in the Squadron ORBs.

Between 11th May 1940 and 31st May 1942, of the principal targets in the Ruhr, Essen had been attacked 89 times, Duisburg 93 and Dortmund 33. Of the main German cities outside that great industrial area Cologne was raided 144 times, Mannheim attacked 68 times and Magdeburg 26 times. The German ports that were most directly concerned with the Battle of the Atlantic were Bremen, Wilhelmshaven, Kiel and Emden, while Hamburg, the Second City in Germany, was a base not only for that battle but also for the Russian front. Bremen had been attacked 115 times.

Bomber Command had accomplished this with Wellington, Hampden, Whitley, Stirling, Halifax, Manchester and Lancaster aircraft designed and built in Great Britain. With the exception of a few Flying Fortresses which operated for a short time in the summer of 1941 and American Bostons deployed in North Africa since March 1942, no aircraft other than British-built had been used by the RAF.

The following night of 1st/2nd June, the second 1000-bomber raid took place. This time 956 aircraft, again with support from the OTUs, crossed the North Sea and headed for the industrial centre of Essen. This raid was a failure on the part of Bomber Command. For though plenty of flares were dropped beforehand to mark the target, the bombing was so widespread that little damage was done to Essen itself. However, with such a large number of aircraft taking part in the attack, damage in the surrounding area was very heavy. As on the previous operation, the cost to Bomber Command in aircraft and air crews was again very heavy. 37 aircraft failed to return following the raid. 85 aircrew were killed, 13 were wounded, with a further 21 becoming POWs. Two of those that failed to return were 78 Squadron aircraft.

Halifax II R9364 EY- was shot down by flak whilst crossing the Dutch coast on the return journey. It crashed into the sea, and the fuselage broke into two sections injuring two of the survivors. After spending two days in a dinghy, they were picked up by a German vessel. The crew was:

Pilot P/O J.S. Lawson MiD RCAF, killed, Runnymede Memorial
Nav F/Sgt T.B. Miller GM. RCAF, POW, Stalag Luft 4 Sagan
B/A Sgt D.E. West, Killed, Runnymede Memorial
W/Op Sgt W. Thompson, Killed, Runnymede Memorial
FÉ Sgt R. McGlen, Killed, Runnymede Memorial
A/G P/O P.J. Jones, POW, Stalag Luft 3 Sagan

The second aircraft collided with a night fighter at 14,000 feet and subsequently crashed at Winterswijk (Gelderland), Holland. The three crew members killed are buried in the Canadian War Cemetery, Groesbeek. It was Halifax II W7698 EY-

Pilot Sq/Ldr G.D. Leyland, POW, Stalag Luft 3 Sagan.
Nav P/O L.G. Geddes RCAF, POW, Stalag Luft 3 Sagan.
B/A Sgt C.G. Pugsley, POW, Stalag 357 Kopernikus.
W/Op Sgt W. Brookes, Killed, Groesbeek War Cemetery
F/E Sgt J.E. Lyons, Killed, Groesbeek War Cemetery
A/G Sgt J. Strang, Killed, Groesbeek War Cemetery

A third 78 Squadron Halifax was lost on this raid while on loan to 10 Squadron at RAF Leeming. There was only one survivor, that being the F/E Sgt W.R. Forbes, who became a POW in Stalag 357 Kopernikus.

In a raid on Essen carried out by 4 Group aircraft during the night of 5th/6th June, 78 Squadron detailed 22 aircraft to take part. One of them had the bad luck to have an engine burst into flames as the bomber was climbing away from the runway. The pilot completed a circuit of the airfield and was lining up with the runway when the bomber's port wing dropped and the plane crashed and burst into flames, it was Halifax II W7669 EY-

Pilot P/O H.E. Bedford, killed, int. Croft Airfield
Nav Sgt J. O'Rourke, killed, int. Croft Airfield
B/A Sgt W.L. Turner, injured but safe
W/Op P/O Alder, injured but safe
F/E Sgt V.G. Musselwhite, killed, int. Croft Airfield
A/G Sgt Phillips and **A/G** Sgt Meller, injured but safe

FOLLOWING THIS OPERATION 78 Squadron moved back to Middleton-St-George, where they were to stay for the next three months. During the night of 19th/20th June their aircraft took part in a raid on Emden. taking off at 23.30 hours, they arrived over Essen, to find 10/10ths cloud obscuring the target. Flares and TIs had been dropped to mark the target area, and crews had only the glow of the flares on the clouds on which to bomb. They carried out the attack, dropping their bombs from a height of 16,500 feet. All the aircraft returned safely to base.

Early on the morning of the 25th June orders were received from 4 Group Headquarters. Operations were on that night and 78 Squadron was to take part. In spite of heavy losses suffered in the first two '1000 bomber raids' Bomber Command took the decision to go ahead with a third and final attack in the series, when it became the turn of Bremen to be visited by a force of 960 bombers. In total, 1,016 aircraft had been mustered, this figure included aircraft that would take part in decoy raids to draw night fighters away from the main target.

When the crews attended the briefing, they were told they would find the target clear of cloud. Taking off at 23.00 hours, they arrived over the target area around 01.15 to find it covered by 10/10ths cloud with a few breaks through which fires could be seen. Bombing took place from a height of 13,500 feet. The Focke-Wulf factory suffered severely, and was left a smouldering ruin, and the shipyards on the River Weser were badly damaged, but the last of the heavy assaults was not the success Bomber Command had hoped for. The cost was very high, for fifty-two aircraft were lost, 199 air crew killed, 3 badly injured and 46 made prisoners of war. 26 men survived when their aircraft crashed whilst they were attempting to return to their bases.

One of the aircraft lost during the raid was a 78 Squadron Halifax that had taken off from Middleton-St-George earlier that night. It was shot down by a night fighter (uffz Heinz Vinke, 11/NJG2) and crashed into the Ijsselmeer, killing two crewmembers. It was Halifax II W1067 EY-

Pilot F/O J.A. Whittingham, Killed, Hemelumer-Oldeferd Cemetery.
Nav P/O G. Gibson, POW, Stalag Luft 3 Sagan.
B/A Sgt D.B. Donaldson, POW, Stalag Luft 6 Heydekrug.
W/Op Sgt H. Dronfield, Killed, Runnymede Memorial
F/E Sgt A.G. Springthorpe, POW, Stalag 357 Kopernikus.
A/G Sgt R.A. Brown, POW, Stalag 357 Kopernikus.

Sergeant Brown died in captivity on 22nd April 1945 but his grave cannot be found. He is commemorated on the Runnymede Memorial.

Two further attacks on Bremen took place, the first on 27th June, from which all the 78 Squadron aircraft returned safely to base. The second attack was on 29th/30th June, in which aircraft from Nos 3, 4, 6 and 8 Groups took part. Further damage was done to the shipyards and the Focke-Wulf factory, causing a delay to the production of aircraft that Germany urgently required. During this operation, 78 Squadron again lost one of its aircraft, Halifax II W1062 EY- It had been badly shot up by a night fighter and crashed-landed at Dorking airfield in Norfolk. A fire broke out, which injured five of the air crew.

Pilot Fl/Lt Woodroffe, Escaped uninjured.
Nav F/Sgt L. Geddes RCAF, Injured but safe.
B/A P/O Lebeau, Injured but safe.
W/Op F/Sgt V. Fulton RCAF, Injured but safe.
F/E Sgt David, Injured but safe.
A/G Sgt E.C. Summerfield, Badly injured.

Sgt Summerfield later died from his wounds. It is thought he may have been responsible for the destruction of the Ju88 night fighter that attacked them, for when it was last seen, it was diving away steeply, with flames streaking from its starboard engine.

In July 1942 Wing Commander Tait, later to become C.O. of 617 Squadron, became the Commanding Officer of 78 Squadron.

Vegesack became the target for 78 Squadron on 19th July. Taking part in this operation were aircraft from Nos 1, 3 and 4 Groups. Bombing took place from a height of 15,000 feet, and scattered fires could be seen through breaks in the cloud. Fortunately there were no casualties on this raid.

Duisburg was attacked on 21st, 23rd and 25th July, with bombing carried out from 15-16,000 feet. Many fires were started in the docks area, and when the bombers departed at 02.00 hours on the 25th three large fires could be seen, with a column of smoke rising to over 1,000 feet being observed in the target area.

A force of 403 bombers attacked Hamburg on the night of 26th/27th July, the primary target being the shipyards that were engaged in building U-Boats. 78 Squadron detailed 21 Halifaxes to take part in the operation, and they began taking off at 22.45. As the bombers approached the target area the crews could see the wall of searchlights that awaited them, then the heavy flak began. It was inevitable that losses would again be high. They bombed from a height of 16,000 feet, with the docks clearly visible below them. A number of hits were seen to be right on target and when they left the area many crews reported seeing large fires burning furiously. Altogether 33 aircraft were reported missing after the raid. 120 air crew were killed and 54 made prisoners of war. A further thirteen survived from aircraft crash-landing while returning to their bases. One aircraft that did not return, was Halifax II W1184 EY- it was lost without trace, probably having been hit by flak before its bombs had been dropped. If this was the case, there was little hope of anyone surviving. The crew's names are recorded on the Runnymede Memorial:

Pilot F/O C. Mitchener | **Nav** Sgt W.J. Taylor | **B/A** Sgt W.K. Daniel
W/Op Sgt D. Morgan | **F/E** Sgt E.A. Tweedale
A/G Sgt G.A.R. Bissonette RCAF | **A/G** Sgt L.G. Dowling

THE MONTH ENDED FOR 78 Squadron with a raid being mounted on Saarbrucken by 16 Halifaxes. They took off from Middleton-St-George at 23.00 hours on the night of 29th/30th July, and after a trouble free outward journey, they bombed from a height of 15,000 feet, and explosions caused by their bombs were seen to start large fires in the target area. At a point 80 miles from the Belgian coast Halifax II W1059 EY-L was attacked four times by a night fighter. The gunners returned fire and the mid-upper gunner saw a big red flash come from the enemy aircraft.

The captain found it impossible to maintain height owing to the starboard outer and port inner engines having been hit by enemy aircraft and ditched the Halifax off the port of Calais. The crew successfully took to their dinghy and were picked up by an ASR launch after being afloat for fourteen hours. They were all safe.

The RAF Station Middleton-St-George report stated:

'Halifax II W1059 EY-l force-landed in the sea 10 miles off Calais. Pilot and crew picked up and OK. Aircraft attacked by Ju88 which put two engines out of action and pilot decided to ditch. Halifax rear gunner claimed to have destroyed the enemy aircraft.'

FOLLOWING A RAID ON Bochum on the night of 5th/6th August, one 78 Squadron aircraft failed to return to base. As it was turning away after the attack, Halifax II W1180 EY- was hit by flak and crashed near Roermond, Holland, killing three of the crew, who were initially buried at Venlo but later re-interred at Jonkerbos War Cemetery.

Pilot Sgt J.C. Stevens, POW, Stalag 344 Lamsdorf.
Nav P/O B. Shipley, POW, Stalag Luft 3 Sagan.
B/A Sgt D. Willoughby, POW, Stalag 344 Lamsdorf.
W/Op Sgt J.W. Clarke, Killed, Jonkerbos War Cemetery.
F/E Sgt A. Greenacre, POW, Stalag 344 Lamsdorf.
A/G Sgt H.M. Gall RCAF, Killed, Jonkerbos War Cemetery.
A/G Sgt J.R. Gilbert RCAF, Killed, Jonkerbos War Cemetery.

DURING AN ATTACK ON Duisburg by squadrons from Nos 1, 3, 4, 6, and 8 Groups, during the night of 6th/7th August. A 78 Squadron aircraft Halifax II W1237 EY-P, was shot down by a night fighter (Hptm Heinrich Prinz Zu Sayn Wittgenstein, 1/NGJ)[1] and crashed into the sea 10 km west of Hoek-Van-Holland, killing all on board. Only one body was recovered, that of A/G Sgt Hoare which was buried in the local Cemetery.

Pilot F/O J.M.J.A. d'Ursel, Killed., Runnymede Memorial
Chevalier of the order Leopold. C de G Belgium
Nav Sgt W.J. Cole, Killed, Runnymede Memorial.
B/A F/Sgt A.G. Johnstone, Killed, Runnymede Memorial.
W/Op Sgt W.G. Scott, Killed, Runnymede Memorial.
F/E F/Sgt W.E.S. Luck, Killed, Runnymede Memorial.
A/G Sgt G.J.M. Cantwell, Killed, Runnymede Memorial.
A/G Sgt J.G.A. Hoare, Killed, Hoek-Van-Holland War Cemetery

TWO NIGHTS LATER, THE 4 Group squadrons were ordered to carry out a raid on Osnabruck. With several of their aircraft grounded for various reasons, 78 Squadron borrowed Halifax II W1106 from 76 Squadron. It took off from Middleton-St-George at 00.07 hours and nothing further was heard. It was presumed lost over the North Sea, from which three bodies were later recovered. F/E Sgt C.M. Howard in Esbjerg Cemetery, Denmark; B/A F/Sgt E.J. Ironmonger was buried in Bergen op Zoom War Cemetery; Holland. A/G F/Sgt A.C. Porter rests in Sage War Cemetery. The rest of the crew are commemorated on the Runnymede Memorial.

Pilot Sgt W.A. Wilson, Runnymede Memorial
Nav Sgt G.A. Palmer, Runnymede Memorial
B/A F/Sgt E.J. Ironmonger, Bergen op Zoom War Cemetery, N'lands
W/Op F/Sgt D.J. Navin RCAF, Runnymede Memorial
F/E Sgt C.M. Howard, Esbjerg (Fourfelt Cemetery), Denmark
A/G F/Sgt A.C. Porter RCAF, Sage War Cemetery, N'lands
A/G Sgt G.D.L. Humphreys, Runnymede Memorial
All died after ditching in the North Sea

AN ATTACK ON MAINZ took place during the night of 11th/12th August in which Nos 3, 4, 5, 6 and 8 Groups were involved. During the attack 20 aircraft were lost. 116 air crew were killed, 3 badly wounded and 31 made prisoners of war. 12 survived crashes after returning to this country. One man managed to evade capture and with the help of the underground

---

[1] Both pilots were of noble birth, F/O d'Ursel being the son of a Belgian Count.

movement, eventually arrived safely back in England. 78 Squadron lost four aircraft during this operation.

Halifax II W1061 EY- was coned by searchlights while in the target area, and sustained serious damage to both port engines from heavy flak. Several crew members were wounded by shrapnel, then a night fighter attacked them and the Halifax crashed at 03.10 hours at Wommelgem, roughly 5 km from Antwerp. The pilot and navigator both died and were buried in Schoonselhof Cemetery. Air gunner F/Sgt A.E. Fay evaded capture, but the rest of the crew became POWs.

> **Pilot** W/O2 W.E. Lunan, killed, Schoonselhof Cemetery
> **Nav** Sgt F.A. Scotland, killed, Schoonselhof Cemetery
> **B/A** F/Sgt L.C. Jupp RCAF, POW, Stalag 357 Kopernikus
> **W/Op** Sgt J.K. Howes RCAF, POW Stalag Luft 4 Sagan
> **F/E** Sgt J.R. Dickinson, POW Stalag 344 Lamsdorf
> **A/G** F/Sgt A.E. Fay RCAF, Evaded Capture
> **A/G** Sgt J.H. Wyatt, POW Stalag 344 Lamsdorf

Halifax II W1115 EY- took off from Middleton-St-George at 21.42 hours and was shot down by flak, crashing at Igstadt, near Weisbaden. The mid upper gunner Sergeant J. Peart has no known grave, He is commemorated on the Runnymede Memorial. The rear gunner Sergeant J.A. Mitchell RCAF, rests in Durnbach War Cemetery. The rest of the crew were made prisoners of war.

> **Pilot** Sgt E.G.S. Monk, POW, Stalag 344 Lamsdorf
> **Nav** P/O E.H. Bodman, POW, Stalag 344
> **B/A** Sgt H. Corbishley RCAF, POW, Stalag 344
> **W/Op** Sgt D. Kimber, POW, Stalag 344
> **F/E** Sgt D.F.J. Lemon, POW, Stalag 344
> **A/G** Sgt J. Peart, Killed, Runnymede Memorial
> **A/G** Sgt J.A. Mitchell, Killed, Buried in Durnbach War Cemetery

Halifax II W1233 EY- took off from RAF Middleton-St-George at 21.39 hours and nothing further was heard from it. It was presumed lost over the North Sea. The body of Wireless Operator P/O Myrick RCAF was recovered from the water and buried in Esbjerg (Fourfelt) Cemetery, Denmark. The rest of the crew are commemorated on the Runnymede Memorial.

> **Pilot** F/Sgt J. Fleetwood-May, Runnymede Memorial
> **Nav** Sgt L. Kelly, Runnymede Memorial
> **B/A** F/Sgt G.H.D. HigginsRAAF, Runnymede Memorial
> **W/Op** P/O J.F. Myrick RCAF, Esbjerg (Fourfelt) Cemetery.

F/E F/Sgt F.N. Thomasson, Runnymede Memorial
A/G Sgt M.J. Hisley, Runnymede Memorial
A/G Sgt J.O. Harrison, Runnymede Memorial
All died after ditching in the North Sea

Halifax II W1245 EY-B took off at 22.41 hours, from RAF Middleton-St-George and was shot down near Mean (Namur) in Belgium. Five members of the crew were killed and buried at Mean Communal Cemetery. The two survivors became prisoners of war.

Pilot F/O D.A. Kingston, killed, Mean Communal Cemetery
Nav P/O G.W. MacAllister , killed, Mean Communal Cemetery
B/A Sgt J. Stewart, POW, No Camp details available
W/Op Sgt I.B. Griffiths, killed, Mean Communal Cemetery
F/E Sgt P. McCann, killed, Mean Communal Cemetery
A/G Sgt E.F. Burrell, killed, Mean Communal Cemetery
A/G R.G. Kendall RCAF, POW, Stalag 344 Lamsdorf

THE PATHFINDER FORCE CAME into existence in August 1942. Since 1940, flares had been used to identify the target area prior to bombs being dropped. This had been thought up by Wing Commander Staton MC, Commanding Officer of No 10 Squadron, and was taken up by Group Captain S.O. Bufton, who became Director of Bombing Operations at the Air Ministry. In early 1942, Bufton's idea of target finding was put before the new C–in–C Bomber Command Sir Arthur Harris, who less than enthusiastic about it and rejected it. The debate between the two men continued until August 1942, when Sir Charles Portal and other senior officers at the Air Ministry chose to come down on the side of Bufton.

The Chief of The Air Staff decided a target finding force was desirable and Sir Arthur was apprised of the decision without delay. The Commander-in-Chief did have his way, both in respect of the title and the new Group's Commander. It was decided that the new Group would be called 'The Pathfinder Force' and Group Captain D.C.T. Bennett was selected as its Commanding Officer, in preference to Group Captain B.E. Embry.

The first two operations carried out by the PFF did not meet with the success that had been hoped for. However, their fortunes changed on their third attempt on the night of 27th/28th August, when Kassel became the target. Aircraft from every group in Bomber Command took part in the attack and Henschel, one of Germany's major aircraft industries, was very badly damaged, along with all the other factories in the town's industrial area, although this was at a considerable cost. When the last of the bombers had returned to their bases, it was found Bomber Command had lost 33 aircraft, 153 air crew had lost their lives and 20 were prisoners of war. One man succeeded in evading capture and six escaped when their aircraft crashed in this country.

The following night, 28th/29th August, during raids on Nurnberg and Saarbrucken, losses increased to 36 aircraft, with 131 air crew killed, 1 seriously wounded and 32 made POWs. Eight managed to evade capture and 32 escaped from aircraft crashing on returning to their bases. One of the missing aircraft was a 78 Squadron Halifax. It had taken off at 19.41 hours from Middleton-St-George to carry out an attack on the Saarbrucken railway marshalling yards, which was an important link in the enemy's rail system. The flak over the target was very heavy and the aircraft was so badly damaged that they were unable to maintain height and eventually crashed between Overisje and Tombeek (Brabant) 17 km south east of Brussels. All on board were killed and buried at Overisje Churchyard, Belgium. Their aircraft was Halifax II W7809 EY-

> **Pilot** Sgt J.A.B. Marshall RAAF | **Nav** W/O T.M. Manning
> **B/A** Sgt J.P. Martin | **W/Op** Sgt T.H. Miller
> **F/E** Sgt G.E. Dunn | **A/G** Sgt S. Ross, Killed, Overisje, Belgium.
> **A/G** Sgt J.G. Miller, Killed, Overisje, Belgium.

Returning from an operation to attack Frankfurt during the night of 8th/9th September, in which aircraft from Nos 1, 3, 4 and 5 Groups had taken part, the crew of 78 Squadron Halifax II W1252 EY- which had sustained serious damage from the heavy flak encountered over the target. The pilot tried to make an emergency landing but the bomber was proving very hard to handle and the crew were forced to bale out. All escaped uninjured. They were:

> **Pilot** F/O R.E. Atkinson | **Nav** P/O W. Harris | **B/A** Sgt A.E. Thomas
> **W/Op** Sgt C.E.J. O'Keefe RAAF | **F/E** Sgt C.C.W. Crofton
> **A/G** Sgt F. Lister | **A/G** Sgt G. McBride

The second aircraft to be lost that night by 78 Squadron was Halifax II W7782 EY-P. This aircraft was shot down by a night fighter, and crashed near Scalyn (Namur), Belgium. Two of the crew succeeded in evading capture and with the help of the *Comete* (underground resistance movement) they were fortunate in reaching Spain on 24th September, arriving back in England by way of Gibraltar, on 19th October 1942.

> **Pilot** F/Lt P.H. Tippets-Aylmer DFC, Killed, Sclayn(Namur), Belgium.
> **Nav** Sgt T.S. Brandon RCAF, POW, Stalag 344 Lamsdorf.
> **B/A** Sgt J.A. Winterbottom. Evaded capture.

F/E Sgt E.T.H. Hodge RCAF, Killed, Sclayn (Namur), Belgium.
A/G F/Sgt G.R. Yeates RCAF, Killed, Sclayn (Namur), Belgium.
A/G P/O E.W.T. Gibbs, Killed, Sclayn (Namur), Belgium.

Halifax II W1273 EY- had taken off at 19.59 hours but was attacked by an Me110 night fighter and the rear gunner killed before they reached the target area. Realising the danger this put them all in, the captain turned and set course for home, landing at RAF Tangmere in Sussex with a full bomb load. The rear turret and tail unit was found to have been extensively damaged as a result of the attack by the night fighter. The remaining crew escaped uninjured.

Pilot W/O C.G. Dennis | 2ⁿᵈ **Pilot** Sgt R.A. 'Dukes' Riggs
Nav Sgt D.W. Griffiths | **B/A** Sgt E.W. Gamble
W/Op Sgt P.P. Smith | **F/E** Sgt R. Grey | **A/G** Sgt V.R. Robins
A/G F/Sgt W. Dewhurst, killed

As per the Squadron Monthly Summary:

'One aircraft was attacked by an Me110 night fighter and the rear gunner, Flight Sergeant Dewhurst, was killed. The Captain decided to abandon the sortie and landed at RAF Tangmere with a full bomb load. The aircraft was subsequently repaired. Flight Sergeant William Dewhurst 759000 (VR). Air Gunner Aged 24. Buried in Blackpool (Carlton) Cemetery. Poulton-le-Fylde, Lancashire, England.'

Bomber Command again suffered badly on the night of 10th/11th September when their target was the heavily-defended city of Dusseldorf, in the heart of the Ruhr Valley. Among those taking part in this operation were aircraft from 1, 3, 4, 5, 6 and 8 Groups. Added to these, were squadrons in 10, 11, 14, 16, 20, 22, 25 and 26 OTUs. The Pathfinders marked the target with 'Pink Pansies' 4,000lb blast bombs converted into super incendiaries for target marking. Damage to Dusseldorf was widespread, with many thousands of people losing their homes.

The cost of this raid was once more very high, with 38 aircraft lost, 176 aircrew killed, 8 seriously wounded and 19 made prisoners of war. One man succeeded in evading capture. Among the missing aircraft was one from 78 Squadron. After taking off from Middleton-St-George at 20.14 hours, Halifax II DT491 EY- had dropped its bombs on the target before being hit by flak. It crashed near the city of Dusseldorf boundary. There were no survivors. The dead were buried in city's Nordfriedhof cemetery and later reburied at Reichswald Forest War Cemetery.

Pilot P/O C.J. Stevenson | **Nav** Sgt B.B. Warren
B/A Sgt A.E. Arnold RNZAF | **W/Op** Sgt W. Hodgson
F/E Sgt R.J. Roy | **A/G** Sgt W.C.H. Hiscock | **A/G** F/Sgt J.H. Woodward RAAF
All killed near Dusseldorf and buried in Germany

DURING SEPTEMBER 1943 THE Halifaxes of 78 Squadron were taken out of service for modification to the tailplanes, in an effort to cure the rudder stall problem. This work had to be done a couple at a time, so as not to interfere with the squadron operations. In the middle of that month, the squadron were also faced with moving from Middleton-St-George to Linton-on-Ouse. This was to be their home until June 1943. One of the first operations from their new base was on the night of 23rd/24th September, when along with other squadrons in 4 Group, they carried out an attack on the U-Boat base at Flensburg. They met with intense anti-aircraft fire, which claimed several aircraft in the attacking force. 78 Squadron suffered the loss of Halifax II R9447 EY-. It took off at 00.25 hours from Linton-on-Ouse and was lost without trace. All the crew are Commemorated on the Runnymede Memorial.

Pilot F/Sgt C. Pattison | **Nav** P/O A.G.T. Bradley | **B/A** Sgt A. Taylor
W/Op Sgt C.A. Newman | **F/E** Sgt J.H. Hadwen | **A/G** Sgt A.W. Jones
A/G Sgt R.A. Kelly | *all killed, Runnymede Memorial*

A FURTHER ATTACK TOOK place on the U-Boat base at Flensburg on the night of 1st/2nd October 1942. On this occasion, the result was a complete disaster. 27 aircraft had been despatched by 4 Group and 12 of them failed to return. Eight Aircraft took off at 17.58 hours from Linton-on-Ouse. One of them was forced to return early with engine trouble, two others were lost in the attack, the first was Halifax II W1036 EY- shot down near Schleswig. The four fatalities were taken to Flensburg for burial, but later reburied at Kiel War Cemetery. Sergeant Hunt was badly injured and one of his legs had to be amputated.

Pilot Sgt J.K. Gregory | **Nav** Sgt B.W. Johnson | **B/A** Sgt S.S. Waldman
W/Op F/Sgt T.E. Turpin | *all killed, Kiel War Cemetery*
F/E Sgt J.H. Hunt RCAF, POW, Stalag 344 Lamsdorf
A/G Sgt K. Markville, POW, Stalag 344 Lamsdorf
A/G Sgt G.E. Morrison, POW, Stalag 344 Lamsdorf

Halifax II BB236 EY- took off at 17.59 hours from Linton-on-Ouse and while it was carrying out its bombing run, it was badly damaged by the heavy flak. It crashed at Friedenshugel, near Flensburg, where those who died were buried. They now rest in Kiel War Cemetery. They were:

Nav F/O J.H. Carrick RCAF | **B/A** F/O G.M. Gillies RCAF
W/Op Sgt N.R. Jones RAAF | **F/E** Sgt E.H. Tytherleigh
all the above were killed, Kiel War Cemetery
Pilot Sgt E.W. Farr, POW, Stalag Luft 6 Heydekrug
A/G Sgt G.E. Smith, POW, Stalag 344 Lamsdorf
A/G Sgt J. Cunningham, POW, Stalag 344 Lamsdorf

AIRCRAFT BELONGING TO NOS 2, 4, 5 and 6 Groups took part in an operation to raid Krefeld, in the Ruhr Valley, during the night of 2nd/3rd October. Squadrons began taking off at 18.30 hours to commence the 700 mile round trip to 'Happy Valley' as it had become known to the air crews. As usual, the flak started as they crossed the Dutch coast and before they reached the target area several aircraft had been shot down. As the bombers approached the target, crews could see the thick curtain of searchlights and flak that they would have to penetrate in order to drop their bombs. 10 aircraft were lost in this operation, 36 air crew were killed, one seriously wounded and 16 made POWs. 78 Squadron reported one aircraft missing, Halifax II W1275 EY- went down over Germany. The five crew members who lost their lives, rest in the Rheinberg War Cemetery.

Pilot F/Lt G.C. Foers | **Nav** F/Sgt F. Christie
B/A F/Sgt T.A. Stephenson RCAF | **W/Op** Sgt H.M. Clark
F/E Sgt L. Millband | **A/G** P/O V.H. Parry
All the above killed, Rheinberg War Cemetery
2nd **Pilot** G.M. Hobbs, POW, Stalag Luft 3 Sagan
A/G Sgt T.L. Kidd, POW, Stalag 344 Lamsdorf

THE ATTACKS ON GERMANY continued and on the night of 15th/16th October 1942, 78 Squadron were detailed to take part in an attack on Koln. At 18.30 hours they began to take off from Linton-on-Ouse but within minutes Halifax II BB239 EY- developed a failure in its hydraulic system, followed by serious engine problems that necessitated jettisoning the bomb load over the North Sea and returning to base. It crash-landed at 19.40 hours and was completely wrecked but all the crew escaped unharmed.

Pilot Sgt E.A. Williams | **Nav** Sgt H. Beals | **B/A** Sgt L. Trevors
W/Op Sgt L. Masterton | **F/E** Sgt E.C. Jones | **A/G** Sgt R. McReynolds
A/G Sgt R. Creaney – *all escaped uninjured*

THE ITALIAN PORT OF Genoa was the target for 78 Squadron on the night of 23rd/24th October. Among the aircraft taking part in the raid was Halifax II W1018 EY- which was hit by flak over the target and crashed near the Chateau De Montcony in Eastern France, killing all on board. The local

French resistance under the leadership of the 18-year-old chauffeur at the chateau, Gilbert Petiot, took the bodies from the wreckage and placed them in the local school. On 24th October the eight members of the crew were laid to rest in Montcony churchyard, where the war graves have been respectfully tended by the villagers ever since; on the 23rd October each year, local dignitaries place flowers on the graves and a monument has been erected at the spot where the aircraft crashed. A plaque made by Gilbert Petiot was presented to the Officer Commanding RAF Linton-on-Ouse at the Squadron Reunion at York on 6th September 1986.

Pilot F/Lt H. Rhoden | **2nd Plt** F/O Teague RCAF
Nav Sgt F.G. Allen | **B/A** Sgt J. Beveridge | **W/Op** Sgt G.J. Chambers
F/E Sgt A.E. Messer | **A/G** Sgt E. Walton | **A/G** Sgt W.S. Rausch
All killed and interred in Montcony churchyard, France

78 SQUADRON CARRIED OUT many 'gardening' (mine laying) operations. Returning from one such mission on the night of 5th/6th November 1942, Halifax DT525 EY- piloted by Sergeant J.G. Mills made a navigational error and the aircraft crashed on high ground on Byland Moor at 22.30 hours, close to the village of Ampleforth, near Helmsley, Yorkshire. The survivors were taken to York Military hospital. Flight Lieutenant Turner, one of the two fatalities, was the squadron gunnery officer.

Pilot Sgt J.G. Mills | **Nav** F/O H.L. Humphries RCAF
B/A Sgt L. Masterton | **W/Op** Sgt C.M. Edgehill | **F/E** Sgt R. Grey – all injured
A/G Sgt C.F. Clark & **A/G** F/Lt G.T. Turner – both killed

THE ITALIAN PORT OF Genoa again came under attack by aircraft of Nos 4, 5 and 8 Groups, during the night of 7th/ 8th November 1942. Along with the rest of 78 Squadron, Halifax II DT547 EY- took off at 16.52 hours from Linton-on-Ouse, and after an uneventful flight, they arrived over Genoa to find good visibility for the attack. They visually identified the target and a 1,000 bomb was seen to explode in the target area. The jetty, the River and Camogi headland could clearly be seen, also the built up area, and a perfect picture was taken showing Genoa docks. DT547 returned safely to base at 02.00 hours. The crew was:

Pilot Sergeant D. McClelland | **Nav** Sergeant D.W. Griffiths
B/A Sergeant R.W. Church | **W/Op** Sergeant G. Currie | **F/E** Sergeant E. Ackroyd
AG Sergeant J.R. Brown | **AG** C. Stevenson

78 Squadron lost two aircraft during this operation, the first was Halifax II W1063 EY- which took off at 17.00 hours from Linton-on-Ouse. On the

outward journey, one of the engines gave trouble and the pilot F/Lt A.P. Dowse DFC, was forced to shut it down. The crew elected to carry on with the mission and they bombed the target, but realising it was impossible to re-cross the Alps, they set course for Gibraltar. Subsequently, the Halifax was ditched some 8km off the Spanish resort of Valencia. After being rescued, the crew were taken to Albacete where, after a brief period of internment, all were released and allowed to return home via Gibraltar, arriving 5th February 1943.

Pilot F/Lt A.P. Dowse DFC | **Nav** Sgt J. Kershaw | **B/A** Sgt A.H.E. Thompson
W/Op Sgt P. Langsford RNZAF | **F/E** Sgt T.T. Slater
A/G Sgt A.W. Hoare | **A/G** P/O A.N. Orr

The second aircraft to be lost that night was Halifax II DT516 EY-. After taking off at 16.51 hours from Linton-on-Ouse, the crew got ready for the long cold journey over the Alps that would enable them to reach their target. The attack on Genoa was carried out successfully and they turned for home. However, on reaching a point over the North Sea, some 65 miles off Newcastle, they were forced to ditch from lack of fuel. Shortly afterwards they were rescued and returned to base with no one any the worse for their landing in the sea. F/Sgt Newcombe was later commissioned but was killed on operations in May 1944 while serving with 76 Squadron. The crew on the Genoa raid were:

Pilot F/Sgt J. Newcombe | **2nd Plt** Sgt Milan | **Nav** P/O D.R. Vickers
B/A Sgt L.A. Trevors | **W/Op** Sgt D.J. McCoy | **F/E** Sgt F.G. Murphy
A/G Sgt W. Reading | **A/G** Sgt J.R. Coates
All rescued uninjured from the North Sea

A RAID ON TURIN took place on the night of 15th/16th November in which 78 Squadron took part. One of the aircraft successfully completed the bomb run and turned for home, but unfortunately, they ran short of fuel near Martlesham Heath, Suffolk, and were forced to abandon the aircraft. The pilot F/Sgt Martin drowned when he fell into the River Deben, but the rest of the crew survived, though four of them were injured.

Pilot F/Sgt R.F. Martin, drowned in River Deben
Nav Sgt C.L. Morton RCAF, injured but safe
B/A Sgt W.L. Turner, escaped uninjured
W/Op Sgt I.A.L. Lockhart RCAF, injured but safe
F/E Sgt F. Summer, injured but safe
A/G Sgt L. Moran, escaped uninjured
A/G Sgt S.A.E. Parrish, injured but safe

FURTHER ATTACKS TOOK PLACE on Turin were carried out on the 18th and 20th November, when heavy damage was done to the Fiat motor factories. On the night of 28th/29th November, Turin again became the target for an attack. On this occasion a force of 228 aircraft took part. A Halifax belonging to 78 Squadron piloted by Sgt Spragg RCAF ran into difficulties while it was outbound. As the aircraft was climbing in order to gain enough height to cross the Alps, the controls began to ice up and the pilot momentarily lost control of the aircraft. Calling the crew on the intercom, he ordered them to bale out. The mid upper gunner Sgt Evans, recalls:

"I suppose panic stations took over, for I can remember being tangled up for what seemed minutes, though it was probably only seconds. I just could not get myself free. I Finally managed to get out of the turret, and fell in an ungainly heap on the fuselage floor. By now the aircraft was falling away. I must have struck my head on the turret steps when I fell out of the turret, for I was unconscious for a few moments. When I came round, I realised the aircraft was still in the air, but thought everyone had baled out. Putting my head in my hands, I sat waiting for the crash. When it did not come, I looked up and saw the light from a torch winking in the darkness of the forward fuselage. By the time I got to my feet, Sgt Simmonite had reached me, and got me into the rest position, explaining the pilot had managed to regain control of the aircraft, and he had cancelled the abandon aircraft signal. I had been in such a mess that my intercom lead had become disconnected and I never heard the Skipper's call. Unfortunately our rear gunner, P/O Wilbey, had been very quick off the mark and he had jumped out of the aircraft. We heard later that he had landed in France and had reached Spain safely some time later".

RETURNING TO BASE AFTER an attack on Torino, Italy, on the night of 11th/12th December 1942, a serious fire broke out in the port inner engine of a 78 Squadron aircraft. Unable to control it, the crew were forced to ditch in Filey Bay, off the coast of Yorkshire, at 19.00 hours. No injuries were reported. The Aircraft was Halifax II W7764 EY-

Pilot P/O M.P. Matson | Nav Sgt G.E. Coleman | B/A Sgt L. McKinnon
W/Op Sgt G.P. Bailey | F/E Sgt R.G. Head RCAF
A/G Sgt T.R. Galbraith | A/G Sgt W. Bamford
All escaped uninjured

BAD WEATHER DURING DECEMBER curtailed bombing raids substantially, and those that were flown involved a number of losses. During a raid on Duisburg on the night of 20th/21st December, one of the 78 Squadron aircraft was badly damaged by flak. Whilst on the return journey, it sent out calls for help at 21.15 and 21.19 hours, moments later, both engines on the port side failed, and the bomber began to lose height. Eventually it came down in the sea at 22.58 hours, roughly 30 miles NE of Great Yarmouth, Norfolk. There were only two survivors and they were taken to the RAF hospital at Ely, suffering from injuries sustained in the crash. Four of the crew are commemorated on the Runnymede Memorial. The body of the seventh member of the crew was laid to rest in Yarmouth. The aircraft was Halifax II DT509 EY-

Pilot F.Sgt J.A. Hunter RCAF, Killed, Runnymede Memorial
Nav P/O A.L. Fox RCAF, Killed, Great Yarmouth (Caister) Cemetery
B/A F/Sgt W.J. Ashworth RCAF, Injured, but safe
W/Op WO2 E.C. Malone RCAF, Killed, Runnymede Memorial
F/E Sgt C.R. Baillie RCAF, Killed, Runnymede Memorial
A/G Sgt A.W. Edwards, Killed, Runnymede Memorial
A/G F/Sgt J.L.R. Kingsley RCAF, Killed, Runnymede Memorial

THESE WERE THE LAST casualties to be suffered by 78 Squadron during 1942. Between January and December 1942, 78 Squadron lost 5 Whitley Mk Vs, and 36 Halifax Mk II on operations, and a further 3 Halifax Mk II in ground incidents. 160 aircrew were killed, 31 injured and 35 made prisoners of war: 3 crew members evaded capture and made it back to England with the aid of Comete (the underground movement). A further seven were interned in Spain, but eventually returned to the UK via Gibraltar. 51 aircrew survived crashes in this country while returning from operations or in air tests while preparing for raids.

By January 1943 most of the main line bomber squadrons had been equipped with the new breed of 4-engine bomber, either the Short Stirling, Handley Page Halifax or Avro Lancaster, though the Vickers Wellington was still being used by some squadrons. Added to this were the trials continually carried out with Oboe, by 49 Squadron, with three raids on Essen over a four-night period. A second electronic aid was H2s. This was a map reading device that could be used not only for blind bombing but also for navigation. An H2s scanner was installed in a bomber, allowing the navigator to differentiate between water and land and between built up areas and open countryside. It did not need to depend on a ground transmitter and proved far superior to Oboe and the existing Gee system.

The Germans had not been slow when it came to finding ways to counter the ever increasing numbers of bombers attacking the heavy industrial area of the Ruhr. Many more of their night fighters were now being equipped with Lichtenstein airborne radar, and this device that enabled their fighters to increase their toll on bombers. Another weapon being installed in the Messerschmitt Bf110 night fighters was a powerful 20mm upward pointing cannon known as *Schrage Musik*.[1] Just a single hit with this lethal weapon on a lightly armoured bomber could prove enough to bring it down, especially if the fuel tanks were hit.

1943 WAS TO BE the year in which the Ruhr Valley became the main target for Bomber Command, commencing on the night of 5th/6th March, and continuing until 18th/19th July, it inflicted destruction on a scale hitherto unknown. There is no doubt that without this setback, the Germans would have been able to hold the Allies at bay for much longer. Though they doggedly carried out repairs to their damaged factories, they could never again achieve the productive capacity they had previously delivered.

During the first weeks of the year, 78 Squadron carried out several raids without incurring any losses, the only incident being on 20th January, when Halifax II DT577 overshot the runway while attempting to land at Linton-on-Ouse, wrecking the undercarriage. Fortunately, none of the crew was injured. The pilot was F/Sgt J.G. Gillow.

On the night of 27th/28th January 78 Squadron joined aircraft from 51, 76 and 102 Squadrons in an attack on Dusseldorf. Pathfinder Mosquitos had already dropped marker flares on the target area, together with coloured flares. The bombing that followed was well concentrated and heavy damage was done to the industrial area of Dusseldorf. Though seven aircraft were lost in the attack, all the 78 Squadron aircraft returned safely to Linton-on-Ouse.

The brief respite without casualties that 78 Squadron had been enjoying was brought to an end when the crews were ordered to attend a briefing on 3rd February. On being told the target that night was to be Hamburg, senior officers warned everyone present that in the coming months many more attacks would be carried out on this important port, with its aircraft industries, oil plants and large submarine construction yards, along with many other factories manufacturing materials that were vital to the German

---

[1] This weapon derives its name from the German term for Jazz Music. Jazz was considered decadent and banned by the Nazis but many Germans tuned in to foreign radio stations in order to hear it. *Schrage Musik* literally translates as 'angular music' and this term was applied sardonically to the upward-angled cannon fitted in the rear of the cockpit of Luftwaffe night fighters, which was fired into the vulnerable underbelly of the RAF bombers after the night fighter had taken up position below, hidden in its victim's blind spot.

War Industry. That night, as the bombers were approaching their target, they saw a wall of searchlights awaiting them. The flak soon commenced and although most of the air crews had experienced flak before, the intensity of this barrage was enough to test the nerves of even the most experienced crew.

Whilst carrying out its bomb run over the target, one of the 78 Squadron aircraft was lost, it was Halifax II W7938 EY-U. After taking off at 18.15 hours from Linton-on-Ouse, it was shot down by a night fighter (Hptm Wolfgang Thimmig, III./NJG1), It crashed at 20.13 hours near Vechta. Five of the crew rest in Sage War Cemetery and two are buried in the Rheinberg War Cemetery. The crew was:

Pilot P/O F. Buchanan | **Nav** F/Sgt H.W. Laughlan RCAF
B/A P/O F.A. Davies | **W/Op** F/Sgt V.R. Wood | **F/E** Sgt C. Milburn
A/G Sgt W.J. Higgs | **A/G** Sgt A.F. McDonald RCAF

During the remainder of the month, all the squadrons in 4 Group took part in raids on Nurnberg and Koln. Fortunately, all of 78 Squadron's aircraft returned safely to base.

On returning to base from a gardening operation on the night of 2nd/3rd March, Halifax II DT770 EY- overshot and crashed some 1,200 yards beyond the runway, after slicing through the tops of nearby trees. One of the crew died in the crash landing and the rest were injured. They were:

Pilot Sgt A.R. Short | **2nd Pilot** F/Sgt A.H. Evans | **Nav** Sgt, R.E.J. White (killed)
B/A Sgt J.B. Brophy | **W/Op** Sgt R.G. Perrett | **F/E** P/O B.W. Ingham
A/G Sgt V. Delaroy-Hall | **A/G** Sgt T. Ellwood

CHAPTER 6

The Battle of the Ruhr

T
WO DAYS LATER THE C-IN-C Air Chief Marshal Sir Arthur Harris
signalled the start of the Battle of the Ruhr. He and his Deputy
Commander, Sir Robert Saundby had under their command 37
heavy four-engine bomber squadrons, giving a strength of 690 aircraft,
and 16 twin-engine bomber squadrons, with a further 250 aircraft.

Sir Arthur stated:

> "At long last we have the new RDF aids and the aircraft. We are now ready
> and equipped. Bomber Command's main offensive and task is to destroy
> the main cities of the Ruhr."

BY MAY THE NUMBER of aircraft in Bomber Command, thanks to the
dedication of workers in the aircraft was well over a thousand. It was a
significant difference to the raid that had taken place on Cologne in May
1942, when the majority of the aircraft that took part, were twin-engine
Wellington bombers, many of them aircraft that had been used by front
line squadrons to carry out bombing raids during 1941, before being used
by OTUs to train new crews who were urgently needed to replace those
lost on the nightly raids being carried out over enemy territory.

Thanks to the efficiency of the Empire Air Training Scheme, hundreds
of new aircrew arrived from OTUs to replace crews who went missing from
the squadrons every time an operation took place. Squadron Leader Gilbert
Howarth later wrote: *"Men went missing during the night but replacements
were on site by 08:00 hours the following morning. No gaps were ever visible
in the ranks."* There was no question or doubt that Bomber Command had
the capacity and the resolve to continue the momentum of the campaign.

78 Squadron was one of ten squadrons in 4 Group to take part in the
raid on Essen on 5th/6th March 1943. 12 Halifaxes took off at 18:00 hours
from Linton-on-Ouse, though two were forced to turn back due to
operating faults. Weather conditions on the way to the target were
reasonably good, and as they got nearer, they could see the Pathfinders
had dropped their markers accurately. The aircraft of 4 Group were in the
first wave to bomb and soon the city of Essen became an inferno. Aerial
reconnaissance photographs taken the following day showed an area of

160 acres destroyed, with Krupp's armament factory and the main power station and the gasworks almost completely destroyed. Thousands of houses were also destroyed or badly damaged, leaving around 30,000 people homeless.

The Ruhr Valley now had the most formidable defence force in Germany and each time it came under attack the bomber crews had to face not only hundreds of searchlights and anti-aircraft guns but also the Luftwaffe night fighter squadrons, for this vast industrial area was surrounded by fighter airfields and their fighters exacted a heavy toll on the bomber force. After this raid it was found that Bomber Command had lost sixteen aircraft and 75 air crew had been killed, with 18 being made prisoners of war. 78 Squadron lost one aircraft, shot down by a night fighter (Hptm Herberet Lutje, III./NJG1). It crashed at 21.35 hours between Rouveen and Staphorst (Overjissel), Holland. The 3 crew members who died were buried in Staphorst (Rouveen) New General Cemetery. The remained of the crew became POWs. The aircraft was Halifax II HR687 EY-

Pilot P/O J.R. Thompson, killed, Staphorst Cemetery, Holland
2nd **Pilot** F/Sgt K.W. Mercer, POW, Stalag 344 Lamsdorf
Nav Sgt A. Loveland, POW, Stalag Luft 3 Sagan
B/A F/Sgt A.C. Layshon, POW, Stalag Luft 3 Sagan
W/Op F/Sgt A.E. Blackwell, killed, Staphorst Cemetery, Holland
F/E F/Sgt O.V. Proctor, POW, Stalag 344 Lamsdorf
A/G Sgt E.C.B. Williams, killed, Staphorst Cemetery, Holland
A/G W/O D.R. Chiswell, POW, Stalag 344 Lamsdorf

78 SQUADRON WERE PART of a large force of bombers to carry out another raid on Essen on the night of 12th/13th March. On this occasion 4 Group supplied the major number of aircraft in the force, which included Halifaxes, Lancasters, Stirlings and Wellingtons. They were led by ten Oboe-equipped Mosquitos, who again, accurately marked out the giant Krupps works for the bombers that followed close behind, several of them soon becoming 'coned' by dozens of searchlights. When this happened, the accurate flak guns were not slow in getting the range and before long bombers could be seen falling away. Nearly 500 tons of high explosives were dropped and over five hundred tons of incendiaries, causing huge fires to break out. Photographic reconnaissance later showed a great deal more damage had been done than on the previous raid. Details later released by the Germans showed that 500 homes had been destroyed, 198 people killed in Essen and 39 killed in Bottrop, a neighbouring town.

The price paid by the RAF was also high: 23 aircraft were lost, 14 by the intense flak, with a further 7 claimed by the night fighters. Two others cannot be accounted for. 132 air crew were killed and 22 made prisoners of war.

78 Squadron lost one aircraft, shot down by one of the night fighters and it crashed at 21.48 hours, close to a farm building near the hamlet of Grafwegen, on the western edge of Reichswald, very close to the Dutch/German border, roughly 3 km from Groesbeek, Holland. The crew were all killed and buried in Uden Cemetery, Holland. The aircraft was Halifax II DT774 EY-E.

Pilot F/Sgt F.A. Marean RCAF | **Nav** Sgt H. Bentley | **B/A** Sgt W.H. Gosnell
W/Op Sgt W.J. McClelland | **F/E** Sgt C.G. Dyer
A/G Sgt G.E. Benson | **A/G** Sgt B.M. Singleton
All killed and buried in Uden Cemetery, Holland

THE BOMBERS RETURNED TO the Ruhr again on the night of 26th/27th March. This time it was the turn of Duisburg to receive the attention of Bomber Command. A force of 455 aircraft took off from their bases in various parts of England. Among them were 112 Halifaxes from 4 and 6 Groups in Yorkshire. This operation was doomed to failure from the very start, for six of the nine Oboe-equipped Mosquitoes had to turn back with faulty sets. With 10/10ths cloud over the target and little or no help from Pathfinder aircraft, the bombing was very scattered. One thing in their favour was that the cloud prevented the searchlights from finding the bombers, but the heavy flak caused severe damage to several of them.

Halifax II W7931 EY-J of 78 Squadron had taken off from Linton-on-Ouse at 19.02 hours and was on the outbound journey when it was crippled by flak. The crew abandoned the aircraft, which crashed at 22.00 hours at Gaanderen-pinneddijk (Gelderland), 5 km SE of Doetinchem, Holland, killing three crew members. They were laid to rest in Doetinchem (Loolan) General Cemetery. The crew was:

Pilot F/Sgt J.M. Tait, killed, Doetinchem Cemetery, Holland
2nd Pilot Sgt J.A. Wilson RNZAF, killed, Doetinchem Cemetery, Holland
Nav F/O S. Hauxwell, POW, Stalag Luft 3 Sagan
B/A W/O G.R. Johnstone, POW, Stalag 357 Kopernikus
W/Op F/Lt R.W. Keen, POW, Stalag Luft 3 Sagan
F/E W/O F.E. Lemon, POW, Stalag 357 Kopernikus
A/G Sgt A. Wilson, killed, Doetinchem Cemetery, Holland
A/G Sgt R.R. Hulleat, POW, Stalag 357 Kopernikus

Berlin was the target for two heavy raids at the end of March. During the first attack F/Lt Dowse and his crew, in Halifax II JB784 EY-S, strayed off track and ran into difficulties, as Sergeant Phil Langsford recalls:

"As I remember, in the early stages of the flight, all went well. However, we came unstuck near Bremen, soon after crossing the coast. We were flying at our maximum height of 19,000 feet over a layer of 10/10ths cloud, which was several thousand feet below us. Presumably, through a navigation error, we flew into the Bremen defences, because all of a sudden, we were being bracketed by predicted flak that was very accurate. Our aircraft was filled with cordite fumes from the nearby bursts.

The skipper did a marvellous job of throwing the Halifax all over the sky, and we managed to shake off the flak, but not before a nearby burst sheared off one of the blades from the port inner propeller, which promptly struck the fuselage, smashing its way into the cabin, not far from my position below the pilot. The aircraft immediately went out of control, due to the disabled motor, and we lost several thousand feet as the skipper struggled to regain control. He ordered us to abandon the aircraft (fortunately, he cancelled the instruction in time, having regained control).

Our bombs had been jettisoned during this episode and we now headed, hopefully, in a direction which would take us back to Linton-on-Ouse. Meanwhile our navigator had lost all his instruments and both of the compasses were unserviceable, the astrodome had been sliced off by a shell splinter, just like taking the top off an egg. In addition, my wireless was on the blink, but with the help of the navigator, who held the internals of the set while I did the necessary repairs, I was able to get it working once more, and then put out a QDM (a magnetic course to steer with zero wind in degrees and time) this entailed contacting three widely spaced D/F stations in England, who took bearings on my signal and then transmitted our position back to us. Whoever those operators were, they did a magnificent job. I gave the bearings to our navigator, who in turn eventually got us safely back home."

DURING THE NIGHT OF 29th/30th March, 78 Squadron became part of a force that set out to attack Berlin. However, severe icing and electrical storms encountered over the North Sea forced 95 aircraft to return to their bases. Those that struggled to get through to the target found it devoid of cloud cover. The route markers that had been dropped to enable the bombers to do a timed run to the target were too far to the south, due to bad weather encountered whilst en route. Many of the crews were so far off route, that they made no attempt to go to the datum point at Muggel See, but bombed well south of the markers instead. Altogether six aircraft were lost on this operation and one of them was a 78 Squadron aircraft, Halifax II W7939 EY- which had taken off at 21.36 hours from Linton-on-

Ouse but after climbing to 8,000 feet encountered engine problems, forcing the crew to jettison the bomb load. Shortly afterwards they abandoned the aircraft about three miles from Malton, Yorkshire. All the crew escaped although two of them were injured.

Pilot Sgt K.A. Toon RNZAF | **Nav** Sgt R. Falcus
B/A Sgt H.J. Burridge | **W/Op** Sgt J. Whelan RAAF
F/E Sgt L. Donaldson | **A/G** Sgt G. Campbell | **A/G** Sgt J.R. Sands
All escaped, two injured

THE FOLLOWING NIGHT IT was back to the Ruhr for 78 Squadron. Taking off at 21.30 hours, they joined squadrons from Nos 1, 3, 4, 5, 6 and 8 Groups to attack Essen. Arriving over the target area, the force, which was comprised of Lancasters, Halifaxes and Wellingtons, found there was no cloud cover and conditions were reasonably clear, so they dropped red markers. Unfortunately, some Mosquito crews also dropped red markers, and this double marking caused some confusion among several of the bomber crews that took part in the attack.

Intense night fighter activity was reported, even in the areas of heavy flak and the concentration of searchlights was the greatest they had encountered to date over the Ruhr. That night 466 tons of high explosives were dropped and a further 210 tons of incendiaries. Reconnaissance photographs taken later showed widespread damage in the centre and western half of the city. Losses in 4 Group amounted to eight Halifaxes, three of them being from 78 Squadron. The first was Halifax II W7937 EY-

Pilot F/O T.N. Foster, missing, Runnymede Memorial
Nav W/O G. Sendall, POW, Stalag 357 Kopernikus
B/A F/Lt H. Jamieson, POW, Stalag Luft 3 Sagan
W/Op F/Sgt E.A. Drury, POW, Stalag Luft 6 Heydekrug
F/E Sgt W.F. Hodgson, POW, Stalag 357 Kopernikus
A/G F/Sgt C. Wayte, POW, Stalag 357 Kopernikus
A/G F/Sgt N.V. Thornton, POW, Stalag Luft 6 Heydekrug

The second aircraft lost that night was Halifax II DT780 EY- which crashed near Monchengladbach, killing two members of the crew, who were buried in Stadfriedhof and later re-interred at Rheinberg War Cemetery.

Pilot P/O G. Riach, killed, Rheinberg War Cemetery
2ⁿᵈ Pilot S/Ldr B.J. Bourchier, POW, Stalag Luft 3 Sagan
Nav F/Sgt E.C. Lacey, POW, Stalag 357 Kopernikus
B/A W/O W. Inglis, POW, Stalag Luft 7 Bankau-Kreulberg
W/Op W/O D.H. Howard, POW, Stalag 357 Kopernikus

F/E Sgt A.M. Parker, killed, Rheinberg War Cemetery
A/G Sgt A. Wright, POW, Camp details not known
A/G Sgt L.L. Stas, POW, Stalag 357 Kopernikus

The third aircraft to be lost that night was Halifax II JB845 EY- which was shot down by a night fighter near the town of Nederweert in the Netherlands, killing all on board. Six were buried at Eindhoven (Woensel) General Cemetery. Sergeant Dunlap's remains were laid to rest in the Canadian War Cemetery, Groesbeek, Holland. The crew was:

Pilot F/Lt T.H.O. Richardson | **Nav** Sgt C.R.C.A. Allberry
B/A Sgt R.J. Kernick | **W/Op** F/O L.R.C. Shadwell
F/E Sgt R.O.M. Dunlap | **A/G** Sgt J. McCormick | **A/G** Sgt T.H. Webb

Fifty-five years after the war had ended, a friend of one of the crew members, Miss Betty-Irene Roberts, was taken to visit the site where Halifax JB845 had crashed on that fateful night in 1943, killing her friend, Sgt Jack McCormick, the mid-upper gunner. Miss Roberts related this sad story:

> "Although I had visited the cemetery at Eindhoven twice, I had not visited the crash site in the woods near Nederweert. I was taken there by some men who were only boys on the night that Halifax JB845 was shot down. They saw the plane crash and afterwards gathered shrapnel pieces."

Later she met the Catholic Priest (who by then was 90 years old) who had said the last rites over the wreckage. He told her. "One of those 'boys' is now a well known Dutch Military Historian, who has been decorated by the Queen of the Netherlands."

Miss Roberts continued. "By order of the Dutch Government, the crash site is now entitled a 'Peace Haven' where no cars or radios are allowed, just walkers and cyclists. It really is a lovely place." (Miss Roberts kindly sent me a photograph of the crash site in the woods near Nederweert, that was taken on the occasion of her visit there in 1998).

It appears, Halifax JB845 EY- took off at 20.00 hours from Linton-on-Ouse on the night of 3rd April 1943 to take part in an attack on Essen. Whilst on the return flight it was caught in the beam of a searchlight and reported to the Luftwaffe night fighter base at Venlo, on the Dutch side of the Dutch-German border, and shot down by one of their fighters.

Since receiving that letter from Miss Roberts I have received a letter from Mrs Joan Bayley, sister of Flight Lieutenant T.H.O. Richardson, the pilot of Halifax JB845. I understand the two ladies are friends who correspond with each other from time to time. Mrs Bayley's letter was accompanied by a copy of a Dutch-German report on the shooting down of JB845. A rough translation of this reads:

> Report of crashed airplane.
>
> To: Chief Inspector for the protection of the population against air attack, 23 Heerengracht, The Hague.
>
> Nederweert 4 April 1943
>
> To-day at 1600 hours, the Brigade-Commander of the Mareshaussee at Nederweert reports that in this municipality, locally known as Koolhofdijk, a four engined English airplane (Hurricane)[1] has been found. This airplane has probably fallen during the night of 3 April 1943 at about 0400 hours, in consequence of an air fight.
>
> As the airplane did not burn, it was not possible to ascertain exactly when it dropped. It was found later by the population of the vicinity.
>
> Some Mareshaussees of the above brigade went immediately to the indicated spot and reported the following:
>
> The airplane is totally smashed: Of the crew (probably four to six persons), one was found dead, and another heavily wounded. A guard of German soldiers was already present. Damage to the forest in which the airplane has fallen, could not be stated.
>
> Afterwards another three dead members of the crew were found in the vicinity, so that in total, four dead men and one severely injured man were found.
>
> The local leader of air defence, The Burgomaster.

The second report, from the same address, ran as follows:

> Nederweert 6 April 1943
>
> In connection with the report of 4 April 1943, I have to report that another dead member of the crew has been found by the guard of the airplane. The man who was severely injured, died meanwhile in hospital at Weert, so in total there are six dead men.[2]
>
> The local Leader of air defence,
>
> A.S.O.

THE BATTLE OF THE Ruhr continued, with Kiel becoming the target for an attack on the night of 4th/5th April. A force of 577 aircraft took part in this operation to bomb the important German port. It was followed by a raid on Duisburg on the 8th/9th April, in which 392 aircraft took part. The

---

[1] How the aircraft came to be identified as a Hurricane is somewhat of a mystery.

[2] The number of crew is also wrong; seven men have been officially accounted for.

two operations cost Bomber Command 37 aircraft, 203 air crew killed and 23 made prisoners of war. One airman succeeded in evading capture. No.78 Squadron were fortunate in not suffering any casualties, though they did lose an aircraft, when it returned early from the Duisberg raid and crash landed at 23.05 hours. No injuries to the crew were reported. It was Halifax II JB857 EY-

Pilot P/O D. McClelland | **Nav** F/Sgt J.W. Beals | **B/A** P/O E.E. Tingley
W/Op Sgt E.J. Currie | **F/E** Sgt H. Ackroyd
A/G Sgt J.R. Brown | **A/G** P/O G.C. Stevenson
All escaped uninjured

AN ATTACK ON THE heavily-defended city of Frankfurt by aircraft from 1, 3, 4, 5, 6 and 8 Groups took place on the night of 10th/11th April. The aircraft of 78 Squadron took off at 23.30 hours from Linton-on-Ouse and made their way to the rendezvous point. This operation was badly hampered by low cloud over the target. Nearly 500 tons of high explosive and incendiary bombs were dropped on the target, inflicting serious damage. Losses amounted to 23 aircraft, 100 air crew killed, 2 badly injured and 14 made prisoners of war. Seven men succeeded in evading capture.

78 Squadron lost one aircraft. This ill-fated sortie had begun when Halifax DT775 EY-F, piloted by Sgt Jack Adams, took off from Linton-on-Ouse at 23.34 hours. This account of the flight was written by crewmember Sergeant Stan Reed in 1945:

"Halifax heavy bomber DT775 coded F-Freddie of No.78 Squadron, No 4 Group, Bomber Command RAF, together with 500 odd aircraft comprised of Lancasters, Halifaxes, Stirlings and Wellingtons, were heading for Frankfurt am Main, Germany, on the night of 10th April 1943. All were taking part in the Battle of the Ruhr, Bomber Command's Spring offensive for 1943. We had flown down from our base at Linton-on-Ouse, in Yorkshire, an established pre-war RAF station which we then shared with our sister squadron No 76. We had left the English coast at Dungeness on Kent's south shore, the main force's concentration point that night, and headed across the English Channel for Dieppe, in France.

I was the regular rear gunner of the crew of F-Freddie, which we had christened F-Firkin, and had been with them since we crewed up together at No 10 OTU Abingdon in Oxfordshire, in the previous October. We considered ourselves to be a happy band of airborne warriors, very compatible, all dead keen but alas, still very green operationally.

The crew was:

Pilot; Jack Adams, then 21 years of age. He had worked in the accounts department of London Fire Brigade prior to joining the RAF. A damned good pilot, with a safe pair of hands.

Navigator; Philip Hyden, was an ex-public school type with the looks, charm, manners and accent to go with it. 21 years old and came from a military family who resided in Aldershot, Hampshire. Joined the RAF straight from his public school, a very likeable chap was old Phil. He was a spot on navigator, who was very competent and always managed to get us back to base on time.

Bomb Aimer; Stan Hurrell was from Totnes, in Devon, where he lived with his widowed Mother. A quiet studious type, with a soft Devon Brogue, he had been a Post Office counter clerk before joining the RAF. He was in his 23rd year and known as Grandad, before Joe Enright joined us. Another dead keen character who was most conscientious over his bomb aiming. He brought back the best bombing photos of the St Nazaire operation of 2nd April, which had targeted the U-Boat pens situated there.

Wireless Operator; Clifford Price. Junior as he was known by virtue of his tender years. He was then 19 years old, came from Surrey and was a single man. He had been in a solicitor's office prior to joining the RAF. A nice quiet lad, small in stature then and very boyish. A good footballer, a centre forward who could score goals. An excellent wireless operator too, who could always provide us with some good music on the aircraft's radio when we were on a long cross country exercise.

Flight Engineer; Nobby Clarke whose Christian name was Matthew, which he never used in the RAF. Another single man who came from Bury St Edmunds in deepest Suffolk, with a broad brogue to confirm this. He joined the RAF on the outbreak of war and trained at Halton as an aero engine fitter. A silent type, who was not given to saying very much. He lived for his beloved Rolls Royce aero engines, and was also 21 years of age.

Mid Upper Gunner; Joe Enright. Christian names Jethro Nathaniel, but always known as Joe in the RAF. He was 28 years of age, and he was the oldest man in the crew. A married man with a small Daughter, he came from County Durham and was a taciturn 'Geordie'. The only member of the crew we never got to know. He and Nobby Clarke joined us at the Heavy Conversion Unit at Riccall and neither had been with us all that long.

Rear Gunner; Myself, Stanley George Reed, 21 years of age and recently married (October 1942). Came from Purfleet in Essex, then a straggling riverside village on the Thames, some twenty odd miles downstream from London. I had worked in a local cardboard mill before joining the RAF. Considered myself a very conscientious plodder. I was dead keen and very proud to be a member of the crew of F-Firkin. Like Nobby Clarke, was then very much a country lad.

The particular Halifax we were flying, a fairly new kite which hadn't done too many operations, was a Mk II Series 1 (Special) of which the nose and mid upper turrets had been removed, to help improve the rather poor performance of this mark of Halifax. The mid upper gunner now manned a ventral position while on operations, looking downwards through a small Perspex blister fitted in the floor of the aircraft just aft of the rear door. A position that was not well sought after, as it entailed laying flat on the floor of the kite for some hours with one's head in the Perspex blister.

This ventral position had been brought into being to assist in reducing the heavy losses of Halifax bombers on operations, caused by the deadly below attacks so favoured by Jerry night fighters. Alas, the position was not then armed, as it later became with a point five Calibre Browning machine gun. An intercom point, oxygen outlet together with a signal light and switch had been installed alongside the blister, but no form of heating was provided, and a cold draughty position it was indeed.

On the night in question, I had flown down to the South Coast sitting up alongside our skipper Jack Adams, as a passenger and occupying the second pilot's seat (for when we carried one), whilst Joe Enright manned the rear turret until it was time for me to take over, somewhere out over the English Channel. I very much enjoyed riding up front in the second pilot's seat, in the utter dark of the night, watching avidly all that went on about me with some great interest, it all being so different to my lonely vigil in the rear turret. I remember so well that trip down to the south coast, from our base in Yorkshire, studying Jack At the controls, clad in his leather Irvin flying jacket, helmeted with his face half hidden behind his oxygen mask, in the dim red glow from the instruments on the panel before him, and the sense of being at the very heart of this huge powerful bomber that I felt so privileged to be aboard that night. Well, I have said that I was dead keen in those days, haven't I?

An enormous roar, a deafening constant roar from the four big aero engines. Rolls Royce Merlins dominated everything else up front. I was conscious of Nobby Clarke our flight engineer, Irvin clad and helmeted, behind me, busy as always at his engineer's panel of instruments, but other than those two, no one else could be seen. Phil Hyden, Cliff Price and Stan Hurrell being at their respective positions on the lower deck of the Halifax, beneath and in front of me.

Having left the English coast and soon, well out over the English Channel, I prepared myself to go aft and take up my normal station in the rear turret for the remainder of the operation. I gathered up my parachute pack and the rest of my gear, including a big thermos flask of hot coffee, then discovered that the microphone of my face mask had gone unserviceable and no amount of banging, the usual remedy we employed, would clear the fault, although I could hear perfectly well enough through my flying helmet earphones. We didn't have a spare headset on board unfortunately, and I made a mental note to draw a spare set from stores come the morrow. It was there-upon decided by Jack, that Joe Enright would now remain in the rear turret for the remainder of the trip, and I would take up the ventral position in his place. It being most essential of course that the rear gunner was able to communicate with the pilot in particular. With one's microphone u/s or even if the intercom system on the aircraft became unserviceable, communication was still possible between crew members and their pilot by means of small signal lights fitted at all crew positions. Any trouble for instance aft, would have been passed immediately to the pilot by flashing the appropriate letter in morse code, say the letter 'F' on the signal light smartly. F stood for fighter! The pilot would then immediately take avoiding action by frantically commencing to weave the aircraft until hopefully clear of danger. In an emergency, we could get by with the signal light system only, but under the present circumstances it was most essential that Joe stayed in the rear turret, as it was our sole means of defence.

So I settled down in the blister position aft, laying on some none too clean canvas engine covers, which were stowed in the aircraft adjacent to the ventral blister position. I had done one operation with my head in that Perspex blister which did not suit me at all, but could not do anything about it then, other than make the best of the situation. After all, it was my 'mike' that had gone u/s wasn't it? For I very much appreciated being in the rear turret, I always felt very much at home behind those four Browning machine guns with a little armour plate beneath my seat. I felt rather naked and very vulnerable no laying flat out, so to speak, on the Halifax's thin metal floor. I flashed Jack up on my signal light to let him know that I was in place and received a reassuring acknowledgement in return. Then settled down to gaze upon an awful lot of nothingness below me, and it was damned cold too, laying in this blister position with no heating available.

I could hear the rest of the crew going about their duties, with Jack quietly in command and not saying much. The navigator informed the pilot their Gee set was practically u/s due to enemy interference, and he would have to rely on his D/R plot. Stan Hurrell in his bomb aimers position in the nose of the aircraft was busying himself looking out for Pathfinder flares and markers which should be showing up soon, as we approached our next turning point. To the north of Dieppe I recall. Cliff Price was conscientiously searching his allotted wave band hoping to pick up any Jerry night fighter controllers nattering to their airborne charges, so that he could give them a blast from a microphone positioned alongside one of our Merlin engines and thus interrupt their broadcasts with some lovely aero engine noises. Nobby Clarke was engaged in checking his petrol tank gauges and effecting changeovers in flight as petrol was used, and we used an awful lot of petrol when airborne. Joe Enright in the tail behind me, sought permission from Jack to test the guns in the rear turret. I then heard the familiar rattle as Joe fired off a short burst from the four .303 Browning machine guns. Only that morning with his help, I had harmonised those very guns down to 100 yards.

On approaching the French coast, Jack warned us of this fact; it was always a gut tightening occasion and it had the effect of putting everyone on their mettle Jack then commenced a gentle weave (A winding course on a general heading of intended flight with variations of height) to distract enemy fighters and predicted radar controlled flak. Having announced his intention to do so, and we crossed the French coast just north of Dieppe, per Phil Hyden's calculations. There was no flak near us, at least as far as I could see from my downward looking blister, and no one mentioned seeing any close to us up front either. Stan Hurrell counted the yellow PFF flares I remembered, aloud. I recall that we were next heading towards Metz in eastern France where there was to be another change of course again hopefully on PFF markers. Jack then warned us that we were now in the Jerry night fighter belt, which in those days ran in some depth along the enemy coast from Spain up to the German border proper.

Now, nothing keeps one on one's toes so to speak, than the prospect of being caught by a Jerry night fighter. It certainly tends to concentrate the mind wonderfully.

All however was going well on board F-Firkin, the four aero engines were all roaring on, all was now very quiet up front with just the occasional word from Phil warning Jack of a slight alteration of course. The golden rule among our crew and amongst the majority of all crews in Bomber Command, was that no one spoke on the intercom whilst over enemy territory unless one had to, Jack did however, speak to each one of us individually from time to time with quiet words of encouragement which always went down well amongst us. All was completely dark below me. It must have been 10/10ths cloud cover all over northern Europe that night. We duly turned on our new heading over Metz amid a sprinkling of yellow PFF markers, but other than the markers I saw nothing at all of that French City beneath me. So we flew on, weaving now more vigorously, with everybody on the 'qui vive' maintaining a close vigil of the black sky all about us and not only for Jerry fighters, but also for any of our own aircraft in the bomber stream which although unseen, were all around us, in case one might get too close for comfort.

I was still looking downwards with my head in the Perspex blister, seeing absolutely nothing at all, when out of the utter nothingness below me and a little astern of us came several blinding lines of very bright green lights, tracer and lot of it. Christ! I remember crying out. A bloody night fighter has caught us from below. The lines of tracer tore into us at a terrible speed. We were raked from our tail to the nose of the Hali', it did then so appear in just one long savage burst which could not have lasted for more than two perhaps three seconds. The noise was considerable, above the roar of the engines too, it was as if a giant was tearing up sheets of corrugated iron by hand and doing it very fast indeed. It was 20mm cannon fire in fact that was hitting us, and some of the cannon shells were exploding on impact in bright little splashed of light. How I was not hit I just do not know for the tracer appeared to go round me as it flashed by, with me laying there on the engine covers on the floor of the Hali' as if frozen stiff. I heard faintly over the intercom that someone had been hit, and was not surprised considering the amount of cannon fire we had taken.

Fire must have broken out immediately amidships where the main petrol tanks were located and also our bomb load, which consisted mainly of incendiary bombs in their metal containers, and streamed back underneath the aircraft.

I saw nothing of the night fighter that had caught us, the Jerry pilot obviously knew his profession very well, creeping up on us as he had done so, quite unseen beneath us, entirely on his airborne radar no doubt, and then hit us plumb amidships, where he could do the most damage, and all in the one short burst too.An 'Experten' for sure. He must have stood off and watched our demise with great satisfaction. I was later told by the Germans, after my capture, that a Me BF110 night fighter had shot us down and that we were just one of the twenty bombers that had been brought down during the night of the Frankfurt raid.

Cliff had been hit in the leg I could now hear over the intercom, and Nobby was saying he had badly burnt his hands. No one else fortunately appeared to have been hit in the attack. Which seemed miraculous to me then, considering what had gone by me and struck up front. There was some shouting going on, and a bit of flap but no real panic at all was evident. I heard nothing from Joe in the turret behind me, but that was not unusual as Joe never did say much, nor had I heard his guns firing. He couldn't have seen the fighter either, then.

I gathered quickly from what was going on up front that we were now well alight and that it was impossible to control the fire let alone put it out. All this happened within a few brief seconds, though at the time, it appeared to last for an age. Whereas in actual fact, from the moment of the attack to the time Jack time Jack Adams our Skipper, and the last to leave our doomed Halifax, baled out, Less than twenty seconds only, was to pass.

Time, then I recall, certainly did seem to stand still as far as I was concerned. The cannon shells had whizzed past me, all hell seemed to break loose up front and we were on fire whilst I still lay on the engine covers just two degrees from being absolutely petrified. I do know I found it all very difficult to take in. I still couldn't believe it was all happening to us, it was so unreal, or so it then seemed to me. Was this all a nightmare, I asked myself? This is what happened to other crews – it just could not happen to us, I kept telling myself. I came back to reality rather abruptly when I heard Jack plain and clear over the intercom saying very calmly. 'This is it chaps, better get out quickly, we've had it'. Phil then shouted something about Switzerland, but I had by then pulled my intercom plug out and was making my way to the rear door on the port side of the Halifax, only a few feet away from me, having grabbed my parachute pack from where I had placed it earlier on taking up the ventral blister position, where I could then bale out smartly.

I remember opening the rear door, it opened inwards up to the roof of the aircraft, and then seeing fully for the first time the whole mass of flames tearing past underneath me. CHRIST! I recall saying. It was damned noisy too, with the aircraft door now open. I could plainly see that we had really had it all right. I must get out fast though, before the whole kite exploded. At the now open door, I paused looking down into all that blackness I was about to jump into. Beyond the tearing flames, I saw two bodies flash by, so I knew that at least two members of the crew had managed to get out OK. I wondered which two it might be.

I then remember sitting down on the floor of the plane with my legs out of the doorway preparing myself to abandon the Hali' when I must have been either sucked or drawn out by the rushing slipstream tearing past outside our stricken aircraft. In the mere seconds from receiving Jack's 'bale out' call I found myself out in the cold night air, with the huge tail of the stricken Halifax shooting past over my head. She was certainly well on fire amidships and diving away to the ground, obviously out of control. I saw no more bodies leaving her. Was I then the last one out I wondered?

All this flashed through my mind as I sat there, up in the black night and still with no sensation of falling at all, just the bitter cold air all around me. It was time I pulled myself together I thought, and pulled the rip cord of my parachute, for I could easily have counted up to one hundred whilst sitting up here in the sky, and the good book stated that a count of ten would be adequate after leaving an aircraft before pulling the ripcord.

I reached across my chest for the parachute pack that should have been clipped onto stout metal hooks attached to my parachute harness, and in position flat on my chest. I was also seeking in the pitch darkness the metal 'D' ring that I had to pull to operate the ripcord to open the parachute, and found to my utter horror and dismay that there was no familiar pack in place as there should have been. My chest was totally bare, just the naked straps of my parachute harness greeted my groping hands.

The parachute just had to be there – where was it? I there upon died several painful deaths as I realised that I must have left the bloody parachute pack on the floor of the Hali' when I had opened the rear door. So this is it I thought! My bloody lot! Missed all that cannon fire from the Jerry fighter only to buy it like this. Well at least it didn't hurt as yet and I knew that it would not take all that long before it would be all over. There was just sweet nothing I could do about it anyway, but what a way to go. I remember shouting to myself, "… and all, my so-and-so fault for leaving my parachute in the Hali! What a prat I am!" I do recall telling myself this at the time, while sitting up there in the night sky and experiencing no sensation of falling.

Then I became aware of two long straps hanging up in the air above me. These white straps ran from my parachute harness as if attached to my shoulders and I hurriedly grabbed them as a lifeline. I pulled the straps down and 'CHRIST ALMIGHTY!' there was my parachute pack firmly clipped to the hooks at the end of the straps. It was as if the Good Lord in his charity had taken pity on me in my hour of need and had given forth a parachute pack when I so badly required one.

I realised at once what had happened. Due to my rapid exit from the kite, I must have broken the stitching on the two long straps, which were about 5 to 6 feet in length and normally folded neatly onto the front of the parachute harness on one's chest and firmly stitched to keep them in position. Large metal clips were attached to the end of the straps, to which the parachute pack was duly connected. When a parachute was opened by pulling the D-ring of the ripcord, the stitching would break as the 'chute commenced to 'stream' and the long straps unfolded immediately, leaving the parachute pack, now empty, above one's head with the canopy of the fully opened parachute above, connected to its many nylon ropes.

So I clutched my parachute pack firmly to my chest, now that it had been fortuitously returned to me, and thanked the Lord for sparing me. I then pulled the D-ring, thinking as I did so of a sardonic corporal back in the parachute section on the base who delighted in saying, when he handed out the parachute packs to us air crew chaps, "If it doesn't work when you bale out – just bring it back and I'll be pleased to give you another one."

Then – wham – my 'chute opened all right – smack in my face as I clutched my pack even tighter to my chest now that I had got it back, thus giving me an airborne nosebleed. Thus I sustained my first injury on this ill-fated operation. It was hardly a war wound, was it?

I continued to descend, or at least I presumed I was descending, for I had no sensation at all of doing so. Instead of just sitting up there in the dark night sky, as I had been prior to opening the 'chute. I felt now as if I was suspended in the cold night sky, just sitting up there and it was cold, bloody cold in fact, but I must confess that sheer fright had quite a lot to do with my coldness.

Our old Halifax had now disappeared from sight. I couldn't even see it burning on the ground beneath me, as I thought I ought to be able to do. Of course it may have crashed in a lake or river, that would have extinguished the fire immediately, but the cloud cover must have been dense to hide a burning crashed aircraft. A thought then entered my head, that my present predicament certainly put paid to the coming weekend I was going to spend with my wife in York. It was coming up to Easter and we, the crew that is, were due for a 48-hour leave, to be taken over a weekend. My wife and I were looking forward very much to that weekend with our son Jack. Now that had all gone for a Burton, hadn't it?"

Amazingly, there was only one fatality among the crew, that being Sergeant Joe Enright, who had taken Stan Reed's place as the rear gunner. Two members of the crew were injured, Clifford Price, who had been hit in the leg and Nobby Clarke, whose hands were badly burned. Along with four other members of the crew, Stan Reed was taken prisoner and spent the remaining two years of the war in Stalag 357 Kopernikus. Phil Hyden was also taken prisoner but, being an officer, was taken to Stalag Luft 3 Sagan, Silesia. This was a camp that was later to become notorious for the murder of 50 RAF officers by the Gestapo following a mass breakout by 79 prisoners.

Halifax II Mk B2 Series 1 DT775 EY-F
Pilot W/O H.J. Adams, POW, Stalag 357 Kopernikus
Nav F/O P. Hyden, POW, Stalag Luft 3 Sagan
B/A W/O S.V.F. Hurrell, POW, Stalag 357 Kopernikus
W/Op F/Sgt C.J. Price, POW, Stalag 357 Kopernikus
F/E F/Sgt M. Clarke, POW, Stalag 357 Kopernikus
A/G F/Sgt S.G. Reed, POW, Stalag 357 Kopernikus
A/G Sgt J.N. Enright, killed, Briey, France

A RAID ON STUTTGART took place during the night of 14th/15th April, which involved aircraft from Nos 1, 3, 4, 5, 6, and 8 Groups. A force of 462 aircraft comprised of 98 Lancasters, 135 Halifaxes, 83 Stirlings and 146 Wellingtons was assembled, of which 74 aborted their missions for various reasons. Bomber Command Headquarters were becoming very concerned at the high number of aircraft failing to carry out their attacks. Though many had good reason for aborting, the numbers returning were becoming intolerable and Station Commanders were ordered to keep a close eye on the squadrons under their command, the inference being that the top brass believed aircrews to be abandoning their missions for spurious reasons due to unwillingness to run the gauntlet of enemy firepower.

Weather conditions for the Stuttgart raid were very good, with no cloud. Bright moonlight and clear visibility enabled the Pathfinders to mark the target area well for the bombers following close behind. More than 700 tons of high explosive and incendiary bombs were dropped, inflicting widespread damage to the city. But the cost was once again high: 23 aircraft were lost in the attack, 96 air crew were killed and 41 became prisoners of war. Twelve airmen managed to evade capture and eventually made their way back to the United Kingdom.

Pilsen in Czechoslovakia was attacked on the night of 16th/17th April. It was a was a long, boring flight for the crews involved in the attack on the Skoda armament factory, which was the primary target. Taking part in the raid were 327 aircraft, comprised of 197 Lancasters and 130 Halifaxes. This number was reduced when 48 aircraft turned back prematurely, for various reasons. The weather conditions en route were good and the crews found bright moonlight over the target with a layer of high, medium cloud cover at 2-3,000 feet. The Pathfinders dropped 32 target indicators and a large number of flares. A large mental hospital at Dobrany suffered some damage and a German barracks was severely damaged, killing 200 German soldiers. However, the factory they had gone all that way to attack was not touched by the 522 tons of high explosive and incendiary bombs dropped by the bombers. A total of 37 aircraft were lost in the raid, two of which were from 78 Squadron.

The first was Halifax II DT773 EY- which was shot down by a Me110 night fighter and crashed near a Luftwaffe base 10 km SSW of Gieslingen-an-der-Steige. The pilot, F/Lt Dowse, who was on his second tour of operations, was the only fatality.[1] The rest of the crew became POWs. The Bomb Aimer, Sergeant H.E. Thompson, was subsequently repatriated after German surgeons had to amputate his leg to save his life.

> **Pilot** F/Lt A.P. Dowse, killed, Durnbach War Cemetery
> **Nav** W/O R. Des-Jardins, POW, Stalag 357 Kopernikus
> **B/A** Sgt H.E. Thompson, POW, later repatriated
> W/O , F/O P. Langsford RNZAF, POW, Stalag Luft 3 Sagan
> **F/E** F/Sgt T.T. Slater, POW, Stalag 357 Kopernikus
> **A/G** F/Lt A.N. Orr, POW, Stalag Luft 3 Sagan
> **A/G** W/O A. Hoare, POW, Stalag 357 Kopernikus

The second aircraft lost that night was Halifax II HR659 EY-A, which took off at 20.51 hours from Linton-on-Ouse and was outward bound when intercepted and shot down by the joint attentions of a Me109 and a Me110. It crashed near Trier in Germany. The two air crew members who died were buried in the Rheinberg War Cemetery. The crew was:

> **Pilot** F/Lt E.G. Mortenson, killed, Rheinberg War Cemetery
> **Nav** P/O R.C.W. Dennis, POW, Stalag Luft 3 Sagan
> **B/A** F/Lt W.G.F. Fisher, POW, Stalag Luft 3 Sagan
> **W/Op** Sgt A. Steven, POW, Camp details not known
> **F/E** Sgt J.A. Bell, POW, Stalag 357 Kopernikus
> **A/G** Sgt D.A. Pitman, killed, Rheinberg War Cemetery
> **A/G** Sgt L.C. Minshaw, POW, Stalag 357 Kopernikus

ON THE SAME NIGHT as the Pilsen raid, aircraft from 78 Squadron joined a force of 271 bombers to raid Mannheim, although 53 of them abandoned

---

[1] This same crew had previously survived after ditching, following an attack on Genoa in November 1942.

their missions and returned early to their bases, of these 34 were twin-engine Wellingtons, many with engine problems. To continue with a doubtful engine when your aircraft only had two of them, could put the crew in worse danger than they already faced. Weather conditions for the raid were good, with bright moonlight and no cloud cover over the target. The Pathfinders dropped 71 target indicators and 233 flares, which helped the main bomber stream to visually identify the rivers Rhine and Neckar and deliver 220 tons of high explosive and 78 tons of incendiary bombs, which inflicted severe damage to the industrial area. But this operation was costly, for 18 bombers failed to return, one of them being 78 Squadron Halifax II JB870 EY- on loan to 76 Squadron, which shared the same base (Linton-on-Ouse). The crew was:

Pilot Sgt W. Illingworth | **Nav** Sgt C.G. West | **B/A** F/O H.D. Dixon
W/Op Sgt E.G. Thomas | **F/E** Sgt R. Woodhall
A/G Sgt S.W. Patton | **A/G** Sgt D.A. Watkins
All killed and interred at Roye New British Cemetery, France

AFTER THE UNSUCCESSFUL ATTACK on Pilsen in mid-April, Bomber Command Headquarters immediately issued orders for another long range operation to be carried out. This time the target was to be Stettin, which called for a flight of over 550 miles to reach the target, well out of range of Oboe. On the night of 20th/21st April, a force of 339 aircraft left their bases and it is worth noting that the number of aircraft (13) to return prematurely was much lower than it had been for some time.

On arriving over the target area the bombers found the city illuminated by the Pathfinders, who had dropped 95 target indicators and 248 flares. Their marking was perfect in the clear visibility and this enabled the bombers to identify the ground features of the River Oder and the dock area and deposit 477 tons of high explosive and incendiary bombs accurately on the target. The fires started were so fierce that the photo reconnaissance aircraft reported them to be still burning 36 hours later. Over a hundred acres of the city was devastated. Severe damage was caused to a chemical factory, with production being completely halted. The human cost was also high with 586 civilians killed and countless others injured. For Bomber Command too it was a costly night, with 21 aircraft being lost in this operation. 81 air crew were confirmed killed and a further 48 were never found. 21 became POWs and seven were temporarily interned in Sweden before being repatriated. One lucky airman evaded capture and eventually escaped via Sweden.

The following night 30th April/1st May, the Squadron took off at 2330 hours from Linton-on-Ouse to take part in a raid on Essen. Whilst over the target, Halifax II W7929 was hit by flak and badly damaged. The pilot, Sgt J.C. Rudd DFM RAAF fought to keep control and succeeded in reaching the East Anglian coast but while attempting an emergency landing at Docking airfield in Norfolk, he lost control and crashed at 0447 hours. Five of the crew were killed, including Sgt Rudd,[1] who is buried nearby at Great Bircham (St Mary's) Churchyard. The crew was:

Pilot F/Sgt J.C. Rudd DFM, RAAF, killed, Great Bircham, Norfolk.
Nav , Sgt J.E, Wilson, killed, Hammersmith, Kensal Green
B/A Sgt R.J. Pike, killed, St John's Skewen, S.Wales
W/Op Sgt H. Mason, killed, St Chad's, Prees, Salop
F/E Sgt R. Davies, injured but safe.
A/G Sgt W. Oldroyd, killed, Hanging Heaton, Batley
A/G Sgt J. Rashbrook, injured but safe

FOLLOWING A THREE DAY respite, the Ruhr offensive continued. This time it was the turn of Dortmund to be the target for Bomber Command. During the night of 4th/5th May, a force of 596 aircraft comprised of 255 Lancasters, 141 Halifaxes, 80 Stirlings, 110 Wellingtons and 10 Mosquitos belonging to the PFF, took off from their bases and set course for the Ruhr. Visibility over the target area was good and Pathfinder marking was extremely accurate. It was the city's first attack of the war and it was an experience that the local population would never forget. Well over a thousand tons of high explosive and incendiary bombs were dropped on the target. It was ideal weather for the raid, with little or no cloud cover at first, but things changed when smoke from decoy fires obscure the view. This was a ploy being used with greater frequency by the Germans to prevent the bombers finding the correct aiming point. Many of the crews reported seeing an exceptionally large explosion during the raid. The glow from the fires could be seen by the crews for 150 miles after leaving the target area.

The losses for this raid amounted to 31 aircraft lost, 104 aircrew killed, 38 missing and 62 prisoners of war. A further seven aircraft crashed on returning to their bases, killing 20 airmen and seriously injuring another 15. When the last surviving aircraft landed at Linton-on-Ouse, 78 Squadron realised that they had lost three Halifaxes.

---

[1] Sgt Rudd was awarded a DFC, gazetted on 13th May 1943, for his spirited display of skill and determination during a previous operation to Stettin.

Morale among the ground crews was always badly affected when the aircraft in their charge failed to return, but replacement planes would arrive just hours later, to which they needed to give their full attention, so they were unable to dwell on the loss of their aircrew colleagues for long, which was just as well. The fight must go on and there would be another aircrew whose lives depended on the work of the groundcrews.

The first of the three aircraft lost that night was Halifax II JB973 EY- which took off at 22.30 hours from Linton-on-Ouse and was intercepted and shot down by a night fighter (Hptm Wolfgang Thimmig 111/NJG1) while on its way to the target. It crashed near Gronau, Germany. The pilot F/Sgt Burns was the only fatality and has no known grave. The remaining members of the crew became prisoners of war.

> **Pilot** F/Sgt A. Burns, missing, Runnymede Memorial
> **Nav** W/O H. Gamble, POW, Stalag Luft 6 Heydekrug
> **B/A** F/Lt J.B. Thompson, POW, Stalag Luft 3 Sagan
> **W/Op** Sgt J.R. Heslop, POW, Repatriated May 1944
> **F/E** F/Sgt F.G. Hockin, POW, Stalag Luft 3 Sagan
> **A/G** F/Sgt W. Ashley, POW, Stalag Luft 6 Heydekrug
> **A/G** F/Sgt H. Tyler, POW, Stalag Luft 6 Heydekrug

Halifax II JB903 EY- took off at 22.38 hours from Linton-on-Ouse and failed to return. No trace of the aircraft or crew was ever found:

> **Pilot** Sgt A.C. Leppard | **Nav** Sgt V.C.G. Moody | **B/A** Sgt R. Boydell
> **W/Op** Sgt P.E. Mellish | **F/E** F/Sgt D.N. Brown
> **A/G** Sgt C. Lewis | **A/G** Sgt F. Moore
> *All reported missing, recorded on Runnymede Memorial*

THE NEXT LOSS WAS Halifax II JB915 EY- which took off at 22.05 hours and was shot down by a night fighter near Ahaus, killing the flight engineer, F/Sgt B. Legg, who was buried at Rheine, approximately 36 km from the scene of the crash. His remains while later reburied at the Reichswald Forest War Cemetery. The remaining members of the crew became POWs.

> **Pilot** S/Ldr J.H.B. Chapple, POW, Stalag Luft 3 Sagan
> **Nav** F/Lt B.A.G. Campbell, POW, Stalag Luft 3 Sagan
> **B/A** F/Lt H.J. King, POW, Stalag Luft 3 Sagan
> **W/Op** F/Sgt E.K. Blackweall, POW, Stalag 357 Kopernikus
> **F/E** F./Sgt B. Legg, Killed, Reichswald Forest War Cemetery
> **A/G** F/Sgt R. Hillary, POW, Stalag 357 Kopernikus
> **A/G** F/Lt E.W. Barnes, POW, Stalag Luft 3 Sagan

THE FOURTH HEAVY RAID on Duisburg took place during the night of 12th/13th May 1943 and when it was over the citizens of Duisburg understood what their counterparts in the city of Essen had suffered on a previous occasion. A force of 572 aircraft from Nos 1, 3, 4, 5, 6 and 8 Groups had taken off off from their bases in Yorkshire, Lincolnshire, Suffolk and Huntingdonshire, with Duisburg's city centre and port area, just off the Rhine, as their target for a concentrated attack. On this occasion 50 bombers aborted their missions and returned early for various reasons. Weather conditions all along the outbound route were very good and the early arrivals were able to see quite clearly the whole of the built-up areas and the river Rhine. Nearly 900 tons of high explosives and over 248,000 incendiaries were dropped. Damage was considerable, especially to the port area. Records show that 21 barges and 13 ships totalling 18,921 tons were sunk and 60 other ships were damaged, making this a successful mission, although it came at a high cost. Bomber Command lost 34 aircraft in this operation, 149 aircrew were killed, 44 were missing and 27 taken prisoner. Two airmen successfully evaded capture.

Halifax II DT777 EY-T from 78 Squadron, captained by Sergeant G.E. Clay, returned to base minus the mid-upper gunner. After bombing the target they were 'coned' by a group of searchlights and during the moments that followed, the pilot was heard to say over the intercom, "We have to get out of this lot quick!" He put the aircraft into a steep, diving 'corkscrew' manoeuvre and as he did so the crew felt a pronounced shuddering. When eventually clear of the searchlights and flak, the skipper called up each member of his crew in turn to check on their safety. There was no reply from the mid-upper gunner, so he sent the flight engineer back to see if their colleague was okay. When he returned the F/E told the pilot the rear escape hatch was open and the gunner was missing. When they landed back at base, the bomber was found to have a deep score mark under its port wing, probably caused by an anti-aircraft shell that scored a hit but failed to explode. This was the probable explanation for the aircraft shuddering when it dived. Sgt Scott parachuted to safety and became a prisoner of war at Stalag 357 Kopernikus. The Squadron ORB record states: *Halifax DT777 EY-T A/G A. Scott POW. Stalag 357 Kopernikus. Misunderstood the captain's intercom message and baled out.*

On the following night of 13th/14th May the town of Bochum was again the target, this time by a force of 442 aircraft which consisted of 135 Halifaxes, 98 Lancasters, 95 Stirlings and 10 Mosquitos. During this operation 530 tons of high explosives and 165,000 incendiaries rained down on the target. German records reveal 349 buildings were destroyed and 302 people killed. 24 aircraft failed to return from this operation and of the crews that manned them, 82 were killed, 16 were missing and 56 became POWs. One man evaded capture, he was Sergeant R.G. Goddard, the Navigator of Halifax JB873 of 78 Squadron. His aircraft was intercepted and shot down by a German night fighter piloted by Lt Schnaufer (11 NJG1). The squadron lost three aircraft during the raid, these were:

Halifax II JB777 EY-T which took off at 23.15 hours from Linton-on-Ouse and was shot down and crashed near Cologne. The only fatality was Flight Engineer Sgt L. Jakes, who was buried locally and later re-interred at Rheinberg War Cemetery. The rest of the crew became POWs:

Pilot W/O G.E. Clay, POW, Stalag Luft 1 Barth Vogelsang
Nav F/Sgt J. O'Reilly, POW, Stalag Luft 4 Sagan
B/A W/O L.D.E. Marriott, POW, Stalag 357 Kopernikus
W/Op F/Sgt E.A. Coates, POW, Stalag Luft 1 Barth Vogelsang
F/E Sgt L. Jakes, Killed, Rheinberg War Cemetery
A/G Sgt C. Leverett, POW, Stalag Luft 3 Sagan
A/G W/O W.J.H. Perry, POW, Stalag Luft 3 Sagan

The second aircraft lost that night was Halifax II JB873 EY-J which took off at 23.29 hours from Linton-on-Ouse and was intercepted by a night fighter (Lt Heinz Wolfgang Schnaufer 11.NJG/1) and crashed near Leuven, Belgium,resulting two fatalities who were buried in Haasrode Churchyard.

Pilot P/O G.H. Dane MiD, killed, Haasrode, Leuven, Belgium
2nd Pilot Sgt J.H. Body, killed, Haasrode, Leuven, Belgium
Nav Sgt R.G. Goddard, evaded capture (later awarded DFM)
B/A W/O L. Adams, POW, Stalag 357 Kopernikus
W/Op F/Sgt J.W. Pople, POW, Stalag Luft 4 Sagan
F/E F/Sgt A.C.P. Minnitt, POW, Stalag Luft 4 Sagan
A/G F/Sgt A. Beatson, POW, Stalag Luft 1 Barth Vogelsang
A/G F/Sgt F.W. Webb, POW, Stalag Luft 6 Heydekrug

Earlier that night, when the crew of Halifax JB873 EY-J had arrived at their aircraft in the dispersal bay at Linton-on-Ouse airfield prior to take-off, they had discovered that somebody had painted over the 'Saint' motif on the side of their aircraft fuselage. Sgt Beatson, the mid-upper gunner, was the first to notice that the good luck motif was missing and being somewhat superstitious, a common trait amongst bomber command aircrew, he forecast trouble on the forthcoming trip accordingly. He was right to do so, for on its outbound flight the bomber lost the use of one of its starboard engines due to a mechanical fault. The pilot, Sgt G.H. Dane, found the heavily-laden bomber was having difficulty maintaining height and speed and was slowly falling behind and below the main stream, thereby becoming a 'sitting duck' for a fighter attack. Realising it was wiser to abort the mission, the pilot ordered the bombs to be jettisoned and turned for home. A few minutes later there was a brief burst of exploding cannon shells inside the aircraft. Prior to this, there had been no flak or searchlight activity and the gunners had not seen any fighters in the vicinity.

They must have been located by radar and a night fighter had attacked them from underneath, the blind spot in a Halifax. The shells set fire to both engines and made a hole in the starboard wing, from which spewed flames that reached back past the tail. The aircraft suddenly went into a diving starboard turn and although the pilot struggled in vain to hold the control column back to his chest and over to port, the angle of the dive increased and the centrifugal force was such that the flight engineer, Sgt Arthur Minnitt, was unable to reach across to press the fire extinguisher buttons in an effort to control the flames.

Deciding that conditions were hopeless, the captain gave the order to abandon the aircraft. As there was a second pilot on board that night, the flight engineer realised there were too many crew members to leave by the front hatch. Handing his captain a parachute pack, he informed him he would go aft to the rear escape hatch.

Struggling from the front to the back of a Halifax was a very difficult task, for the aircrew had to climb over the main spar in the centre of the fuselage and then negotiate many projections and the mid-upper turret which hampered the way. On this occasion, in spite of the angle at which the bomber was diving and the bulky parachute firmly clipped to his chest, the flight engineer managed to make the distance back to the rear hatch in double quick time, to find the mid-upper gunner had already opened the hatch and was in the process of baling out. Sgt Minnitt needed no persuasion to follow him through the open hatch. As he pulled on his ripcord, after counting to 10, he saw pieces of the burning Halifax falling away and just seconds later the aircraft exploded in mid-air. The crew's successful exit was due entirely to the two pilots, who had continued to struggle with the controls in order to give their comrades time to bale out, before losing their own lives in the explosion that followed. An exceedingly brave and selfless action, of which there are many similar instances recorded in the annals of RAF Bomber Command.

After landing safely, Sergeant Minnit was handicapped from the start due to losing his left flying boot and was captured by a German army squad later in the day. The navigator, Sgt R.G. Goddard, was luckier, for upon landing he was fortunate enough to call at the house of a member of the resistance and, with the help of the underground movement, was able to make his way back to the UK.

The third aircraft to be lost that night was Halifax II JB924 EY-M 'Mother'. The crew were flying a replacement aircraft because their own aircraft, E-Easy, had been damaged in a previous raid. They also had a 2nd pilot aboard, Sergeant E. Pritchard (an acclimatisation flight prior to him being assigned his own crew). The journey had been uneventful until they were near the German night fighter base at Leewaurden. The Wireless operator, Sgt Matches, was listening in to the German wavelength and heard that a fighter had been sent after them. Within moments the Halifax was under attack, with bullets causing heavy damage to the controls. The captain gave orders for everyone to bale out as the aircraft went into a steep dive and broke into pieces before hitting the ground. All but one of the crew were killed and buried at Wijnaldum in Friesland.

Pilot P/O R.E. Bragg | **2nd Pilot** Sgt E. Pritchard | **Nav** W/O J.M. Farrell RCAF
W/Op Sgt R.D. Matches | **F/E** F/Lt R. Grey | **A/G** Sgt D. Baxter | **A/G** F/Sgt A.A. Kew
All of the above were killed and interred at Wijnaldum, Friesland
B/A W/O H.E. Gell, POW, Stalag 357 Kopernikus

ON THE NIGHT OF 23rd/24th May 1943, it was back to 'Happy Valley' for a force of 826 aircraft. For some it was their visit to the Ruhr but others had been there before and it was a place they had come to hate and fear due to the ferocity of the anti-aircraft fire and night fighter attacks that could be relied upon as a welcoming party. Former aircrew would freely admit in later years that their hearts sank whenever they attended a briefing and were told that the operation was going to involve another trip to the Ruhr. On this occasion, the target was to be the city of Dortmund.

Orders were received from Bomber Command HQ for the best 250 crews from every group taking part in this operation to be in the first wave after the target had been marked. They were instructed to bomb on the target indicators and if none were visible, they were to orbit the target and come in again and carry out another bomb run, by which time a further salvo of target indicators would have been dropped.

During this raid 1,000 tons of high explosive bombs along with 86,500 incendiaries rained down on the city, in what was to be its last raid for a year, though it would take a lot longer than that for the city's population to forget it. Large areas were devastated. Nearly 2,000 buildings were destroyed and Hoesch, the biggest steelworks in Germany and the primary target, was put out of action. 595 people were killed and 1,275 injured.

Bomber Command losses were also considerable: 38 aircraft lost, 144 air crew killed, 44 missing and 69 made prisoners of war.

That night 78 Squadron suffered the loss of three aircraft.

After completing it bombing run Halifax II JD122 EY-A turned for home, but was intercepted by a night fighter (Hptm Wolfgang Thimmig 111./NJG1) and crashed at Zuna (Overijssel) in the Netherlands, killing the entire crew who were buried at Wierden General Cemetery.

Pilot Sgt G.E. Schubert | **Nav** Sgt D.C. Oliver | **B/A** F/O A.B. Orme
W/Op Sgt P.J. Wood | **F/E** Sgt R.E. Goodyear | **A/G** Sgt J. Redman
A/G Sgt J. Goldflust
All were killed and interred at Wierden Cemetery, Netherlands

HALIFAX II JD160 EY- was a victim of the heavy flak over the target and crashed approximately 7 km south-east of Rheinberg. Sergeant Chaffey, who was struck by a shell splinter while descending by parachute, was the only fatality. He was interred at Rheinberg War Cemetery. The remaining crew members all became prisoners of war.

Pilot W/O G.H. Tinniswood, POW, Stalag 357 Kopernikus
Nav F/Lt P.H. Bear, POW, Stalag Luft 3 Sagan
B/A F/O R. Donovan, POW, Stalag Luft 3 Sagan
W/Op F/Sgt G.J. Wallace, POW, Stalag 357 Kopernikus
F/E Sgt F.M. Chaffey, killed, Rheinberg Cmy, Germany
A/G W/O E.F. Harries, POW, Stalag 357 Kopernikus
A/G Sgt J.O. Mander, POW, Stalag 357 Kopernikus

HALIFAX II W7926 EY-P was shot down and ditched into the sea near the Dutch coast on its homeward leg. An SOS was sent out at 01.56 hours. The two gunners had baled out over land and the remaining five crew members were picked up by a German convoy after being in a dinghy for ten hours. They all became prisoners of war:

Pilot W/O B.W.T. Horn, POW, Stalag 357 Kopernikus
Nav W/O G. Irving, POW, Stalag Luft 6 Heydekrug
B/A F/Sgt W.H. Allely, POW, Stalag 357 Kopernikus
W/Op Sgt D.R. Wilcox, POW, Stalag 357 Kopernikus
F/E F/Sgt R.F. Cumming, POW, Stalag 357 Kopernikus
A/G F/Sgt F. Churchyard RCAF, POW, Stalag 357 Kopernikus
A/G W/O G.J.U. Stevens, POW, Stalag 357 Kopernikus

With Bomber Command's Ruhr offensive now in its third month, the city of Dusseldorf became the target on the night of 25th/26th May, followed by Essen on the 27th/28th and Wuppertal on the 29th/30th. Although 83 aircraft were lost on these operations, 78 Squadron did not incur any losses. However, this run of good luck came to an end on the night of 11th/12th June, when they became part of a force of 783 aircraft consisting of 326 Lancasters, 143 Halifaxes, 99 Stirlings, 143 Wellingtons and 13 Mosquitos. Of these, 86 aborted their missions and returned prematurely with various problems. When the remaining aircraft arrived over the target, they found visibility was good, though there was a strong crosswind. During the attack 11,065 tons of high explosive bombs and 351,235 incendiaries were dropped, causing a great deal of devastation to the city centre. The industrial suburbs also suffered damage, much of it caused by incendiaries. The attack was deemed successful but the cost was high. Losses amounted to 38 aircraft, with the Halifaxes of 4 Group bearing the brunt of the casualties. 145 air crew were killed, 55 were missing and 52 made POWs. Three men evaded capture and later returned to the UK.

78 Squadron lost two aircraft in this operation.

After completing it bomb run Halifax II W7932 EY- was attacked by a night fighter and crashed on farmland near Flushing in the Netherlands, killing all the crew, they were:

Pilot W/O F. Hemmings | Nav Sgt J. Stone | B/A P/O W.C.R. Foale
W/ Op Sgt A. Shaw | F/E Sgt J. Muir
A/G Sgt T.W.R. Daniel | A/G Sgt D. Montgomery
All were killed and buried near Flushing, Netherlands

The second aircraft was Halifax MkII Series B1 Special HR684 EY- which had taken off at 22.41 hours from Linton-on-Ouse and crashed on the east bank of the River Rhine, killing all on board. The crew were buried at Nordfriedhof, Dusseldorf and later re-interred at Reichswald Forest War Cemetery. This aircraft had a six-man crew:

Pilot F/Sgt J.M. Gavagan | Nav Sgt L.J. Jeal | B/A P/O J.B. Binns
W/Op Sgt T.A. Davies | F/E Sgt A.E. Hayes | A/G Sgt P. Hollyer
All killed near Voerdre, Germany

Following a raid on Bochum during the night of 12th/13th June, Halifax II JD145 EY- was reported lost in the North Sea, just off the Dutch coast. Only two bodies were recovered and buried in Dutch cemeteries. The rest of the crew were never found and their names are commemorated on the Runnymede Memorial. The crew was:

Pilot **F/Sgt** M. Baxter | **Nav** Sgt W.H. Jordan | **B/A** Sgt J. Angus
F/E Sgt A.McD Young | **A/G** Sgt E.G. Westall
All of the above lost without trace, Runnymede Memorial
W/Op Sgt C.W. Payne, killed, Vredenhof Cemetery, Holland
A/G Sgt E. Wright, killed, Westerschelling Cemetery, Holland

THIS WAS THE LAST operation undertaken by 78 Squadron from RAF Linton-on-Ouse. They moved to RAF Breighton on 16th June 1943 and this station became their home for the rest of the war.

One of the first raids to be carried out from their new home was on 22nd/23rd June 1943, when they became part of a force of 557 aircraft that set out to attack the German city of Mulheim, though this force was drastically reduced when 58 of the participants returned prematurely to their bases due to various problems. The remaining aircraft proceeded to the target, where they dropped 755 tons of high explosive bombs and 300,000 incendiaries, causing an inferno that raged completely out of control, in spite of the valiant efforts of the German fire services who fought to rescue victims trapped in the remains of their homes. German records show that 578 civilians were killed and 1,200 injured. Bomber Command losses on this operation amounted to 35 aircraft lost, 165 air crew killed, 38 missing and 33 made prisoners of war. Three men evaded capture. One of these evaders was Sergeant John Duffee the 2nd pilot of Halifax JB885 captained by F/Lt L. Knight, mentioned below.

No.78 Squadron lost two aircraft during the operation, they were:

Halifax II W7930 EY-H which took off at 23.16 hours from Breighton and was shot down by flak over the Netherlands, crashing in a wooded area on a farm south of Utrecht. All the crew members were killed and buried at Amersfoort General Cemetery, they were:

Pilot **F/Sgt** E. Tipler | **Nav** Sgt J.E. Woodward | **B/A** Sgt W. Anderson
W/Op Sgt C.P. Johns | **F/E** Sgt L.D. Lingwood
A/G Sgt T.H. Bell | **A/G** Sgt D.E. Tuddenham
All were killed and interred at Amersfoort Cemetery, Netherlands

The second aircraft lost was Halifax II JB885 EY-H which was shot down by a night fighter (Hptm Wilhelm Herget 1./NJG1). It crashed at Beugt (Noord Brabant) in the Netherlands. Five crew members were killed and buried at Eindhoven General Cemetery, including Sgt Simons, who died from his wounds on 28th June 1943. The crew was:

Pilot **F/Lt** L. Knight | **B/A** F/O R.D. Caldercourt | **W/Op** F/O S.A.C. Cutler
F/E Sgt F.C. Simons | **A/G** Sgt F.J.R. Bain

All the above were killed and interred at Eindhoven Cemetery, Netherlands
2nd Pilot Sgt J. Duffee, evaded capture
Nav F/O H.J. Standfast, POW, Stalag Luft 3 Sagan
A/G F/Sgt J.H. Lee, POW, Stalag 357 Kopernikus

A TOTAL OF 630 bombers took off from their bases on the night of 24th/25th June at around 23.00 hours, their target the German town of Wuppertal home to the Goldschmitt adhesives firm, which made *Tego-Film* wood adhesive used in wooden airframe components in German aircraft such as the Ta 154 Moskito and He 162 Spatz. This large force comprised 251 Lancasters, 171 Halifaxes, 98 Stirlings, 101 Wellington and 9 Mosquitos. The proportion of pilots aborting their missions prematurely was still very high and on this occasion 79 aircraft failed to reach the target. The small town of Wuppertal demanded a great deal of accuracy but in spite of accurate marking by the Pathfinders, many bombs went astray and inflicted catastrophic damage to residential areas with significant loss of life, although the industrial district of Elberfeld was also destroyed by more than 815 tons of high explosive bombs and 332,000 incendiaries dropped by the bombers. The searchlights and flak were very active between Cologne and Dusseldorf and many bombers encountered night fighters on their return journey.

The persistent high casualties suffered by many of the squadrons was beginning to have a demoralising effect on the crews. Air crew casualties on this raid alone were 116 killed, 63 missing and 44 made prisoners of war. One man did manage to evade his captors and eventually returned to this country.

78 Squadron lost one aircraft, Halifax II JB962 EY- which has taken off at 23.00 hours from Breighton and was shot down by flak near Dormagen in Germany. There were no survivors. Only five bodies were recovered and interred at Rheinberg War Cemetery. The names of the two gunners are commemorated on the Runnymede Memorial.

Pilot F/Sgt K.F. Morrison RNZAF | **Nav** Sgt P.A. Kennedy
B/A SgtSgt I. Macrae | **W/Op** Sgt W. Cox | **F/E** Sgt W. Barry
All of the above interred at Rheinberg War Cemetery, Germany
A/G F/Sgt E.W.J. Collingwood | **A/G** Sgt T.S. Payne
Missing presumed dead, Runnymede Memorial

THE FOLLOWING NIGHT OF 25th/26th June, 78 Squadron took part in an operation mounted by aircraft from Nos 1, 3, 4, 5, 6 and 8 Groups to attack Gelsenkirchen. This area was noted for its oil refineries and was therefore a very important target. After the Dutch coast had been crossed, the crews encountered 10/10 cloud all the way to the target, which was completely cloud covered on arrival, preventing the bombers from carrying out a concentrated attack and resulted in only minor damage being done. The loss of 33 aircraft was a high price to pay for such an ineffective attack. The casualties amounted to 118 killed, 50 missing and 36 made POWs.

78 Squadron lost one aircraft in the raid, Halifax II JB 928 EY-S which was shot down by a night fighter and crashed near Bergen (Noord Holland). All of the crew members survived and became prisoners of war. The wireless operator, Flight Sergeant A.J. Guy, was repatriated in February 1945 aboard the RMS *Arundel Castle*. The crew was:

Pilot F/O M.H. Oddie, killed, Bergen General Cemetery, Holland
Nav F/Sgt A.A. J. Hutchinson, POW, Stalag 357 Kopernikus
B/A F/O P. Daulby, POW, Stalag Luft 3 Sagan
W/Op F.Sgt A.J. Guy, POW, Repatriated 6/2/45
F/E F/Sgt A.D. Gillespie, POW, Stalag Luft 6 Heydekrug
A/G Sgt T.L. Roberts, POW, Stalag 357 Kopernikus
A/G F/O D.W. Lusty, POW, Stalag Luft 3 Sagan

FOLLOWING THE GELSENKIRCHEN RAID the aircrews were given a 24-hour break before the next operation. This gave the ground crews extra time to bring the Squadron up to full strength. On the morning of 28th June the air crews were ordered to attend a briefing, where they were informed that the target for that night's operation would be Cologne. Bomber Command despatched 600 aircraft on this raid and the force consisted of 267 Lancasters, 169 Halifaxes, 75 Stirlings, 77 Wellingtons and 12 Mosquitos. Once again a large number of aircraft aborted their missions and returned to base prematurely and only 534 arrived over the target area. Sky markers dropped by the Mosquitos were swallowed up by thick cloud that did not allow even the slightest glare to help the bombers following behind. In spite of the bad visibility, the bombers carried out the raid to the best of their ability and Cologne had its worst raid of the war. Several crews reported seeing a terrific explosion that turned the sky scarlet and lasted a few seconds. Though the searchlights were ineffective, due to the thick cloud, the flak was intense and the night fighters were also very active.

A total of 839 tons of high explosive bombs and 318,000 incendiaries fell on the city, causing considerable damage to industrial premises and residential areas. The casualty figures were exceptionally high. German sources put them at 4,337 killed and 10,000 injured. Cologne Cathedral was damaged by high explosive bombs during the raid. Fortunately, it was not hit by incendiaries, for these would have caused irreparable damage. After the war some people claimed the bomber crews had been instructed to ensure bombs were dropped well away from the cathedral, which was to be used only as a reference point, but this was refuted by Bomber Command. After this operation 25 aircraft failed to return, one of them being from 78 Squadron. It was Halifax II JB907 EY- which had taken off from Breighton at about 23.30 hours. It is uncertain whether it was shot down by flak or a night fighter, as both were extremely active that night. It crashed at Valkenberg in Belgium, killing all the crew, who were laid to rest in Maastricht General Cemetery. They were:

Pilot F/Sgt P.W.J. Rendle | **Nav** Sgt G.J. Samuel
B/A Sgt C.A. Morris | **W/Op** Sgt T.I.L. Dagg
F/E Sgt L. Howarth | **A/G** Sgt F. Hill | **A/G** F/Sgt W.R. Townsend
All killed and interred at Maastricht Cemetery, Belgium

THE WEARY AIR CREWS were this time given a three night stand down, to help them recover from the strain of facing searchlights, flak and night fighters night after night. Many were on the verge of breakdowns, yet one rarely heard of any crew members refusing to fly. To be accused of LMF (Lack of Moral Fibre)[1] was something nobody wanted, yet it could, and did occur from time to time, especially as crews were approaching the end of a tour of 30 operations, after which they knew they would be 'rested'. Every time they took off on an operation there was the nagging thought that this would be the one where their luck ran out and they knew that the odds were stacked against them completing a tour without being shot down. The closer they got to achieving this goal, the more their anxiety increased until, with just one or two ops to go before becoming 'tour expired', the mental pressure could become unbearable.

Though it is perfectly understandable that Commanding Officers could not allow genuine cases of cowardice to go unpunished, more should have

---

[1] Lack of Moral Fibre or LMF was a punitive designation used by the Royal Air Force during the Second World War to stigmatise aircrew who refused to fly on operations. By early 1940, RAF commanders were concerned about mounting psychological casualties in Bomber Command and Coastal Command. A letter circulated to commands on 22 April 1940 recommended that squadron commanders identify men who had forfeited their confidence, distinguishing medical cases from those 'lacking moral fibre'. By the summer of 1940, senior commanders became concerned that medical officers were removing too many men from flying duty. More detailed guidance was given in the *Memorandum on the Disposal of Members of Air Crews Who Forfeit the Confidence of Their Commanding Officers* S.61141/S.7.C(1) issued on 28 September 1940, signed by Charles Evans, Principal Assistant Secretary for Personnel in the Air Ministry. This 'LMF memorandum' was revised in 19 September 1941, 3 February 1943 and 1 March 1945.

been done to help good men whose nerves had cracked under the extreme pressure that bomber crews had to face night after night. There is something very wrong when a man who has given everything he possibly can in the service of his country, finds himself facing the degradation of having his badges of rank forcibly removed, quite possibly in front of his own comrades, before being sent to another station where he is not known and there given the most humiliating jobs possible. It did not end there either, for when that airman was discharged, his record followed him, leaving him to face a lifetime of shame, which is totally unjustified after all that he had endured.

AT A BRIEFING ON 3rd July, bomber and pathfinder crews heard their Station Commanders inform them the target that night would again be Cologne. Little did they realise that on this raid they would encounter a new experimental tactic from the Luftwaffe given the name *Wilde Sau* (Wild Boar), which involved free roaming Messerschmitt 109's acting on their own initiative and not controlled by ground communications, on which they knew the RAF were eavesdropping.

The target of this raid was the eastern bank of the Rhine, where most of the industrial plants were situated. Having been accurately marked by the Oboe-equipped Mosquitos and ably supported by the Pathfinders backing them up, the main force was able to carry out a successful attack, in spite being attacked by night fighters over the target, who claimed to have shot down 12 bombers, a boast which was hotly disputed by the flak batteries. At their debriefings the RAF crews were inclined to concur that on this occasion the flak had done more damage than the night fighters. A total of 34 aircraft were lost during this operation, 124 air crew were killed, 37 were missing and 35 made POWs. Four managed to evade capture.

On this last day before a four-day stand down, 78 Squadron lost one aircraft when Halifax II JD203 EY-Z crashed near Ashstead in Surrey. The crew all survived this escapade without injury.

Pilot S/Ldr P. Bunclark | **Nav** Sgt J. Moore | **B/A** Sgt R. Dixon
W/Op F/Lt D. Bradford | **F/E** F.Sgt E.F.C. Matthews
A/G F/Sgt L. Mallory | **A/G** P/O J. Castle
All survived uninjured

AFTER A WELL-EARNED FOUR-NIGHT break, the crews were assembled for briefing on the afternoon of 9th July. Another attack was to be carried out on a target they had visited several times before, the city of Gelsenkirchen.

At 22.30 hours the crews of 78 Squadron took off to join the rest of the bomber force that numbered 418 aircraft. It consisted of 218 Lancasters, 190 Halifaxes and 10 Mosquitos. Unfortunately, the raid was a complete failure, with very little damage to show for the loss of 12 aircraft, 39 air crew killed and 27 made prisoners of war, though six men did succeed in evading capture. The Squadron lost one aircraft, Halifax II JD157 EY-T, which ditched 150 yards from the shore at Seaford in Sussex. The crew survived without injury; one was picked up by an air-sea rescue launch and the rest waded ashore. The crew was:

> **Pilot** F/Sgt S. Liggett | **Nav** Sgt L. Trowbridge | **B/A** Sgt S. Watt
> **W/Op** Sgt J. Birrell | **F/E** Sgt E.A. Gosling
> **A/G** Sgt L.E. Hughes | **A/G** Sgt K.W. Smith
> *All escaped uninjured*

AACHEN BECAME THE TARGET for 374 aircraft of Nos 3, 4, 6 and 8 Groups on the night of 13th/14th July 1943. This force consisted of 214 Halifaxes, 18 Lancasters, 55 Stirlings, 76 Wellingtons and 11 Mosquitos. A strong tailwind that had not been forecast was responsible for the bombers arriving early in the target area. By the time the Pathfinders had marked the aiming point, a large number of bombers were already over the target. It appears they all decided to commence their bomb runs at the same time, which caused a few hair-raising moments for some crews when they looked up and saw bombs falling from aircraft above them. No doubt, some of the bombers lost in that raid were due to mid air collisions.

Twenty aircraft failed to return that night and losses among air crew personnel amounted to 83 killed, 9 missing, 37 made prisoners of war and 9 who evaded capture. As usual 78 Squadron had played its part in the operation and lost three aircraft.

Halifax II JD801 EY-G crashed at Peursum (Zuid Holland) with no survivors. The crew were buried in Crooswijk Cemetery, Rotterdam.

> **Pilot** W/O P. Horrocks | **Nav** F/O C.D. Hosken RCAF | **B/A** Sgt A.S. Jelfs
> **W/Op** Sgt J. Chaplin | **F/E** F/Sgt W. Harries
> **A/G** Sgt G. Bowden | **A/G** Sgt W. Rouse
> *All killed and interred at Crooswijk Cemetery, Rotterdam*

Halifax II JD108 EY-U was shot down at Froidchapelle in Belgium after becoming the victim of a night fighter flown by Oblt Rudolf Altendorf. (11./NJG4). The five fatalities were buried at Gosselies Cemetery

> **Pilot** W/O K.A. Toon RNZAF | **B/A** F/Sgt H.J. Burridge
> **F/E** Sgt L. Donaldson | **A/G** F/Lt J.D. Nesbit | **A/G** F/Sgt G.M. Campbell

All the above were killed and interred at Gosselies, Charleroi
2nd Pilot D.W.G. Cowell, evaded capture
Nav Sgt R. Falcus, evaded capture
W/Op P/O J. McDonald, POW Stalag Luft 3 Sagan

HALIFAX II JD175 EY-F crashed in the vicinity of Koln, killing all the crew, who were buried at Rheinberg War Cemetery. Sgt Yonker is also listed on the Runnymede Memorial. The crew was:

Pilot W/O C.M. Colbourn | **Nav** W/O A.R. Lutes RCAF
B/A Sgt Z. Yonker RCAF | **W/Op** Sgt A. Slack
F/E Sgt F. Oakley | **A/G** Sgt W.V. Gerrard | **A/G** Sgt W. Robinson
All killed and interred at Rheinberg War Cemetery, Germany

THE CONCLUDING RAIDS OF the Ruhr offensive started with a force of 165 Halifaxes from 4, 6 and 8 Groups which attacked the Puegeot Motor Factory in the Montbeliard suburb of Souchaux, near to the Swiss border, during the night of 15th/16th July. Five bombers were lost in a raid that caused little damage to the factory but was responsible for the deaths of 123 civilians. In addition 13 air crew were killed and 7 were missing, 5 were made prisoners of war and 10 managed to evade capture.

78 Squadron lost two aircraft that night.

The crew of Halifax II DT771 EY-D had a very narrow escape before the operation had got under way. D-Dog was an old aircraft and not renowned for its reliability and the crew were not overjoyed at being assigned to fly it on this raid. Things began to go wrong soon after final preparations for take off had been completed, as Flying Officer Gerry Carver recalls:

"We pounded down the main runway into the gathering dusk and reached the half way mark, with approximately 1,000 yards of runway to go, and assuming a tail up flying position, I noticed that the air speed indicator gauge still registered zero. We were now in a critical situation that called for a 'go or no go' decision.

Having first established the airspeed indicator was not just stuck, by giving it a sharp rap, I made that decision. I closed the throttles and applied the brakes and full flap. Unfortunately, D-Dog did not respond. The momentum of such a heavily laden aircraft defied the braking action. We rumbled on, overshooting the end of the runway, the overshoot area, then through a hedge, across a country lane, and finally came to rest in a potato field. Fortunately, the emergency drill eliminated any risk of fire and no injuries were sustained, we were lucky. Much good humoured 'Mickey' taking resulted and the spot where D-Dog came to rest became known as "Gerry's potato patch dispersal".

It eventually came to light that the cause of the unserviceable airspeed indicator was that the air pressure pipe leading from the pitot head to the ASI on the instrument panel had become bent, restricting the flow of air."

The second aircraft to be lost that night was Halifax II DT768 EY-W. It crashed at Nogent-le-Rotrou (Eure-et-Loir) in France, killing two of the crew. The cause of the crash was engine trouble. The crew was:

Pilot P/O O.P. Marshall, Killed, Nogent-le-Rotrou, France
Nav F/Lt D.J. Gibson, POW, Stalag Luft 3 Sagan
B/A F/O N.S.M. Reid, Killed, Nogent-le-Rotrou, France
W/Op , Sgt I.J. Sansum, Evaded capture
F/E F/O A.D. Ablett, POW, Stalag Luft 3 Sagan
A/G Sgt A.J. Stevenson, POW, Stalag 357 Kopernikus
A/G Sgt B.A. Lee, POW, Stalag Luft 7 Bankau-Kruelberg

During their term of captivity, most, if not all prisoners of war received promotion and in the case of Sergeant B.A. Lee, he became a flight Sergeant and later a Warrant Officer. In his postwar interrogation report, he related his experiences.

"My chute got entangled in a tree, so I never bothered about it. I left all my flying gear at the bottom of the tree and started walking in a southerly direction until I came to a road. I continued to walk until 05.00 hours, when I was surprised to see a young woman coming along on a cycle so early in the morning. She stopped and made me to understand that I was to go into a hedge and hide and that she would be back to bring me some food and clothing. After an hour she returned with some bread and meat and a blue blouse. She told me to keep hidden and that she would return after a short time, but as I considered that I was too close to where my plane had crashed, and I now had a blouse as some sort of disguise. I now decided to push on a little further.

I walked for several days and nights, resting for a few hours in the early mornings. One day I was walking along a country lane and feeling rather tired and very foot sore, and I decided around noon to rest in a hedge. Just as I was about to lay down, two men on cycles overtook me, so I waited until they were well past me before I scrambled into the hedge. However, one of the men came back. He sat beside me and asked in French if I was English, at the same time, he pulled up my trouser leg and revealed my flying boot.

We talked in a kind of sign language and I made him understand that I had come down by parachute. He told me to keep walking to within a kilometre of Mondoubleau, where he would meet me with some clothes and food. By now, the thought of food was tantalising, as I had lived for several days on Horlicks tablets and apples I had taken from an orchard. I walked for about an hour before the second cyclist returned and brought me clothes and food. I changed into the civilian clothes and the man walked along the road and allowed me to ride his bike to a farm. Here I was told to go to bed, which I thankfully did. When I got up it was getting dark and the man then served me a meal. The cyclist returned at 22.00 hours and we walked into Mondoubleau, where I was taken into a house. I was there for about two days when a man and his married daughter came to visit. She could speak English and it was obvious that her visit was to check and prove that I really was English.

These people came to visit a few days later and this time they brought me some maps. I suggested that I should leave and get away to Spain, but they told me to stay where I was, as they expected an invasion soon. I listened to their advice and just helped around the house to keep myself occupied. Owing to the frequent comings and goings from the house, and my looking in drawers and finding many different kinds of maps, I thought this might be the meeting place of a resistance group. I asked the lady of the house if this was so and, with great reluctance, she admitted that it was a resistance headquarters.

One day a cyclist arrived and asked me if I would like to send a radio message to my people in England. I took up the offer and I gave him a brief message. He went away with it and when he returned he confirmed the message had been sent.

Another man turned up during this period and told me he was the head of a resistance movement in another area. He spent most of his time typing and looking at maps, but no one was allowed to see what he had written. He occasionally went off to Paris.

Another day he said he was meeting a girl at the station, she would be wearing feathers in her hat so that she would be recognised. She duly arrived and was brought to the house. She told me I could write a letter to my people in England and she would take it and see that it went by plane, which would be leaving from somewhere in the Paris area. I wrote a letter saying I was all right, but I found when I did return to England neither the radio message nor the letter ever got through. This same girl told me that if I liked to go to St Nazaire that I could go on a fishing boat with two or three intelligence officers and be picked up by submarine and taken to England. When I asked how I could get to St Nazaire, that I knew was a highly protected U-Boat base, she just shrugged her shoulders.

The people who I was staying with had no confidence in the man or the girl. The man was always very frightened that the Gestapo were coming, and spent a lot of his time watching people arrive by bus. They were very strange people.

One day he came in and said there were Gestapo people in the town and he just went off and I did not see him again. The cyclist also heard this rumour of Gestapo in the area and as a precaution I was taken to another farm somewhere east of the town. As there were several scares in Mondoubleau about Gestapo in the area, I went to this farm each for a few days.

In October 1943 the cyclist told me he was expecting some arms to be dropped by the RAF and showed me some batteries and coloured glass. He asked me if this would do for signalling to the aircraft. As it was all he had, I agreed it would do, but nothing happened as the code word had been discovered.

In the middle of November I was awakened in the early morning by the lady of the house, as she had heard cars coming into the town. About 08.00 hours I saw German troops and was told they were looking for a parachutist, which I presumed was me. I went to hide in the garage and, although the house was searched three times and the garage once, I was not discovered.

In the evening a man arrived and took me to another house and I stayed there for two nights and returned to the first house during the day. On December 15th I was taken to a chateau near Lunay, but I stayed there only ten days as the owner of the chateau received information that the Gestapo were coming to the area on Christmas night. To get me away, he took me on the pillion of a motorcycle to Mazange, where he met a Priest who supplied me with identity papers and ration cards, then took me to a house.

Here I met a man called Harry Gregory, a soldier from the 'Loyals' who had been there since the time of Dunkirk. I stayed at the house until June 1944, and nothing of any great importance happened until just before the Invasion, when the owner of the chateau told me there may be a chance of getting me away by plane. During my long stay at this house, I also met another Dunkirk soldier named Brierley, also from the Loyals, who was not particularly friendly with his army colleague Gregory.

One morning both Brierley and I were warned to be at a certain place to be picked up by car. We travelled about three hours in the car, being told that we were going to get on a plane. En route we stopped at another chateau and went in, but the owner said he knew nothing about us or our plane, and he would have nothing to do with us. The driver of the car left us after giving us 1,000 Francs.

Not knowing where we were and the chateau owner not being very helpful in not giving us our position, except that we should cross a river and go to a village, we left as instructed. On the way we were stopped by some Frenchmen and asked for our identity cards. While the cards were being examined, more Frenchmen turned up and we were taken to a local café and searched. We declared ourselves as we thought they were members of the Maquis. We were given pistols and put in a car and driven to a lodge where, for some reason, our pistols were taken from us. At the lodge we met an English woman who told us she had been dropped by parachute a little time before. Both of us were a little unhappy at the situation we were now in, as the Maquis were a careless lot, shooting off their pistols haphazardly. The day after we arrived we were taken to see a German prisoner who the Maquis had captured and who was being kept prisoner in the chateau attic. We met up with two other English airmen and an American, at this chateau.

We were awakened the next morning, Sunday, to the sound of rifles and grenades. The five of us, who were all evaders, took to the woods at the back of the chateau, but a German patrol quickly rounded us up and we were taken to Romorantin and, as we alighted from the lorry, we were beaten up with the rifle butts of the German guards. They also tried to smash our faces against a wall. Our wrists were tied with wire and then we were all tied to each other and knocked down and beaten with a whip. I was eventually cut loose, kicked into a room and interrogated by two German army officers. I was beaten up so badly that I can hardly remember what I said to them. We were then all taken to Orleans, where we suffered another interview, by the Gestapo this time. I was finally sent to Stalag Luft VII at Bankau on July 11th 1944 and was liberated by the Russians in April 1945. Since my return to this country I have heard that some of my helpers in France were put into concentration camps."

THE FLIGHT ENGINEER, FROM Lee's crew, Flying Officer P.D. Ablett, also had bad luck in his evasion attempt, for he was captured crossing the Pyrenees on 29th August 1943. He fell ill in the mountains of Andorra, where he had been taken by a guide. He lost his way, then spent six weeks in Fresnes prison in Paris, before being transferred to a prison camp in Germany. The wireless operator, Sergeant I.J. Sansum was the only one of the crew to successfully escape back to the UK, and his interrogation report shows how this was achieved.

"On landing I badly sprained my ankle and after getting rid of my flying gear I started to hobble, with the faint hope of finding other members of my crew. After about two hours and having no success, I lay down in a straw stack in a farmyard and went to sleep around 02.30 hours. The following morning I was discovered by a young boy. As I speak only a few French words, I had difficulty in explaining who I was, but I finally managed to make myself understood. He went to his mother, who brought me some milk and then told me I must move on as the Gendarmes would soon be arriving. I took her advice and painfully hobbled on. As my ankle was by now badly swollen and giving me a lot of pain, I had no alternative but to lay down in a field. While I lay there, a woman drove some cows into the field and saw me. She did not offer any help, but told me to shut the gate when I left.

About half an hour later a man came and told me it was important that I should be hidden, as there were a lot of Germans about. He then carried me across his shoulder into a nearby wood and later returned with some food and wine. He then went away and returned later with a note written in bad English which asked me if I had any means of getting away, or whether I had any friends or any other means of helping myself. I wrote on the back of the note stating that I had 2,000 Francs and a map. A reply came back saying that this was not much and that I had better give myself up.

I explained to my helper the contents of the last note and he went away, returning with a horse and cart. Carrying me into the cart he covered me with straw and drove into Nogent-le-Rotrou, where he drove to the back of a house. He carried me inside and gave me some food, then introduced me to the author of the notes, she was a young girl who spoke a little English. After I had eaten, she left the house and came back with a man who spoke good English. He told me it would not be safe to remain there as there was a German garrison in the town. I was given an old mackintosh to cover my uniform and was again put onto a horse-drawn cart and this time driven by another man to his farm about two kilometres out of town, where I remained for three weeks while my ankle improved.

During my time at this farm I was constantly visited by the young girl that wrote the notes; she brought me English books to read and told me she was trying to get in touch with someone else who could maybe help me. After two weeks she managed to contact an organisation in Paris, who arranged the rest of my journey for me. I finally reached Gibraltar on Wednesday November 10th 1943 and was flown back to the United Kingdom on the following day."

SO ENDED THE BOMBER Command campaign over the Ruhr. It had lasted from March until July 1943 and for 78 Squadron alone it had meant the loss of 35 aircraft, 123 aircrew had lost their lives, 17 were missing and 88 made prisoners of war. Fortunately 13 men had evaded capture and been able to make their way back to this country.

~ CHAPTER 7 ~

Hamburg & Peenemünde

ON THE NIGHT OF 25TH/26TH July 78 Squadron took part in a raid on Hamburg, Europe's biggest port and the home of Germany's largest U-Boat building yards. The Battle of the Atlantic was slowly being won by the Royal Navy, but U-Boats continued to be built at a high rate. The type IX now being produced in the Hamburg yards had a displacement of 1,200 tons and had fuel tanks with a capacity of over 200 tons, giving the submarine a range of over 10,000 nautical miles.

These large submarines were in great demand by Admiral Doenitz for long range attacks on shipping off the American Eastern seaboard, as well as the West African coast. They could carry as many as twenty torpedoes, putting a great many ships at risk every time a one of these U-boats left its home port. This made it imperative that the yards where these submarines were being built received the full attention of Bomber Command, if the Allies were to have any chance of winning the Battle of the Atlantic.

The bombers were issued with packs of metallised paper known as 'window'. Each of these packs contained about 2,200 pieces per bundle, they measured 27 centimetres long and 2 centimetres wide with black paper on one side and aluminium foil on the other. The length of these pieces was important because it was the wavelength of the German radar used to track the aircraft. As the strips of window fluttered to the ground they jammed the German radar frequency and completely disabled it. Although window was an unqualified success, the Hamburg defences still claimed 14 aircraft in this raid. 78 Squadron were fortunate in not suffering any losses, though several of their aircraft had wounded men aboard when they landed back at Breighton.

On reaching their dispersals the ground crews immediately began the task of repairing battle damage and in some cases, cleaning up the inside of the aircraft following the removal of any wounded or dead by the station medical staff. It was not a pleasant task, but one that had to be done before repairs could commence. A half crown for cleaning out a rear turret after a gunner had been killed was the average added to an airman's daily rate.

The night of 25th/26th July saw an attack carried out on Essen. This was a target that most of the crews had experienced previously, and none of them were looking forward to the reception that awaited them, for Essen was surrounded by searchlights and flak units, and there was also the inevitable night fighter presence to contend with.

The aircraft of 78 Squadron took off at 22.00 hours from RAF Breighton to rendezvous with aircraft from other squadrons before setting course for the target, but for one of the Breighton aircraft it was to be its last sortie. Halifax II JD330 EY-F was shot down by a night fighter at 01.00 hours in the vicinity of Duisburg. The four fatalities were initially buried the and later re-interred at Reichswald Forest War Cemetery.

Pilot P/O E.R. Carrington, POW, Stalag Luft 3 Sagan
Nav F/O F. King, killed, Reichswald Forest War Cemetery
B/A Sgt H.W. Marshall, POW, Stalag 4B Muhlberg-Elbe
W/Op Sgt C.H.G. Daft, killed, Reichswald Forest War Cemetery
F/E Sgt R.T. Davies, POW, Stalag 4B Muhlberg-Elbe
A/G Sgt T. Morris, killed, Reichswald Forest War Cemetery
A/G P/O A.E. Gale, killed, Reichswald Forest War Cemetery

LOSSES ON THIS OPERATION were heavy with 30 aircraft being lost, 143 air crew killed and 39 made POWs. One man succeeded in evading capture.

The population of Hamburg experienced their second heavy raid within 48 hours when on the 27th/28th July Bomber Command again bombed the port. From the moment the first target indicator was dropped, hundreds of tons of high explosive bombs and incendiaries rained down on the city, generating a firestorm of such gigantic proportions that all attempts by the city's firefighters were completely overwhelmed. German records estimate that 40,000 people perished in circumstances never previously experienced. Most died of suffocation caused by the intense firestorm sucking all the oxygen out of the air.

One aircraft from 78 Squadron failed to return, Halifax II JD148 EY-A which was reportedly shot down by flak over Wilhelmshaven, resulting in the deaths of two crew members and the remainder becoming POWs.

Pilot Sgt L.E. Maidment, killed, Sage War Cemetery
Nav Sgt J. Sowter, POW, Stalag 4B Muhlberg-Elbe
B/A Sgt L.H. Croad, killed, Runnymede Memorial
W/Op Sgt C.W. Robertson, killed, Sage War Cemetery
F/E Sgt J. Fagan, POW, Stalag 4B Muhlberg-Elbe
A/G Sgt J.E. Roberts, POW, Stalag 4B Muhlberg-Elbe
A/G Sgt T. Ferguson, POW, Stalag 4B Muhlberg-Elbe

BOMBER COMMAND LOSSES ON this op were once again heavy, with 22 aircraft failing to return to their bases, 101 air crew killed, 16 injured and 21 made prisoners of war.

On the afternoon of 29th July 78 Squadron air crews were called to a briefing. When they were all assembled the curtains were drawn back to loud groans from many in the room on seeing where the tape ended, for their target was once again the port of Hamburg. The general feeling among the crews was. "How many of us will return this time?"

At 22.00 hours that night the aircraft of 78 Squadron took off. After forming up in the very congested skies over Yorkshire and Lincolnshire, they took their places among the many other squadrons who were setting course for the German port.

How anyone had survived after the pounding Hamburg had received during the past week defies imagination, but when they arrived over the city, the flak guns and searchlights were still as active as ever. Oboe equipped Mosquitoes dropped target indicators and the Pathfinders lit up the target with flares ready for the first wave of bombers to drop their loads of high explosive and incendiary bombs, causing the sky above Hamburg to glow with the huge fires. Hamburg had once again suffered tremendous damage when this raid was over, but it was not without heavy losses to the bomber squadrons: 32 aircraft lost, 177 air crew killed and 117 made POWs. Two of 78 Squadron's aircraft failed to return.

Halifax II JB798 EY-P was hit by flak and crashed at Bad Oldesloe, 20 km SW of Lubeck with no survivors. The fatalities were buried in Hamburg Cemetery, in the city's Olhsdorf district. They were:

Pilot F/Sgt F.A. Fraser RAAF | **Nav** Sgt W.M.T. Hetherington RCAF
B/A F/Sgt R.C. Baille RCAF | **W/Op** Sgt W.E. Goodacre
F/E Sgt J.R. Nicholls | **A/G** Sgt T. Campbell | **A/G** Sgt G.H. Woodcock RCAF
All killed and interred at Oldsdorf Cemetery, Hamburg

HALIFAX II JD252 EY-W was lost over the North Sea. One body was recovered by an ASR launch the following day, identified as that of Sgt G.M. Gibb and taken to Driffield Cemetery for interment. The rest of the crew are commemorated on the Runnymede Memorial.

Pilot Sgt P.F. Snape | **Nav** P/O K. Wilson | **B/A** F/O C.E. Burns
W/Op Sgt G.M. Gibb | **F/E** Sgt L.J. Dugard | **A/G** Sgt E.G. Nickels
A/G Sgt C.R. Langley
All died in the North Sea after ditching

THE NEXT NIGHT 30TH/31ST July 1943, a large force of bombers attacked Remscheid in the Ruhr Valley. This city may not have been visited as often as others in this area, but it was still well protected by flak and night fighters. As a result Bomber Command lost 17 aircraft, 74 air crew killed and 32 made prisoners of war. One man managed to evade capture. Two of the 17 aircraft lost were 78 Squadron Halifaxes.

After being badly damaged by flak, Halifax II JD329 EY-G was shot down by a night fighter, crashing at Uedesheim on the west bank of the Rhine, about 7km from Nuess. Five crew members were killed and two became prisoners of war:

Pilot Sgt R. Shelton | **Nav** Sgt A.H. Marshall
A/G F/Sgt G.A. Rourke RAAF | **W/Op** Sgt J.F. Harper | **F/E** Sgt D. Williams
All the above were killed and interred at Reichswald Forest War Cemetery
B/A F/O G.I. Whitehouse, POW, Stalag Luft 3 Sagan
A/G F/Sgt K.A. Skidmore RAAF, POW, Stalag 4A Hohenstein

HALIFAX II JD375 EY-P crashed at Rengen with the loss of all on board, who were buried in a local cemetery and later moved a collective grave in Rheinberg War Cemetery. They were:

Pilot Sgt D. Hadwin | **Nav** Sgt A.B. Cresswell | **B/A** Sgt G.H. Irons
W/Op Sgt A.B. Radcliffe | **F/E** Sgt B.J. Bond | **A/G** Sgt J.C. Gibson
A/G Sgt J.A. Suffield | *All killed and interred at Rheinberg War Cemetery*

FOR THOSE SQUADRONS THAT took part in the fourth attack on Hamburg on the 2nd/3rd August, the operation began with heavy cloud over the North Sea, added to which severe icing problems were experienced. This caused several crews to abort the mission and turn for home. Those that persevered met with fierce flak from the time they entered enemy territory and it continued all the way to the target. Once more, it was a night of terror for the citizens of Hamburg as hundreds of tons of high explosive bombs and incendiaries rained down, destroying all that was left of the city. The morale of the German people must have been at an all time low, and this was what Sir Arthur Harris had intended when he issued orders for the 1,000 bomber raids to commence.

However, it had been another bad night for Bomber Command with 37 aircraft missing, 92 air crew killed, 14 injured, 21 made POWs and 7 interned in Sweden. 78 Squadron had contributed 23 Halifaxes to this operation and on this occasion they all returned safely to base, though most of them suffered varying amounts of damage.

A week later 15 Halifaxes of 78 Squadron took off at 21.00 hours on the night of 9ᵗʰ/10ᵗʰ August to take part in a raid on Mannheim. They all returned safely to base. The next night an attack was mounted on Nurnberg and this time 21 aircraft took off from Breighton. Returning from the raid, Halifax II JD151 EY-M was approaching for a priority landing, due to shortage of fuel, when it crashed at 06.19 hours between the villages of Wressell and Breighton, resulting in the deaths of three of the crew. The flight engineer, Sgt W.J. Brown, died of his injuries on 13ᵗʰ August.

Pilot F/Sgt J. Jenkinson, injured but safe
Nav Sgt H.Binns, killed, Liverpool (Allerton) Cemetery
B/A Sgt W. Eyles & | **W/Op** F/Lt G.J. O'Neill,[1] injured but safe
F/E Sgt W.J. Brown, injured, died later, Liverpool (Allerton) Cemy
A/G Sgt T. Gillicker, killed, Southport (Birkdale) Cemetery
A/G Sgt L.J. Richard, injured but safe

DURING THE NIGHT OF 12ᵗʰ/13ᵗʰ August 1943, 26 aircraft were detailed by 78 Squadron to take part in a raid on the Italian city of Milan. They were to rendezvous with aircraft from No's 1, 5 and 8 Groups. Their targets were the Alfa Romeo motor works and the main railway station. The attack was carried out successfully with severe damage being inflicted on both of the targets. This operation resulted in Italy deciding to capitulate, leaving the Germans to carry on the fight alone. Though six aircraft were lost during this operation, all 78 Squadron aircraft returned safely to base.

ON 17TH AUGUST, 78 Squadron air crews were called to a briefing at which they were informed that an attack was to be mounted by a large bomber force against an important target located on the shores of the Baltic. The crews were not informed what was taking place at the target, a place called Peenemünde, but they were left in no doubt that if this operation was not successful, they would be ordered to carry out another raid immediately.

A force of 25 Halifaxes was despatched from RAF Breighton. One of the aircraft taking part was commanded by F/O James Keirl; he and his crew had just completed a heavy conversion course at RAF Riccall and on the morning of 17ᵗʰ August they arrived at their new squadron to be informed they were on 'Ops' that night. Flying Officer Keirl was to fly as 2ⁿᵈ pilot with another crew and Sergeant Greet was to be mid-upper gunner with Pilot Officer Ferguson. During the briefing the crews were told the target was an experimental station on the Baltic coast and the attack would take

[1] Flight Lt G.J. O'Neill was the squadron's signals leader.

place from a height of 6,000-10,000 feet. It was once more impressed upon the crews that in the event of the operation being unsuccessful, they would be sent back repeatedly until it was destroyed.

The force despatched to attack Peenemünde comprised 324 Lancasters, 218 Halifaxes (145 from 4 Group) and 54 Stirlings. The bombing plan for the attack was to be on three separate aiming points. 4 Group Halifaxes with 3 Group Stirlings and Lancasters would open the main force attack by bombing the first aiming point, the workers housing estate. Lancasters of 1 Group were allocated the second aiming point, the production works, while aircraft of 5 and 6 Groups would strike at the experimental works. The thinking behind the decision to bomb the workers housing was clear from the Bomber Command operation order, which stated: *'All available Halifaxes are to attack the living and sleeping quarters in order to kill or incapacitate as many of the scientific and technical personnel as possible.'*

The officer responsible for organising and controlling this vital operation was Group Captain J.H. Searby[1] of 83 Squadron. He was the obvious choice for command of the force that would attack Peenemünde.

At 21.00 hours 25 Halifaxes from 78 Squadron began to take off for the long haul to their destination but Halifax JD370 EY-F was destined not to join the rest of the squadron. After taking off at 21:14 hours from the west to east runway, it crashed at Willow's Garth, practically astride the main road running SSE to the village of Howden. The only crew member injured was the pilot, W/O V. McKinley. The rest of the crew escaped, they were:

Pilot W/O V. McKinley (injured) | **Nav** Sgt A.J.K. Steven | **B/A** Sgt A. McKenzie
W/Op Sgt Sgt F. Cartwright | **F/E** Sgt A. Scrivens
A/G Sgt J. Winchester | **A/G** Sgt D.G. Cummings

IN THE EVENT, THE raid on Peenemünde was a complete success, though at a high cost of 46 aircraft, 253 air crew killed, 4 injured and 16 made prisoners of war. All the 78 Squadron aircraft returned safely to base.

LEVERKUSEN BECAME THE TARGET for the Halifaxes of 78 Squadron when they took off from Breighton on the night of 22nd/23rd August and, once again, they all returned safely to base.

---

[1] G/Cpt Searby joined the RAF in 1929 and was commissioned in 1939. In March 1943 he was awarded the DFC and given command of 106 Squadron. Shortly afterwards he was given command of 83 (Pathfinder) Squadron, leading his Lancasters during the battles of the Ruhr, Hamburg and Berlin and developing the 'Master Bomber' technique.

~ CHAPTER 8 ~

The Battle of Berlin

O N MONDAY 23RD AUGUST 1943 Air Chief Marshal Sir Arthur Harris took the decision for the Battle of Berlin to commence. It was to a memorable decision that was meant to herald the end of the war in Europe, a war that had been going on for nearly four years, although at this stage there was no sign whatsoever of it ending.

Just after mid-day a Mosquito was despatched from 1409 Meteorological Flight at Oakington. It flew as far as Kassel, from where the crew could check the weather conditions and gauge whether it was suitable for the bombers to carry out a raid that night. The cloud was low but scattered. As soon as the Mosquito arrived back at Oakington, Harris gave the order for the attack on Berlin to commence. Teleprinters began to send out the plan that had already been prepared by the operations staff. Groups received the orders a little before 16.30 hours, which did not leave much time for each squadron to prepare, for the first bomber was due to take off only three hours later.

The force that was to raid Berlin that night consisted of 719 aircraft: 335 Lancasters, 251 Halifaxes, 124 Stirlings and 9 Mosquitos. It was the responsibility of No.4 Group to provide the greatest number of aircraft from the squadrons under their command. They rose to the challenge by despatching 156 Halifaxes: 158 Squadron sent 28, with 51 Sqn and 78 Sqn each sending 27. 158 Squadron's contribution that night would not be exceeded by any other squadron throughout the Battle of Berlin.

The total tonnage of bombs being carried on this raid amounted to 1,812. It consisted of 962 tons of high explosives and 850 tons of incendiaries. However, the tonnage dropped on the target was below that amount, due to 75 aircraft aborting their missions due to various problems.

In company with all the other squadrons taking part in the operation, the aircraft of 78 Squadron crossed the Dutch coast around 22.00 hours. It was a clear night,, which made it easier for the searchlight and flak crews to locate the bombers. Night fighters were also busy and shot down a Halifax near Groningen. The bombers flew on and crossed the German frontier, leaving 90 minutes flying time still remaining before they reached the outskirts of their target, known to the aircrews as 'The Big City'.

Many of the crews taking part in this raid would not return to their bases, for as the force progressed toward their goal the flak grew thicker, with hundreds of searchlights combing the night sky. Occasionally a dreaded blue master searchlight would pick out a bomber and immediately a dozen others would lock onto the hapless victim. Before the pilot could throw his aircraft into a 'corkscrew' dive to escape the clutches of the searchlights, all too often a shell would score a hit and the night sky would be illuminated as the aircraft's bomb load exploded. Moments later, a black void would be left, with nothing to mark the spot where moments before, an aircraft had been flying.

On reaching Berlin, the bombers met with intense flak from hundreds of guns sited all over the city. Many had been situated in concrete bunkers specially built to house them. Though the operation was deemed 'successful' it was to prove very costly for Bomber Command, with the loss of 63 aircraft, 257 air crew killed, 9 seriously injured and 101 made prisoners of war. One man succeeded in evading capture.

During this raid 78 Squadron suffered its heaviest loss since the Dortmund raid on 23rd/24th May (when they had lost three aircraft). When the last surviving aircraft had landed at RAF Breighton after the first Berlin raid, five of the squadron's Halifaxes were missing. Two had been shot down over the target, one had ditched into the North Sea and two collided with each other on their return. On returning to Breighton these two aircraft had been instructed to divert to Leconfield, near Beverley in Yorkshire but while circling the airfield in readiness for landing, they collided, killing 14 crew and badly injuring one. In total the squadron's losses were 29 aircrew killed, 4 injured (one seriously) and two made prisoners of war.

The first of the two planes that collided was Halifax II BB373 EY-K

Pilot Sgt G.G. Bell RNZAF | 2nd **Pilot** F/Sgt R.R. Gilbert | **Nav** P/O E. Platt
B/A Sgt W.L. Clarke | **W/Op** Sgt A. Lee | **F/E** Sgt A.E. Lester
A/G Sgt D.C.M. Walton RAAF | **A/G** Sgt R.B. Fletcher
All killed in a collision near Beverley, Yorkshire

The other aircraft involved was Halifax II JB874 EY-E:

Pilot F/O C.J. Keirl | **Nav** F/O H.W. Baylis | **B/A** Sgt H.R. Jones
W/Op Sgt C.H. Hilton | **F/E** Sgt E..B.F. Scorey | **A/G** Sgt F. Roberts
A/G Sgt J. Greet, seriously injured
All but one killed in a collision near Beverley, Yorkshire

Sergeant Greet was admitted to Beverley Base Hospital, suffering from fractures to the base of his skull and right femur. His injuries were so serious that nearly five years were to pass before he was fully recovered and able to leave hospital. When their daughter was born, Sergeant Greet and his wife Christened her Beverley.

The other three aircraft lost by 78 Squadron that night were:

Halifax II JD248 EY-J, which was shot down by a night fighter and crashed at Havelberg in Germany. There were no survivors.

> **Pilot** W/O J.H. Lowery | **Nav** Sgt R.F. Avis | **B/A** Sgt J.F. Egan
> **W/Op** Sgt D.P. Martin | **F/E** Sgt C.W. Moore
> **A/G** Sgt D. Lamb | **A/G** Sgt T.A.T. Williams
> *All killed and interred at Berlin 1939-45 War Cemetery*

Halifax II JD305 EY-C was badly shot up by night fighters, which inflicted serious damage to the engines. The pilot, F/O Austin, made a gallant attempt to reach base but ditched into the North Sea. As the bomber sank, an empty fuel tank broke free, onto which the air gunner, Sgt Russell, assisted his three injured colleagues. In the 16 hours before help arrived, Sgt Winn fell into the water and drowned and sergeants Rowen and Thewlis died from their wounds soon after being taken aboard the air-sea rescue launch which eventually found them.

In recognition of his gallant actions that night, Sgt Russell was awarded the DFM, gazetted on 24th September 1943.

> **Pilot** F/O J. Austin, killed, Runnymede Memorial
> **Nav** Sgt F.R. Rowen, died on ASR launch
> **B/A** Sgt R.A. Winn, drowned, Runnymede Memorial
> **W/Op** Sgt A.C. Thewlis, died on ASR launch
> **F/E** Sgt S.W. Kent, killed, Runnymede Memorial
> **A/G** Sgt R. Askwith, killed, Runnymede Memorial
> **A/G** Sgt G.E. Russell, Rescued by ASR Launch, awarded DFM

Halifax II JD310 EY-Z was shot down at Klosterfelde, 30 km NNE from the centre of Berlin. There were no survivors.

> **Pilot** S/Ldr P. Bunclark DFC, DFM | **Nav** Sgt J.S. Moore | **B/A** Sgt K.T. Dixon
> **W/Op** Sgt V.A. Robins DFC | **F/E** F/Sgt E.F.C. Matthews
> **A/G** Sgt L.A. Mallory RCAF | **A/G** Sgt J.G. Castle RCAF
> *All killed and interred at Berlin 1939-45 War Cemetery*

NURNBERG BECAME THE NEXT target for a large force of bombers from Nos 1, 3, 4, 5, 6 and 8 Groups on the night of 27th/28th August. The planes of 78 Squadron took off at 21.00 hours from RAF Breighton to join the force that was to raid the giant Siemens-Schukert factory, which manufactured the diesel engines for U-Boats. This factory had been attacked and badly damaged in a raid on Nurnberg during the night of 8th/9th March, but it had since been rebuilt and was once again producing the vital engines needed to keep the 'wolf packs' operational in the Atlantic, where they persistently attacked the Allied convoys bringing food, war materials and thousands of troops to join those steadily being massed all over Britain, ready for the long-awaited invasion of Europe.

The result of the attack on Nurnberg was successful, though Bomber Command lost 36 aircraft, 178 air crew were killed and 49 were made POWs. 15 men evaded capture and returned in due course to the UK, thanks to the help received from the underground organisations.

Two aircraft failed to return to RAF Breighton following the raid, they were Halifax II JD406 EY-P which crashed at Souilly (Muesse) in France. The crew members who died lie in Souilly Churchyard. They were:

Pilot P/O R. Orr RCAF | **Nav** P/O W. Gregson | **B/A** Sgt P.J. Wenmoth
W/Op Sgt I. Illingworth | **F/E** Sgt E.J. Williams | **A/G** Sgt H. McGill
A/G Sgt W.A. Dunleavy RCAF
All killed and interred at Souilly churchyard, France

The second aircraft lost on this mission was Halifax II JD414 EY-M, which exploded in mid-air over the target after a fire had started in the main fuel tanks. The six crew members who died were buried in the Durnbach War Cemetery. The crew was:

Pilot P/O S. Norris | **2nd Pilot** F/O J. Birtles RAAF | **Nav** P/O T. Tabberer
B/A P/O H. McTernaghan | **F/E** Sgt D.J. Purcell | **A/G** Sgt R.S. Payne
A/G P/O F.R. Sanderson
All killed and interred at Durnbach War Cemetery, Germany
W/Op F/Sgt B. Crompton, POW Stalag Luft 3 Sagan

Two nights after the attack on Nurnberg a force of 660 bombers were sent to attack Monchengladbach and Rheydt. This target was just over the Dutch-German border and therefore well within range to be Oboe directed. It was also well backed up by excellent Pathfinder marking, enabling the bombers to drop their bombs accurately on the target, causing serious damage to both towns. In all 32 bombers were lost on this operation, of which three were from 78 Squadron.

Halifax II JD201 EY-Y took off at 00.03 hours from Breighton and at 01.00 hours it crashed near Murrow station, Wisbech, Cambridgeshire, killing the entire crew. They were:

Pilot F/Lt A.R. Short | **Nav** P/O F. Street | **B/A** F/O T.D. O'Boyle
W/Op P/O M.H. Davies | **F/E** Sgt W.G. Onion
A/G Sgt E.A. White | **A/G** Sgt L.J.V. Cotton
All killed in crash near Wisbech, Cambridgeshire

Halifax II JD409 EY-D was shot down by a night fighter (Hptm Rupprecht Stab.11./NJG). It crashed 4 km SW of Westmalle (Antwerpen) WSW of Turnhout. Six of the 7 crew members were killed. They were:

Pilot Sgt A.D. Johnstone | **Nav** Sgt W.P. Williams | **B/A** Sgt A.H. Peadon
W/Op Sgt K.W. Smith | **F/E** Sgt A.A. Reeves | **A/G** Sgt T.I. Goodwin
All killed and interred at Schoonselhof Cemetery
A/G Sgt H.T. Street, survived and evaded capture

The third aircraft to be lost that night was Halifax II JD453 EY-C. After suffering heavy damage from intensive flak, it was intercepted and shot down by night fighters. Three crew members were killed and the rest became POWs:

Pilot Sgt R.G. Collins MiD, killed, Rheinberg War Cemetery
Nav Sgt W.H. Evans, killed, Rheinberg War Cemetery
B/A Sgt C.F. Jaggard, POW, Stalag 4B Muhlberg-Elbe
W/Op Sgt N. Simpson, POW, Stalag 4B Muhlberg-Elbe
F/E Sgt C. Hunt, POW, Stalag 4B Muhlberg-Elbe
A/G Sgt J.E. Ward, POW, Stalag Luft 3 Sagan
A/G Sgt E.E. Deverell RAAF, killed, Rheinberg War Cemetery

DURING THE NIGHT OF 31st August/1st September Berlin was raided again, this time by a force of 622 aircraft, consisting of 331 Lancasters, 176 Halifaxes, 106 Stirlings and 9 Mosquitos acting as route markers. It was the second time in nine nights that the German capital had been the target. 86 pilots prematurely aborted their missions, a number reported being unable to gain the required operating height due to engines overheating.

With the raid on Monchengladbach having taken place less than 24 hours earlier, many of the crews were tired, having had only a few hours sleep, and this, combined with being instructed to fly seventy miles beyond Berlin before turning back to carry out the attack from the south-east, had caused a feeling of great dissatisfaction among those taking part in this raid. The raid itself was bad enough, without adding a 140-mile detour before reaching the target.

The bomber force had been tracked by German radar ever since crossing the Dutch coast and en route to the target lost at least twenty aircraft. By the time Berlin was reached, German night fighters were waiting to drop bright flares to reveal the bombers in the event of cloud obscuring the searchlights. This second of the Berlin raids was one never to be forgotten by any of the bomber crews who took part in it. It was a failure, and a very expensive one: 50 aircraft were lost, 238 aircrew were killed, 4 were badly injured and 101 became POWs. Three men managed to evade capture.

During the debacle 78 Squadron lost two of its aircraft.

Halifax II JD 328 EY-O was lost over Berlin after becoming a victim of the flak, killing three members of the crew, with the remainder becoming prisoners of war:

Pilot Sgt R. Chisholm, POW, Stalag 4B Muhlberg-Elbe
Nav Sgt N.Schnier RCAF, POW, Stalag 4B Muhlberg-Elbe
B/A Sgt S.W.Chapman, killed, Runnymede Memorial
W/Op Sgt H.S.H.Quinn, POW, Stalag 4B Muhlberg-Elbe
F/E , Sgt D.R.Spencer, POW , Stalag 357 Kopernikus
A/G Sgt C.C.Stenning, killed, Runnymede Memorial
A/G Sgt M.J.Bovacanti RCAF, killed, Berlin 1939-45 War Cemetery

Halifax II JD377 EY-G was badly damaged during the attack and crashed at Kleitzen, Germany, killing one crewmember, who is buried in the Choloy War Cemetery in France. The rest of the crew became prisoners of war.

Pilot F/Sgt C. Rowlands RNZAF, POW, Stalag 4B Muhlberg-Elbe
Nav Sgt P.R. Terry, POW, Stalag 4B Muhlberg-Elbe
B/A Sgt A.R. Robinson, POW, Stalag 4B Muhlberg-Elbe
W/Op Sgt J. Marshall, POW, Stalag 4B Muhlberg-Elbe
F/E Sgt G.W. Bloomfield, Killed, Choloy War Cemetery
A/G Sgt S.N. Heavisides, POW, Stalag 4B Muhlberg-Elbe
A/G Sgt D. Wade, POW, Stalag 4B Muhlberg-Elbe

THE SQUADRON WAS PLACED on stand-by for operations on September 1st, but in the event, they were stood down. Whilst on a training flight on the night of 2nd/3rd September 1943, Halifax II JD306 EY-X, piloted by F/O J.C. Smith was mistaken for an enemy aircraft and damaged by anti-aircraft fire from a battery on the Welsh coast at 23.02 hours and abandoned near Haycastle, 6 miles north of Haverfordwest, Pembrokeshire. No injuries were reported among the crew (no crew names are available).

The third raid on Berlin took place on the night of 3rd/4th September carried out by 316 Lancasters aided by 4 Mosquitos. This was due to the high losses suffered by the Halifax and Stirling squadrons. The raid was pronounced a success, with severe damage to parts of the city, but given the vast area which Berlin covers, damage inflicted was less than expected.

The total losses during the three raids on Berlin since 23rd August amounted to 137 aircraft lost, 736 air crew killed, 14 injured and 305 made prisoners of war. Four men evaded capture and 10 were briefly interned in Sweden (but repatriated shortly afterwards).

The next mission for 78 Squadron was on the night of 5th/6th September, when orders were received from Bomber Command HQ for a double attack to be launched on Mannheim and Ludwigshafen. At 21.13 hours 22 aircraft took off from RAF Breighton and were soon on course for the Dutch coast, being part of a force of over 600 aircraft from Nos 4, 5 and 6 Groups. As the first wave of bombers was crossing the coastline, the German coastal defences opened up and the air was thick with explosions and the smell of cordite. Several aircraft quickly became victims of the intense flak, with still more being shot down by night fighters. The bombers had been tracked by Freya radar ever since approaching the Dutch coast.

Weather conditions over Mannheim were extremely good, with high patchy cloud, which gave the Mosquitos an opportunity to mark the target area so that the bombers following close behind were able to see the target clearly. They were not slow in moving in to start their bombing run. A total of 1,500 tons of high explosive and incendiary bombs were dropped. The Blue Master Searchlight picked up several aircraft and they could be seen twisting and turning, doing their utmost to get out of its clutches, but all too often the flak was accurate and the bomber would be seen going down in flames or exploding with a bright flash as its bomb bay was struck by a shell.

In all 37 aircraft were lost in the attack on Mannheim, 169 air crew were killed, 2 were injured, 63 made POWs and 10 managed to evade capture. 78 Squadron lost four aircraft, these were:

Halifax II HR874 EY-B, which had taken off at 19.01 hours from RAF Breighton and was shot down over Mannheim, killing four members of the crew, who rest in the Durnbach War Cemetery. The crew was:

> **Pilot** Sgt F.J. Edser, killed, Durnbach War Cemetery
> **Nav** Sgt S.J. Muldoon, POW, Stalag 4B Muhlberg-Elbe
> **B/A** Sgt G. Jones, POW, Stalag 4B Muhlberg-Elbe
> **W/Op** Sgt P. Hinson, killed, Durnbach War Cemetery
> **F/E** Sgt H. Mott, POW, Stalag 4B Muhlberg-Elbe
> **A/G** Sgt A.N. Moore, killed, Durnbach War Cemetery
> **A/G** Sgt D.T.F. Doyle, killed, Durnbach War Cemetery

Halifax II JB872 EY-Q took off at 19.33 hours from RAF Breighton. It was intercepted and attacked by a night fighter when approaching the target at 19,000 feet. Though badly damaged, the pilot P/O F.C. Ebeling RAAF, decided to continue on course, jettisoning the bombs just short of the aiming point. While on its homeward journey, flying at 16,000 feet, both the port engines failed and almost immediately the Halifax spun and crashed at St Hilaire-le-Grand (Marne) in France. One crew member survived, the rest were buried at Choloy War Cemetery.

Pilot P/O F.C. Ebeling RAAF | **2nd Pilot** F/Sgt V.R. Baker
Nav Sgt H.W. Milligan | **W/Op** Sgt P. Groom | **F/E** Sgt W. Sheffield
A/G Sgt W.R. Huntley | **A/G** Sgt H.J. Pratt
All above killed, interred at Choloy War Cemetery, France
B/A Sgt H. Salter survived and evaded capture

Halifax II JD475 EY-Z took off at 19.46 hours from RAF Breighton and crashed at Lindenberg, killing four crew members who were interred at the Rheinberg War Cemetery. (At 42 years of age F/Lt Hunter was well above the average age for pilots on operational duty.) The crew was:

Pilot F/Lt R.T. Hunter, killed, Rheinberg War Cemetery
Nav P/O M.W.B. Walsh, killed, Rheinberg War Cemetery
B/A Sgt R.H. Caldwell, POW, Stalag 4B Muhlberg-Elbe
W/Op Sgt C. Miles, POW, Stalag 4B Muhlberg-Elbe
F/E Sgt J.A.G. Buchanan, POW, Stalag 4B Muhlberg-Elbe
A/G Sgt J.G. Mein, killed, Rheinberg War Cemetery
A/G , Sgt J.C. Gibney RAAF, killed , Rheinberg War Cemetery

Halifax II LW229 EY-Y took off at 19.48 hours from RAF Breighton and was shot down over Mannheim, killing four members of the crew, who were interred at the Rheinberg War Cemetery. The rest became prisoners of war. It was reported that a fire had started in the flight engineer's station and rapidly spread to the entire port wing. The crew was:

Pilot F/Lt A.E. Ferguson, killed, Rheinberg War Cemetery
Nav F/O A.C. Beales, POW, Stalag Luft 3 Sagan
B/A P/O H.C.S. Hamley, POW, Stalag Luft 3 Sagan
W/Op Sgt A.R. Fleming, Killed, Rheinberg War Cemetery
F/E Sgt R.A. Davies, POW, Stalag 4B Muhlberg-Elbe
A/G Sgt F.O. Dwyer RAAF, killed, Rheinberg War Cemetery
A/G Sgt J. Trace RAAF, killed, Rheinberg War Cemetery

The night of 6th/7th September 1943, saw an attack carried out on Munich by a force of 404 Lancasters and Halifaxes. The raid was successful with heavy damage being reported. The Luftwaffe once again made use of flares to enable the bombers to be seen by the fighters waiting to attack them.

When the last of the surviving bombers had landed back at their bases, it was found that 19 were missing, 88 air crew had been killed, 6 injured and 29 made POWs. One 78 Squadron Halifax had been lost over Munich, shot down by a night fighter, killing four members of the crew who were interred at Durnbach War Cemetery. This was Halifax II JD454 EY-E:

Pilot P/O A.J. Beazleigh, killed, Durnbach War Cemetery
Nav F/Sgt C.M. Edghill, POW Stalag 4B Muhlberg-Elbe
B/A F/O W.J. Cameron, killed, Durnbach War Cemetery
W/Op Sgt M. Emerson, killed, Durnbach War Cemetery
F/E F/Lt W.D. Merriment, POW Stalag 4B Muhlberg-Elbe
A/G P/O G.A. Scarcliff, killed, Durnbach War Cemetery
A/G Sgt W.D. Anderson RCAF, killed, Durnbach War Cemetery

FOLLOWING A SHORT BREAK which allowed the crews to get some well earned rest, 78 Squadron took part in an attack on Montlucon on the night of 15th/16th September and on the next night they raided Mondane. All the aircraft returned safely after both raids.

For the next week the squadron was stood down from operations, though air tests were still carried out on aircraft that had been repaired and serviced. New aircrews had been arriving at RAF Breighton to replace those lost in recent operations and for this, Bomber Command was indebted to the Empire Air Training Scheme for providing a steady supply of trained aircrews to fill the vacancies.

On the morning of 22nd September a briefing was held and the crew were told that operations were 'on' for that night. At 18.30 hours that evening the Halifaxes of 78 Squadron took off to rendezvous with aircraft from 1, 3, 4, 5, 6 and 8 Groups to take part in attacking the 'target for tonight', which in this instance was the German city of Hanover. Before long the large force of bombers was approaching the Dutch coast and, in spite of large quantities of 'window' being dropped to confuse the German radar, the searchlights in their hundreds soon picked up the bombers, after which the flak guns opened fire and began putting up a deadly curtain of explosions through which the crews had to fly their bomb-laden aircraft.

Once they had fought their way through the seemingly impenetrable wall of flak, a multitude of single-engine and twin-engine night fighters would be waiting take their turn. The larger twin-engine aircraft would drop flares to illuminate the bombers, then all the other fighters would swarm in to carry out their attacks. Many of the twin-engine fighters were now equipped with Mauser MG 151/20 heavy calibre cannons using 20mm shells. They became known as *Schrage Musik* and were mounted at an angle at the rear of the cockpit of the Me110, Ju88, Do217 and Me410 night fighters. This enabled them to underfly the unsuspecting bombers and fire the guns upwards into the vulnerable underbelly of the bomber above them. It took only a short burst of fire to set the bomber ablaze, then the fighter would dive away, leaving the bomb load to finish the job.

In spite of this carnage, the bomber force continued relentlessly on their way to their targets, where the aim was to inflict heavy damage to factories and steelworks in Hanover's industrial areas. Thousands of homes were also destroyed in the process, leaving hundreds of civilians dead and many more badly injured or homeless. When the attack was over, Bomber Command was left to count the cost: 31 aircraft lost, 156 aircrew dead, 3 injured and 45 made POWs.

In this raid 78 Squadron had lost one aircraft, Halifax II LW232 EY-O which was badly damaged by flak over the target area and span out of control. The order to bale out was given but the rear gunner, Sgt Spiers was trapped in his turret. The flight engineer and mid-upper gunner went to the aid of their comrade and the captain, F/O Thompson remained at the controls in order to give them time to do so. This selfless act cost him his life, because he went down with the aircraft, as did the tail gunner and his two would-be saviours. Their graves are in the Hanover War Cemetery. Pilot Officer Kaye was a Polish national serving in the Royal Air Force. At 18 years of age, Sgt West was among the youngest airmen to be killed on bomber operations. The crew was:

Pilot F/O P. Thompson, killed, Hannover War Cemetery
Nav P/O M.M. Kaye, POW, Stalag Luft 3 Sagan
B/A Sgt W.G. Yeo, POW, Stalag 357 Kopernikus
W/Op Sgt J. Knox, POW, Stalag Luft 6 Heydekrug
F/E Sgt B. West, killed, Hannover War Cemetery
A/G Sgt L.J. Grange, killed, Hannover War Cemetery
A/G Sgt W.R. Spiers, killed, Hannover War Cemetery

THE 23RD/24TH SEPTEMBER SAW an attack mounted on the German city of Mannheim by a large force from Bomber Command. As had been the case in a raid earlier in the year, one of the most important targets was the I.G. Farben works. When the raid was over a great deal of damage had once again been done to the factory. Bomber Command casualties from this raid were 36 aircraft lost, 179 air crew killed, 5 seriously wounded and 41 made prisoners of war. 10 men succeeded in evading capture.

In this operation 78 Squadron lost two aircraft.

Halifax II LW266 EY-V was shot down at a height of 19,000 feet by a night fighter, killing three members of the crew, who were buried at the Rheinberg War Cemetery. The survivors became POWs:

Pilot W/O F. Poole RNZAF, killed, Rheinberg War Cemetery
Nav P/O F.N. Scott RCAF, POW, Stalag Luft 3 Sagan
B/A Sgt A.E. Sturgeon, POW, Stalag 357 Kopernikus[1]
W/Op Sgt J.S. McDonald, killed, Rheinberg War Cemetery
F/E Sgt R.L. Schelsher, POW, no camp details available
A/G Sgt C. Gibson, POW, Stalag L6 Heydekrug
A/G Sgt H. Entwhistle, Killed, Rheinberg War Cemetery

Halifax II LW273 EY-L crashed at Colombey-les-Belles (Meurthe-et-Moselle), 15 km south of Toul, France, after being badly damaged by flak during its bomb run over Mannheim. All the crew survived and five of them succeeded in evading capture, including the Wireless Op, F/Lt Jones DFC, who was on his second tour of operations. The crew was:

Pilot F/O K.E. Cooper RCAF, POW Stalag Luft 3, Sagan
Nav F/O R. Isherwood, evaded capture
B/A Sgt A.D. Galloway, evaded capture
W/Op F/Lt J.R. Jones DFC RAAF, evaded capture
F/E Sgt J. Rimmer, POW, Dulag Luft, Wetzler
A/G Sgt K.W. Thorpe, evaded capture
A/G Sgt A.F. Chapman, evaded capture

FOUR NIGHTS LATER, ON 27th/28th September, Bomber Command carried out the second of four raids on the city of Hanover, but despite the heavy damage to the industrial area of the city, the raid was considered a failure due to the heavy losses incurred: 47 aircraft lost, 238 aircrew killed, 5 injured, and 66 made prisoners of war. One man evaded capture.

78 Squadron had despatched twenty aircraft that night and three of them failed to return.

Halifax II JD416 EY-F took off at 19.06 hours from RAF Breighton and was shot down over the target area; there were no survivors. The crew members were all buried at Hanover War Cemetery.

Pilot F/Sgt C.R. Skerrett RAAF | 2nd **Pilot** Sgt P.J. Elson
Nav Sgt J. Strachan | **B/A** Sgt R.W. Dando | **W/Op** Sgt R. Hill
F/E Sgt P.R. Fox | **A/G** Sgt N.E. Weighell | **A/G** Sgt R.M. Telfer
All killed and interred at Hanover War Cemetery

---

[1] In the closing days of the war, Sgt Sturgeon managed to escape from Kopernikus and reached home on 23rd April 1945.

Halifax II JD476 EY-M took off at 19.05 hours and was hit and badly damaged by the intense flak over Hanover. It caught fire and the order to bale out was given by the captain. A report made later by Sergeant Preston, who was the only survivor, stated: *"I opened the escape hatch and immediately made my exit, after which I heard no further news of the crew."* His six comrades were interred at Hanover War Cemetery.

Pilot F/Sgt H. Ferme RAAF | **B/A** Sgt F.W. Hucker | **W/Op** Sgt T.A.C. Dorn
F/E Sgt R.J. Drinkwater | **A/G** Sgt L.E. Hughes | **A/G** Sgt E.J. Bream
All the above were killed and interred at Hannover War Cemetery
Nav Sgt G.W. Preston, POW, Stalag 357 Kopernikus

Halifax II LW230 EY-G took off at 19.05 hours from RAF Breighton and was shot down over the target area with no survivors. The crewmembers were all buried at Hanover War Cemetery. (F/Lt G.G. Paul's parents lived in Argentina at Temperley, Buenos Aires.) The crew was:

Pilot F/Lt W.B. Smith RNZAF | **Nav** F/Lt G.G. Paul | **B/A** P/O A.B. Cocking
W/Op Sgt J. Norman | **F/E** P/O G.E. Hickling
A/G Sgt R.A. Smith | **A/G** F/Sgt J.S. Wilkins RAAF
All were killed and interred at Hanover War Cemetery

DURING THE NIGHT OF 29th/30 September, Halifaxes of 78 Squadron joined aircraft from several other 4 Group squadrons in an attack on Bochum. The operation was successful and many buildings were severely damaged. The flak over the target area was intense and resulted in the loss of thirteen aircraft. Two 78 Squadron aircraft failed to return after the raid.

Halifax II LW225 EY-C was presumed lost in the North Sea. The bodies of four crew members were recovered and interred at Sage War Cemetery, and three are listed on the Runnymede Memorial. The crew was:

Pilot P/O G.W. Wilson | **F/E** Sgt H. Kirkham | **A/G** Sgt L.W. Nichols
A/G Sgt H.E.St.H. Goom – *all listed on Runnymede Memorial*
Nav F/Sgt S.G. Mills | **B/A** P/O A.G. Corsby | **W/Op** P/O S.T. Wariner
All interred at Sage War Cemetery

The second aircraft lost that night was Halifax II LW263 EY-E. On regaining the east coast of England, the crew were unable to pinpoint their position and, after searching for some time, they crashed into a wooded area on the Foxhill Road, near Scunthorpe, Lincolnshire, killing two of the crew. On the 10th December 1943 the *London Gazette* announce the award of the DFM to Sgt Cherry. The crew was:

Nav P/O D.J. Polman | **B/A** Sgt T.H. Sharpe
both the above killed in crash landing, Scunthorpe, Lincolnshire
Pilot P/O E.E. Kitchen DFC | **W/Op** Sgt H.E.M. Watson
F/E Sgt R. Cherry | **A/G** F/Sgt D.F. Booth | **A/G** P/O G.T. Gilby DFC
escaped uninjured

THE 4 GROUP HALIFAXES were called upon to attack Kassel on the night of 3rd/4th October 1943. Following their usual course, they made their way out over the North Sea. As the bomber force were approaching the Dutch-German coastline, the crews could see hundreds of searchlights beginning to sweep the sky, and immediately they were over the mainland, the flak began. Guns of all calibres began to form a wall of smoke and flame from roughly 17,000 to 20,000 feet. It was enough to make even the most experienced of the air crews feel terrified. All around them, aircraft started to go down, yet seemingly miraculously, a large number of them got through to reach the target area. They lost no time in releasing their bomb loads, before turning onto a course that would get them away from the main barrage of flak and night fighters.

28 aircraft failed to return to their bases that night, 113 air crew were killed, 10 were injured and 53 made prisoners of war, with one evasion.

78 Squadron lost one aircraft, Halifax II LW262 EY-Z. It was hit by flak while over the target and immediately went out of control. Seconds after the order to bale out was given, the bomber exploded and crashed at Melgerhausen, about 4 km from Melsungen. Those who died were buried in Hanover War Cemetery. The crew was:

Pilot P/O R.S. Bussey | **Nav** Sgt H.E. Parsons | **B/A** Sgt D.B. Polson
W/Op Sgt E.C. Wadsworth | **A/G** Sgt C.C. Davison
All the above were killed and interred at Hannover War Cemetery
F/E Sgt J.F. Baker, POW Stalag Luft 3 Sagan
A/G Sgt H.F. Trowell, POW Stalag Luft 3 Sagan

DURING THE NEXT THREE nights, raids were carried out on Frankfurt and Stuttgart without loss of any 78 Squadron aircraft or injury to any aircrew. However, this changed on the night of 8th/9th October when once more Hanover was the target for a large force of bombers from Nos 1, 3, 4, 5, 6 and 8 Groups which set out from their bases in Yorkshire, Lincolnshire and Suffolk. After crossing the North Sea, they reached the German coast south of Heligoland, where they had to run the gauntlet of the searchlights and flak that awaited them. Inevitably, a number of bombers failed to make it through the intense barrage of flak put up by the German gunners but the rest continued on their way. On approaching Hanover, crews could see many fires already burning ferociously below, which had been started by the first wave of aircraft to attack. Each of the crews dropped their bombs as near to the target as possible before turning to get away from the flak. This operation resulted in the loss of 31 aircraft, 161 air crew killed, 8 injured and 54 made prisoners of war. Three 78 Squadron aircraft failed to return to RAF Breighton.

Halifax II JD455 EY-K suffered heavy damage over the target area and crashed at 01.45 hours at Stocksdorf in Germany, killing four members of the crew, who were interred at Rheinberg War Cemetery. The remainder of the crew became prisoners of war.

Nav Sgt F. Madden | **W/Op** SgtJ.P. Todd | **F/E** Sgt L. Harrett | **A/G** Sgt W. Voss
All the above were killed and interred at Rheinberg War Cemetery
Pilot Sgt J.E. Swindin, POW Stalag Luft 3, Sagan
B/A Sgt C.A. Walsh, POW Stalag Luft 3, Sagan
A/G Sgt W. Robertson POW Stalag 4B, Muhlberg-Elbe

The second loss that night was Halifax II LW236 EY-Q, which crashed at Strohen, again a victim of the heavy flak. The six fatalities were initially interred locally but reburied post-war at Hanover War Cemetery.

Pilot Sgt W.H. Scott | **Nav** Sgt C.N. Boutle | **B/A** Sgt G.H. Styler
W/Op Sgt F.G. McVey | **F/E** Sgt A.N. Griffiths-Buchanan | **A/G** Sgt S. Smith DFM[1]
All the above were killed and interred at Hannover War Cemetery
A/G Sgt L.W. Coleman, POW Stalag 4B, Muhlberg-Elbe

Halifax II LW315 EY-G was the third of the squadron's aircraft to be lost in this raid. It crashed at Harsewinkel, 12 km NW of Gutersloh, after being badly damaged by flak. The six crew members who died were laid to rest in the Reichswald Forest War Cemetery. The crew was:

Pilot F/Lt R.F. Williams | **Nav** P/O L.G. Heaney
B/A P/O S. McManus RCAF | **W/Op** Sgt R.T. Johnson
F/E Sgt W. Quinn | **A/G** P/O G.L. Hughes RCAF
All of the above were killed and interred at Reichswald Forest War Cemetery
A/G Sgt N.F. Page, POW, Stalag 4B Muhlberg-Elbe.

In a statement regarding the raid, Sgt N.F. Page later reported:

"My period at RAF Breighton was very short, our crew arrived on 30th September and we were shot down on the night of 8th/9th October in Halifax

---

[1] Sergeant Smith previously served with 61 Squadron, where he gained his DFM in most hazardous circumstances on 24th/25th September 1942.

Crew members of 'A' Flight 78 Squadron who took part in
the squadron's first operation of World War II
on the night of 19th July 1940, an attack on the marshalling yards
at Gelsenkirchen and Recklinghausen.
(*left to right*) Back row: first three unknown, F/O Robinson, P/O Denny, Sgt Roberts.
Front row: Sgt Heyworth, Sq/Ldr Wildey ('A' Flight commander) and P/O Webb. [D WEBB]

Sgt Wilson's 78 Squadron crew and their Whitley,
Autumn 1940
(*left to right*) Sgt Astle (rear gunner);
Sgt Clark (navigator); Sgt Wilson (pilot);
Sgt Tarrent (wireless operator);
P/O Glover (2nd pilot). [D. WEBB]

78 Squadron crew with
Whitley N1486 EY- July 1940
(*left to right*) Sgt Roberts (W/Op); P/O Webb
(rear gunner); P/O Denny (pilot); Sgt Wilson (2nd
pilot); Sgt Walker (observer). [D. WEBB]

Pilot Len Broadhurst in Halifax III LV869 EY-G 'George' at RAF Breighton, July 1944
The crest represents four local pubs: the Bowman, the Swan, the New Inn and the Seven Sisters. The 37 beer glasses signify night operations; the six glasses of milk daylight sorties and the bottle of whisky the 21st operation. After 53 'ops' LV869 was lost over Kiel, 15th Sept 1944.

The crew of G-George preparing for a flight, 1944.

F/O Johnny Freemantle and F/O Taffy Evans.

The crew of G-George, 1944. (*left to right*)
F/O G. Larkworthy (flight engineer), F/O Andy Jamieson (bomb aimer), F/O J. Freemantle (mid-upper gunner), F/Lt L. Broadhurst (pilot), F/O Taffy Evans (rear gunner).

[All photos: LEN BROADHURST]

FO Larkworthy, flight engineer.

Halifax III LV869 EY-G George at RAF Breighton, 1944.

The crew of Halifax III G-George, 1944. (*left to right*) F/Lt L. Broadhurst (pilot), F/O
A. Jamieson (bomb aimer), F/ O G. Larkworthy (flight engineer), F/Lt Saunders

Stan Hurrell, bomb aimer.

Cliff Price, Wireless Op.

Sgt Jack Adams, pilot.

Phil Hyden, navigator 1942.

**The crew of
Halifax Mk II
DT775 EY-F-Freddie
78 Squadron RAF**

Nobby Clarke, F/Eng 1942.

Joe Enright, air gunner 1941.

The grave of Sgt Joe Enright.

Stan Reed, tail gunner.

Halifax II DT775 EY-F-Freddie (renamed F-Firkin by the crew) was shot down over Briey, France on the night of 10/11 April 1943. All the crew became POWs, with the exception of air gunner Sgt Joe Enright, who lost his life [STAN REED]

Former aircrew chums Cliff Price, Stan Reid and Stan Hurrell meet up in 1992.

Wing Commander Guy Lawrence, commanding officer of 78 Squadron, chats with his crew before departure to Berlin on 31st August 1943. In the background is their Halifax II (Series 1a) JD173EY-V 'Victor', displaying a score of seven completed operations. This aircraft went on to complete a total of 23 'ops' with 78 Squadron before passing on to No 1658 HCU. It was finally struck off charge in February 1945. [GUY LAWRENCE]

Halifax II LW271 EY-S being prepared for a raid over enemy territory. It took off from Breighton at 16.29 on 2nd December 1943 for a raid on Frankfurt. It was shot down over Germany and six of the seven crew members were killed and interred at Rheinberg War Cemetery. They were: **Pilot** W/O P.R. Waller, **Nav** F/Sgt B.L. Purvis, **B/A** Sgt S.P. Mirams, **W/Op** Sgt K. Perkins, **A/G** Sgt K.W. Smith MiD, **A/G** Sgt T.R. Derrington (all killed); the only survivor was **F/E** Sgt K.R. Babbage (POW).

The Air / Ground Crew of Halifax 'C' Charlie after completing 30 sorties.

The crew of 78 Squadron Halifax C-Charlie, pose for a photo after completing a 'full tour' of 30 operations over hostile territory. Very few crews achieved this goal.

Dutch civilians pay their respects at the crash site of Halifax JB845, a 78 Squadron aircraft shot down by a night-fighter from the Luftwaffe base at Venlo on the night of 3rd April 1943. All the crew were killed. The location is near Nederweert, Holland, where a total of six RAF aircraft crashed.
[photo: MISS BETTY IRENE ROBERTS]

Air and ground crew of S-Sugar, 'C' Flight, 78

Air and ground crew of S-Sugar, 'C' Flight, 78 Squadron. (*from left to right*) Flt/Sgt Larry Coates RCAF
(mid-upper gunner), P/O Eric Prichard (flight engineer), Flt Lt Bill Rodney, DFC RCAF (Pilot),
Flt Lt Ted Jones (navigator), Flt Lt Art Hicks (bomb aimer) [photo: C. RICHARDS]

Ground crew standing near rear turret of Halifax U-Uncle, RAF Breighton 1944 'Polly' Perkins, Les Fellows, 'Jonah' Jones, Henry Wilkins, Cpl Rowe and unknown.

Corporal Rowe, LAC Ernie Jones and LAC Cliff Richards, ground crew of Halifax II U-Uncle, RAF Breighton 1943.

Radar Section Staff, RAF Breighton, 1943/44. ®

[all photos: C. RICHARDS]

78 Squadron Halifax EY-B on a flight test over East Yorkshire.

78 Squadron Halifax E-Easy on a daylight test from RAF Breighton, late 1943.
[GUY LAWRENCE]

Aircrew personnel of 78 Squadron assembled prior to the squadron's transfer from
Bomber Command to Transport Command, RAF Breighton 1945. [E. RICHARDS]

LW315 EY-G on our first operation. I was the rear gunner and the only survivor, the remaining six perished with the plane.

After bombing Hanover a Ju88 got us and we were going down in flames. I hand rotated the turret (the hydraulics were gone), exited backwards and parachuted from 16-17,000 feet. Although it was night-time (01.30 hours or thereabouts) I was captured immediately on landing near to the village of Harsewinkel, to the west of Gutersloh.

The pilot F/Lt R.F. Williams, joined the RAF pre-war as a ground wireless operator. Early in the war he retrained to become a rear gunner on Whitleys, completing a full tour of 31 operations, and ending up as Gunnery Leader on his squadron (No. 78). He later took a Navigator's course and passed as a navigator instructor. He was then posted to a squadron in Algeria as Navigation Officer. With further career development and training, he became a pilot with the rank of Flight Lieutenant and we crewed up in July 1943 at Lossiemouth No.20 OTU. From there we went to Marston Moor, then to Breighton."

At 12.30 hours on 16th October 1943, Halifax II JD161 was taking off from Hartford Bridge on a training flight when it crashed into a Boston IIIa BZ276 of 342 Squadron, operated by the Free French Air Force. Both aircraft were damaged beyond repair and four airmen were reported to have been injured. The Halifax was a 78 Squadron aircraft, whose pilot was Flight Sergeant G.R.L. Cunningham. The names of those injured are not available.

Another accident involving a 78 Squadron aircraft occurred on 20th October when Halifax II LW294 EY-O crashed on Breighton airfield. Its pilot was trying to go round again after a misjudged approach. No injuries to any of the crew were reported. The pilot was Sergeant J.J. Rolfe.

The night of 22nd/23rd October saw 78 Squadron take part in a raid on Kassel when 130 Halifaxes from 4 Group joined aircraft from Nos 1, 5, 6 and 8 Groups for the raid. The marking of the target by Pathfinders was excellent and the bombers, following close behind, were able to carry out a concentrated attack on the target. By the time the last aircraft had departed, a firestorm was raging. Photographs taken by reconnaissance aircraft showed that Kassel had been dealt a severe blow. Large areas of the city's residential district were completely destroyed and the Henschel aircraft factories, which were preparing for the full scale production of the V1 flying bomb, were seriously damaged.

That night Bomber Command also suffered very heavy casualties, losing 48 aircraft, 243 air crew killed, 7 injured and 80 made prisoners of war.

78 Squadron lost two aircraft, they were:

Halifax II LW293 EY-L which took off at 17.31 hours from Breighton and crashed at Vorden in Germany, killing all the crew, who were laid to rest at Hanover War Cemetery. They were:

Pilot S/Ldr G.A. Sells DFC | Nav F./Lt D.R. Rogers | B/A F/Lt C.H. Abbot
W/Op P/O G. Simpson | F/E P/O S. Greenlees | A/G P/O J.W. Hardcastle
A/G F/Sgt J.S. Ferris RCAF
All killed and interred at Hannover War Cemetery

Halifax II LW301 EY-C Took off at 17.27 hours from RAF Breighton and crashed at approximately 21.00 hours at the town of Obervellmar, in the northern outskirts of Kassel, after suffering heavy damage from flak while over the target. Three crew members died and five were taken prisoner.

Pilot W/O B.E.E. Allden | 2ⁿᵈ Pilot Sgt J.A. Buck | A/G Sgt G.A. Nelson
All the above were killed and interred at Hannover War Cemetery
Nav Sgt J. Clingly, POW Stalag 4B, Muhlberg-Elbe
B/A Sgt T.D. Gower, POW Stalag Luft Barth, Vogelsang
W/Op Sgt D.S. Hemelik, POW Stalag 4B, Muhlberg-Elbe
F/E , Sgt R.J. Williams, POW Stalag Luft 3, Sagan.
A/G F/Sgt K.R. Miller RAAF, POW Stalag4B, Muhlberg-Elbe

AN ATTACK CARRIED OUT on Dusseldorf on the 3ʳᵈ/4ᵗʰ November by a large force from Bomber Command resulted in the loss of 28 aircraft. On this occasion 78 Squadron were fortunate and all their aircraft returned safely. This luck soon ran out, however, when a raid on the city of Cannes in the south of France on the night of 10ᵗʰ/11ᵗʰ of November resulted in the loss of Halifax II LW321 EY-T, killing all on board, whose remains were laid to rest at St-Desir War Cemetery, 4 km west of Lisieux. They were:

Pilot F/Sgt A. Berry | Nav Sgt L. Austin | B/A Sgt J.R. Cowen
W/Op Sgt G.N. Cox | F/E Sgt G.H.C. Horne
A/G Sgt J.E. Taylor | A/G Sgt J.H. Barkwell
All killed and interred at St-Desir War Cemetery, France

A DUAL ATTACK WAS mounted on Berlin and Mannheim on the night of 18ᵗʰ/19ᵗʰ November, by a large force of bombers from all seven groups of Bomber Command. The Lancaster squadrons attacked Berlin, whilst the Halifax and Stirling squadrons bombed Mannheim, due to the fact that the Lancaster's carried a heavier bomb load and could operate at a greater height and at a higher speed, which gave them an advantage when attacking such a heavily defended area as Berlin. Even so, 10 Lancasters were lost. Mannheim claimed 24 bombers but on this occasion all the 78 Squadron aircraft returned safely to base.

On the night of 19th/20th November, aircraft from Nos 3, 4, 6 and 8 Groups carried out a raid on Leverkusen. Bad weather was experienced all the way to the target and this kept the night fighters grounded, but the intense flak accounted for the loss of eleven aircraft on this operation, six of which were shot down while on the return flight to their bases. Two of the aircraft lost belonged to 78 Squadron.

Halifax I JD118 EY-U took off at 16.16 hours from RAF Breighton and was badly damaged by heavy flak over the target. In spite of this the pilot, Flight Sergeant W. Hrinkiw RCAF, somehow managed to fly the stricken plane back to England and make a crash landing at North Cave, 10 miles south-west of Beverley, Yorkshire. The navigator, Sgt W.A. Valley RCAF was killed but the remaining crew members escaped unharmed:

Nav Sgt W.A. Valley RCAF, killed, Harrogate (Stonefall) Cemetery
Pilot F/Sgt W. Hrinkiw RCAF | **B/A** F/Sgt L.G. Preece RCAF
W/Op Sgt W. Jones | **F/E** Sgt S. Littler | **A/G** Sgt T. Stump
All escaped uninjured
A/G Sgt G. Creer, injured but safe

A second aircraft to suffer heavy damage from the intense flak over the target area that night was Halifax II LW223 EY-P. It had taken off at 16.24 hours and, after carrying out its bomb run, was hit by a shell. On returning to base, it overshot the runway and finished up astride the railway line south of the village of Bubwith. No serious injuries were reported.

Pilot F/O F.R.Harris, injured but safe | **Nav** Sgt C.Weeks, escaped uninjured
B/A Sgt C.Watt, injured but safe | **W/Op** Sgt J.Everett, escaped uninjured
F/E Sgt I.Bell and **A/G** Sgt E.Hamlyn, escaped uninjured
A/G Sgt W.Langtree RCAF, escaped uninjured

THE NIGHT OF 22ND/23RD November 1943 saw Bomber Command launch the heaviest attack of the war against Berlin. Every Group in the Command took part in this operation. A force of 764 aircraft attacked the Central and Western parts of the city, including 234 Halifaxes of 4 Group. Fifty Stirlings also took part in this operation but it was to be the last time this aircraft would raid the German capital, due to the heavy losses they had consistently incurred. Their short wingspan restricted the height at which they could operate, leading to unnecessary losses. Another design fault was the bomb bay, which was divided into sections, which prevented them from carrying bombs of more than 4,000 lbs in weight.

The weather over the target was 10/10ths cloud but the Pathfinders, relying on their H2s sets, found and accurately marked the aiming point with their yellow and red target indicators set to detonate above the clouds. What followed was the most concentrated and destructive bombing raid so far on Berlin. Many important buildings were badly damaged, these included the Reich Chancellery, the Foreign Office and several foreign legations in Wilhelmstrasse, which included the French and British Embassies and a number of other government buildings. The western suburbs likewise suffered as the bombing extended in that direction from the city centre. The railway system was badly disrupted when the Potsdamer and Stettiner stations were seriously damaged, for no trains were able to enter or leave for some time because of blocked lines.

Due to bad weather over Germany, most of the night fighters were grounded and consequently the bomber losses were not as bad as they might have been. When the last surviving aircraft had returned to its base, 32 were missing, 168 air crew had been killed, 5 were seriously injured and 25 had become prisoners of war.

That night 78 Squadron had despatched 18 Halifaxes from RAF Breighton. Two had returned early, one due to severe icing and the other due to oxygen failure. Of the remaining 16 aircraft that had successfully reached and bombed the target, 15 returned safely to base but one of them, Halifax II LW319 EY-U had suffered serious damage over the target. On regaining the East Anglian coast, the pilot F/Lt R.F. Martin attempted to land at Coltishall, Norfolk but he lost control and crashed at 23.06 hours at Beeston Park, near Norwich, resulting in the deaths of four crew members, including himself. Three were injured but survived:

Pilot F/Lt R.F. Martin, critically injured, died later in hospital
Nav P/O F.E.G. Salmon, critically injured, died later in hospital
B/A F/O B.A. Blackwell, killed, buried in home town
W/Op P/O A. Parlour, Injured but safe
F/E Sgt S.G. Bird, killed, buried in home town
A/G Sgt J. Taylor, injured but safe
A/G Sgt J. Thompson RAAF, injured but safe

WHEN THE 78 SQUADRON aircraft landed after the raid, they found the press waiting to interview them. One behind the other they appeared in the lights of the flare-path and moments later they touched down. As each bomber reached the end of the runway it turned onto the perimeter track and slowly made its way to one of the hard standings. Once the engines had been switched off and the crew had left the aircraft, the ground crew quickly got to work, making a complete check of the bomber from back to front. Until all necessary repairs had been carried out, the aircraft would not be allowed back into the air.

R-Robert was the first to land and its crew the first to tell how remarkably easy it had been to give Berlin its heaviest bombing to date. The pilot was W/O Downs, a Londoner, who spontaneously said:

> "It was wizard. We flew above the cloud all the way. They were certainly shooting the flak up all the way there and back and the kite got hit twice, but nobody got hurt. It was my first time over Berlin. I was surprised it was so easy. We put our load down in the marked area and didn't see a night fighter the whole time."

The crews came straggling out of the darkness into a large Nissen hut where they would be debriefed. A Canadian pilot came in, followed by a Scottish engineer, an English rear gunner and wireless operator, an American bomb aimer and a Canadian navigator, who added:

> "We flew above 10/10th cloud all the way. There was slight icing up, but nothing to mention. The temperature fell to about minus 20 degrees. Our navigation was purely by the stars. On the way to the target we saw periodic flak. Over the target the flak was not very heavy but what there was, was very accurate, and there were no night fighters."

Attacks on Frankfurt took place on the night of 25th/26th November and on Berlin the following night 26th/27th November. The total number of aircraft lost by Bomber Command during both these operations amounted to 68 but 78 Squadron lost no aircraft on either raid.

Bomber Command mounted a raid on Leipzig on the night of 3rd/4th December and to draw attention away from this raid a diversionary attack was made on Mannheim. In spite of this, the aircraft attacking Leipzig were intercepted by hordes of night fighters, which resulted in the loss of 26 aircraft, 128 air crew killed, 2 severely wounded and 14 made prisoners of war. On this operation 78 Squadron lost one aircraft which crashed into the bridge spanning the River Nahe at Bad Munster am Stein, killing four members of the crew. Their bodies lie in the Rheinberg War Cemetery. The aircraft was Halifax II LW313 EY-U

Pilot F/Sgt G.R.L. Gunningham | **B/A** Sgt H.R. Wright RCAF
A/G Sgt E. Evans | **A/G** Sgt P.J. Regan
All of the above were killed and interred at Rheinberg War Cemetery
Nav F/Sgt H. Riley, POW Stalag Luft 3, Sagan
W/Op Sgt H. Kennaby, POW Stalag 4B, Muhlberg-Elbe
F/E Sgt K. Hughes, POW Stalag 4B, Muhlberg-Elbe

DURING THE NEXT TWO weeks bad weather prevented the bombers of 4 Group from operating over Germany, but on the night of 20th/21st December operations resumed and this time the target was Frankfurt. This heralded a period in which Halifax losses were to rise significantly. It commenced when a diversionary raid by Lancasters and Mosquitos to Mannheim failed in its objective of fooling German night fighter controllers and instead the main force suffered numerous attacks while en route to and from the target. Though the operation inflicted considerable damage to Frankfurt, the loss of 44 aircraft was an extremely high price to pay. 205 air crew were killed, one was injured and 97 made prisoners of war. Seven men succeeded in evading captivity and eventually returning to England.

This proved to be the worst night since September for 78 Squadron; five of their aircraft failed to return.

The first was Halifax II JN974 EY-M, which was hit by heavy flak over the target and subsequently attacked by a night fighter (Oblt Werner Baake 1./NJG1 out from Venlo). It crashed at Oirshot (Noord Brabant), 12 km from Eindhoven in the Netherlands. Fortunately, all the crew survived:

Pilot F/Lt J.G. Smith, Evaded capture
2nd **Pilot** Sgt W. Heubner USAAF, POW, Camp details not known
Nav F/O S. Smith, POW, Camp details not known
B/A Sgt W. Boddy, POW, Stalag 4B Muhlberg-Elbe
W/Op F/Sgt J.C. Cash, POW, Stalag 357 Kopernikus
F/E Sgt J.T. Frost, POW, Camp details not known
A/G Sgt F.E.P. Allen, Evaded capture
A/G Sgt G.J. Woods RAAF, POW, Stalag 4B Muhlberg-Elbe

Halifax II LW271 EY-S was shot down over the target, but from this aircraft there was only one survivor. The crewmembers were:

Pilot W/O P.R. Walker | **Nav** F/Sgt B.L. Purvis | **B/A** Sgt S.P. Mirams
W/Op Sgt K. Perkins | **A/G** Sgt K.W. Smith MiD | **A/G** Sgt T.R. Derrington
All the above killed and interred at Rheinberg War Cemetery
F/E Sgt K.R. Rabbage, hospitalised due to injuries, POW

Halifax II LW320 EY-Z took off at 16.24 hours from RAF Breighton and came down in a wood known as Roderbos on the Dutch/Belgian border, near the Hamlet of De Plank. After the war, the body of 1st Lt L.M. Kelly USAAF was returned to the USA for burial in his home town.

Pilot 1Lt L.M. Kelly USAAF, Killed, Margraten Cemetery
Nav F/Sgt J. Rigby, POW, Stalag Luft 3 Sagan
B/A Sgt G.E. Wilson, POW, Stalag Luft 3 Sagan

W/Op P/O A. Boothby, POW, Stal;ag Luft 3 Sagan
F/E Sgt P.A. Westcott, POW, Stalag 4B Muhlberg-Elbe
A/G P/O D.F. Booth, POW, Stalag Luft 3 Sagan
A/G Sgt R.C. Wellard, POW, Stalag 4B Muhlberg-Elbe

After safely returning to base and while awaiting permission to land, Halifax II LW330 EY-O stalled and crashed at 02.00 hours near Howden, about 4 miles from Breighton, bursting into flames on impact and killing all those on board. Their bodies were interred at Harrogate's Stonefall cemetery. The crew members, from four Allied countries, were:

Pilot F/Sgt A. Molloy RAAF | **Nav** Sgt F.E.J. Hothersall RNZAF
B/A F/O B.D. Heading RAAF | **W/Op** F/Sgt F.W. Doonan RAAF
F/E Sgt A.D. Meynell | **A/G** Sgt W.E. Edwards RCAF | **A/G** Sgt J.M. Blake RCAF
All the above killed and interred at Harrogate (Stonefall) Cemetery

After sustaining flak damage over the target Halifax II LW338 EY-Q crashed at Michelbach, Germany, killing all on board. The airmen were laid to rest in Durnbach War Cemetery. They were:

Pilot W/O B. Bolsworth DFM | **Nav** P/O D.A. Hyne | **B/A** Sgt W.M. Gray
W/Op Sgt G. Hampton | **F/E** Sgt W.H. Veale
A/G P/O A.G. Thorne | **A/G** Sgt G.M. Coggans
All killed and interred at Durnbach War Cemetery

THIS WAS 78 SQUADRON'S last operation in 1943. The squadron's losses during the year had been considerable: 87 aircraft lost on operations and a further 4 written off in ground incidents; 354 aircrew killed, 24 injured and 165 made prisoners of war. 19 men had succeeded in evading capture and, with the aid of the Belgian and French underground movements, had eventually made their way back to the United Kingdom.

78 Squadron's first operation in 1944 was on 14th January, when a gardening raid was carried out on the west end of Nordeney. Nine aircraft had been detailed to take part. On arriving at the dropping zone they found the visibility was clear, with a slight haze, though it was very dark. Five of the Halifaxes dropped their mines from a height of 7,000 feet, but the parachutes were not seen to open. Four aircraft returned with their mines due to problems with their H2s sets. All the aircraft returned safely.

Bad weather prevented any bomber operations from taking place in the first few weeks of the year but on the night of 20th/21st January, Nos 1, 3, 4, 5, 6 and 8 Groups mounted an attack on Berlin. 78 Squadron despatched 19 aircraft on the raid. One of them was forced to return early due to generators overcharging, thereby causing a risk of fire. The bomb load was safely jettisoned over the sea.

The main force of bombers was intercepted soon after crossing the German coast and several were shot down. As with the earlier Berlin raids, the 'Big City' once more suffered only moderate damage, but the toll exacted on the RAF was a heavy one: 42 aircraft lost, 174 air crew killed, 8 injured and 69 made POWs. Eleven men evaded capture and in due course returned to the UK.

In this operation 78 Squadron lost one aircraft, Halifax II LW291 EY-M. After taking off at 16.40 hours from Breighton nothing further was heard of the bomber or its crew (according to Squadron ORBs at PRO). It seems the Halifax crashed at Grossmutz, 10 km SE of the small town of Lindow in Germany. There was only one survivor, flight engineer Sergeant H.H. Bennett, who became a POW. The rest of the crew perished and were buried at Grossmutz Cemetery on 22nd January 1944. At the end of the war, their bodies reburied at the 1939-45 War Cemetery in Berlin.

Pilot F/Sgt F.R. Moffat RCAF | **Nav** Sgt N. Legg | **B/A** F/O W.R. McGregor RCAF
W/Op F/O R.G. Selman | **A/G** Sgt J.A. Stewart | **A/G** Sgt H.W. Rudelhoff
All the above were killed and interred at Grossmutz Cemetery
F/E Sgt H.H. Bennett, POW, Stalag 357 Kopernikus

Another 78 Squadron Halifax made an emergency landing at Coltishall, with the port inner engine damaged by flak. It landed safely with no injuries being reported.

The following night 78 Squadron despatched 15 aircraft to take part in a raid on Magdeburg. Four of them were forced to return for various reasons but the rest went on to bomb the primary target at 23.04 hours from a height of 15,000 feet, after it had been identified by H2s and Pathfinder ground and sky markers. A large concentration of fires raging over the target area was reported.

Two 78 Squadron aircraft failed to return from this operation.

Halifax II LW300 EY-H was badly damaged by a night fighter on the way to the target when fuel tanks 2 and 4 were holed. On the return journey, shortage of fuel forced them to ditch in the rough waters of the North Sea, east of Hull. Only two of the crew survived and were later picked up by a Royal Navy destroyer. The crew was:

Pilot F/Sgt D.R.H. Rees | **Nav** F/O C.B. Watt | **W/Op** Sgt E. Moxen
F/E Sgt P. Fowler | **A/G** Sgt M.G. Mulligan RCAF
All of the above lost at sea, names listed on Runnymede Memorial

B/A F/O N.A. Marston and **A/G** Sgt D.W. McMillan
Rescued by a Royal Navy Destroyer

Flight Sergeant Rees was from the small village of Llandybie in West Wales, where his father was the local Station Master. He had one sister and a brother, Wynford, who was later to become Dean of Brecon Cathedral. A memorial on the south wall of *Eglws Santes Tybie* (Llandybie Parish Church) lists the names of no less than twelve local men who gave their lives in service with the Royal Air Force. One of them is F/Sgt D.R.H. Rees.

Halifax II JP117 EY-Y, having taken off at 20.04 hours from Breighton, reached the target area and dropped its bombs at 23.04 hours from a height of 20,000 feet before being badly damaged by flak. The pilot managed to get the aircraft back to England but it crashed near Heslerton, Yorkshire. Sergeant W. Walker was slightly injured but all the crew were declared fit for flying duties the next day. The crew was:

Pilot Sgt W. Hockler | **Nav** F/O F. Sait RCAF
B/A F/O F. Handerson | **W/Op** Sgt S. Howard | **F/E** Sgt W. Walker
A/G Sgt W. McClean | **A/G** Sgt W.G. Baron

DURING THE LAST WEEK of January 78 Squadron was equipped with the new Mk III Halifax. These were an improvement on the earlier aircraft, fitted with Bristol Hercules engines (1615 hp each) which improved the all round performance of the aircraft.

On the night of 2nd/3rd February, 78 Squadron were detailed to carry out a gardening raid on Kiel Bay. As the first Halifax III LV817 EY- began its take off, it swung off the runway and hit another parked Halifax, causing slight damage, before hitting a bank, completely wrecking the undercarriage. No injuries were reported, but the brand new Halifax was a complete write off. The crew was:

Pilot F/Lt B. Denman | 2nd **Pilot** Sgt S. Hampson | **Nav** F/O B.M. Wells
B/A F/O T.J. Cowley | **W/Op** F/Lt T.J. Fudge | **F/E** Sgt E.G. Glibbery
A/G F/Sgt H. Kelter | **A/G** Sgt A. Sinden

ON THE MORNING OF the 15th February, battle orders posted on the squadron noticeboard informed the crews that they would be flying that night, and when the briefing took place, they learned the target was to be Berlin. For this operation 78 Squadron had detailed 26 aircraft but this number was reduced to eighteen for a variety of reasons. One aircraft failed to take off due to technical problems, two returned with engine failure, three were forced to return early when some of the crew were being sick or suffering from lack of oxygen. The captain of another aircraft had to abort due to the rear gunner suffering from extreme cold due to the failure of his electrically heated clothing. An eighth aircraft had to abandon the raid after reaching Sylt, due to a compass failure and being fifteen minutes late reaching the enemy coast. The remaining eighteen aircraft reached and bombed the target, which had been identified with red and green sky markers and H2s. Crews reported the target being well alight, with the bombing being accurate and well concentrated.

The squadron lost one aircraft in this attack, Halifax III LW798 EY-A. While over the target area the undercarriage dropped down and, despite several attempts by the crew, it could not be retracted. The aerodynamic drag this caused increased the aircraft's fuel consumption and on nearing the English coast, with petrol running out, the Captain was forced to turn back out to sea and order the crew to bale out. There was only one survivor. The rest of the crew were never found and their names are commemorated on the Runnymede Memorial:

Pilot F/Lt R.N. Shard DFC.DFM | **Nav** W/O1 J.B. Fowler RCAF
W/Op Sgt J.R. Forder | **F/E** Sgt K.E. Clark
A/G Sgt N. Walton | **A/G** Sgt W. Iddon
All the above were lost a sea and are named on the Runnymede Memorial
B/A F/O W. Uyen RCAF, rescued

22 AIRCRAFT WERE DETAILED for Ops by 78 Squadron on the morning of 16th February 1944, but this was later cancelled. On the 18th February 24 aircraft were detailed for Ops and again it was cancelled. On 19th February 23 aircraft were detailed for operations and this time the raid was on. The squadron were fortunate in having the new Halifax Mk III, for those squadrons still equipped with the Mk II and Mk V had suffered very heavy losses since the beginning of the year. The Bomber Command force for this operation consisted of 823 aircraft in total: 561 Lancasters, 255 Halifaxes and 7 Mosquitos from Nos 3, 4, 5, 6 and 8 Groups.

A pre-briefing for the raid was scheduled for 11.00 hours but when the pilots and navigators had gathered ready for it to begin, a telephone call was received by the Squadron Commander, telling him the briefing had been put back to 17.00 hours. The crews gathered once more for the delayed briefing and when the doors had been locked, it got under way. When the curtain covering the wall map was removed, it exposed the red ribbon indicating their course to and from the target for that night, which was to be Leipzig.

While all the crew members were being made aware of the night's target, the ground crews were hard at work 'fuelling up' and 'bombing up' the aircraft. Each one was loaded with one 2,000 lb high explosive bomb and 4,000 lb of incendiaries in small bomb containers. Mechanics were carrying out the final engine checks and the motor transport drivers were standing by to take the crews out to their aircraft after they had eaten the meal specially prepared for them by the cooks.

After their meal the crews went to the locker rooms to get dressed in their woollen long johns, sweaters, pullovers and wool-lined boots. On top of this they wore their parachute harness, Mae West life-jacket, fleece lined flying helmet and gloves. For the gunners there was extra outer clothing with electrically-heated gloves and insoles for their boots. These latter items were vital, for the gun turrets were notorious for being the coldest places in the aircraft, especially the rear turret, and without these electrically heated garments the gunners would be almost certain to suffer frostbite in their hands and feet. Pilots would abort the mission if the tail gunner reported that this equipment was not working, rather than allowing him to suffer the consequences.

When the time came for the crew to go out to the aircraft, they got into their allotted crew bus and minutes later arrived at the dispersal area where their plane awaited them. There was time for a last cigarette and a chance to relieve themselves (usually on the tail wheel for 'good luck') before boarding the aircraft for the long hazardous journey that lay ahead of them, over some of the most heavily defended areas in Europe.

At midnight the 78 Squadron aircraft began taking off to rendezvous with the rest of the squadrons taking part in the raid, before making their way out over the North Sea to cross the Borkum islands and the Dutch coast, on a course that would take them clear of the defences at Emden. North of Osnabruck, another change of course would point them in the general direction of Berlin. Shortly after crossing the Dutch coast, several aircraft were shot down by flak and night fighters. A further change of course put them onto a south-easterly heading that took them to Leipzig. Suddenly, white target indicators that had been dropped by the Pathfinders lit up the sky, these were followed by green markers. Now the searchlights appeared and the heavy flak guns opened up. The sky was a mass of exploding shells and the acrid smell of cordite filled the aircraft. All over the night sky, aircraft were being shot down, some of them hit before they could drop their bombs, in which case the bomb load would detonate with an enormous explosion. The crews of these bombers stood no chance of survival. Far below, fires were raging out of control and still the bombs continued to rain down. In the light of the fires and explosions the crews could see dozens of bombers all around them and every few minutes another aircraft would fall victim to the never-ending flak.

In the course of this raid, the important target of the railway marshalling yards was hit by high explosive and incendiary bombs, which inflicted serious damage, thus delaying the delivery of vital supplies urgently required by the German arms industry.

But the cost of this operation was extremely high and resulted in the greatest loss of aircraft during a single raid since the bombing of Germany had begun. An unprecedented 82 Bomber Command aircraft were lost, 429 aircrew were killed, 10 seriously wounded and 141 became prisoners of war. Just one man succeeded in evading capture.

Of the 22 aircraft detailed for this raid by 78 Squadron, five failed to take off and a further five returned early for various reasons. Three aircraft were shot down en route, leaving only nine to bomb the target, which made No.78 the only squadron in 4 Group to suffer any losses.

Halifax III LV816 EY-M was intercepted and shot down by a night fighter whilst on the way to the target area. The 2nd Pilot and the navigator were the only ones to escape. The crew was:

Pilot F/Lt B. Denman | **B/A** F/O G.S.Wilson
W/Op P/O R.G. Messer | **F/E** Sgt E.G. Glibbery
A/G F/Sgt H.F. Kelter RCAF | **A/G** W/O2 E.F. McAneeley RCAF
All the above were killed and interred at Berlin 1939-45 War Cemetery
2nd Plt F/Sgt W.A.Lea, POW, Stalag 357 Kopernikus
Nav F/O E.M.Wells, POW, Stalag Luft 3 Sagan

Halifax III LK763 EY-K took off just after midnight from RAF Breighton and was lost without trace. The crew members were:

Pilot Sgt J. Smith | **Nav** F/Sgt E.M. Coulter RCAF
B/A F/O I.R.M. Douglas-Pulleyne | **W/Op** Sgt G.F. Reynolds
F/E Sgt G. Beal | **A/G** Sgt L.E. Mears | **A/G** Sgt R.G. O'Neill RAAF
All were lost without trace and listed on the Runnymede Memorial

The third aircraft to be lost that night was Halifax III LW367 EY-L. After taking off just after midnight from RAF Breighton it suffered heavy damage from flak on the way to Leipzig and crashed near Kallenkote in the Netherlands. Six of the crew were buried at Kallenkote General Cemetery and following the discovery of another body in the wreckage two days later, mid-upper gunner Sgt Hemmings joined his comrades.

Pilot P/O T.H. Smith | **Nav** P/O I.G. Bunn | **B/A** P/O D.A. Riach RCAF
W/Op F/Sgt A.V. Hamilton RNZAF | **F/E** Sgt W.J. Webb
A/G Sgt H. Hemmings | **A/G** Sgt R.J. Chaplin
All killed, interred Kallenkote General Cemetery, Netherlands

THE SQUADRON WAS TO suffer two further losses on the following night of 20th/21st February, when aircraft of 4 Group joined squadrons from Nos 3, 5, 6 and 8 Groups to carry out an attack on Stuttgart. Sixteen of the squadron's aircraft had been detailed for the raid but due to engine problems, three were forced to abort and return early.

In this attack 4 Group lost five aircraft, two of which belonged to 78 Squadron. Halifax III EY- crashed at Dunsfold in Surrey. While touching down, the aircraft swung round and in spite of the pilot trying to take off again, it crashed into some trees. No one was injured, but the Halifax was written off. The crew was:

Pilot F/Sgt W. Hrinkiw RCAF | **Nav** F/Sgt J. Woodward
B/A F/Sgt L.G. Preece | **W/Op** Sgt W. Jones | **F/E** Sgt S. Littler
A/G F/Sgt J. Sands | **A/G** Sgt D. Stump
All escaped uninjured

The crew of Halifax III LV814 EY-C were all killed when it crashed at Recourt-le-Cruex (Meuse), south of Verdun in France. The cause of the crash is not known. They were buried in the Choloy War Cemetery.

Pilot F/Sgt G.M. Storey | **Nav** F/Sgt J.S. Sutherland
B/A F/O P. Kinsella | **W/Op** Sgt A.E. Reeve | **F/E** Sgt W.R. Hales
A/G Sgt E.C. Nott | **A/G** Sgt R.W. Gray
All killed and interred at Choloy War Cemetery, France

ON 24TH FEBRUARY 78 Squadron received orders from 4 Group HQ to take part in a raid on Schweinfurt. Accordingly, 15 aircraft were detailed for the operation, three of which failed to take off and a further four returned early, reasons given included engine problems, tail plane vibration and blind flying instruments going u/s.

Schweinfurt was an important target because it was a manufacturing centre for the ball bearing industry. Without these vital parts, the German war machine would grind to a halt. This was a heavily defended target, so the gunners had to be vigilant in case night fighters were about.

When the 78 Squadron aircraft arrived over the target area they found it had been identified by the Pathfinders with target indicators and red and green markers. A large concentration of fires were already burning, having been started by the first wave of bombers. The flames from the burning buildings clearly lit up the target and greatly assisted the crews in the second wave. The raid was successful but once again the cost to Bomber Command was high: 35 aircraft lost, 166 air crew killed, one seriously injured and 69 became prisoners of war. Three men managed to avoid capture and eventually made their way home.

78 Squadron lost one aircraft when Halifax III LW509 ET-T was shot down by a night fighter. One crew member lost his life and the rest became prisoners of war.

Pilot F/O E. Melin RAAF, POW, Stalag Luft 3 Sagan
Nav F/O C.F. Richens, POW, Stalag Luft 3 Sagan
B/A P/O D. Laver, POW, Stalag Luft 3 Sagan
W/Op P/O K.F. Smith, POW, Stalag Luft 3 Sagan
F/E Sgt M. Bradbury, POW, Stalag 357 Kopernikus
A/G Sgt K. Wisleman RCAF, POW, Camp details not known
A/G Sgt R.W. Airey, killed, Runnymede Memorial

THE ATTACK ON AUGSBURG on the night of 25/26th February, was one in which all groups of Bomber Command took part. For this operation 78 Squadron contributed 13 Halifax aircraft. When all the squadrons had rendezvoused over the North Sea, the total strike force numbered 594 aircraft, although a number of them aborted their missions and headed for home with engine faults, etc. Unknown to the bomber crews, while they were over the North Sea they had been picked up by the powerful long range 'Korfu' detectors now in use by the Germans and the night fighters, fully prepared, fuelled and armed, were waiting to pounce on the slower, heavily-laden bombers as soon as they had made their way across the Dutch coast. Before the night was over, 23 aircraft had been lost, 101 air crew killed, 4 badly wounded, 43 made POWs and 6 interned in Switzerland. Nine men evaded capture, returning to the UK months later. On this operation 78 Squadron lost one aircraft, Halifax III LV794 EY-O, which was attacked and set on fire at 20,000 feet by a night fighter over Augsburg. Four of the seven crew members lost their lives and were buried at the Rheinberg War Cemetery and the survivors became prisoners of war.

Pilot F/Lt W.M. Carruthers | **F/E** Sgt I. Bell
A/G F/Sgt C.W. Sisley RAAF | **A/G** F/Sgt B. Janke RAAF
All the above were killed; interred Rheinberg War Cemetery
Nav F/Sgt A. Collins, POW, repatriated 6/2/45
B/A F/Sgt E.C. Hocking RNZAF, POW, Stalag 357 Kopernikus
W/Op Sgt A.R. Flexman, POW, Stalag 357 Kopernikus

On the night of 1st/2nd March 22 aircraft were detailed for operations by 78 Squadron. Time for take off was scheduled for midnight and the target tonight was to be Stuttgart. However, prior to take off, snow fell and froze hard on the aircraft surfaces, making it impossible for the majority of them to take off. Only six aircraft managed to get airborne and of these only four reached the target, two having been forced to abort the flight due to ice preventing them from climbing. When the remaining four arrived over the target, 10/10ths cloud prevented any results of the bombing being observed. Having done their best, the four aircraft returned safely to base.

From 2nd to 5th March, there were no operations.

THOUGH A DATE FOR the long anticipated invasion of Normandy had yet to be made known, Bomber Command were given the task of attacking important railway marshalling yards, which contained vital equipment ready to be transported to wherever the invasion might take place along the coast of France. Orders were given for the major of railway marshalling yards and the workshops that kept the rolling stock in good working order to be attacked, but without giving the enemy any idea where the invasion would take place. These raids would continue right up to the day when the landing took place.

On 6th March orders were issued by 4 Group Headquarters for 116 aircraft from 4 Group to rendezvous with 119 aircraft from 6 Group to mount an attack on the large marshalling yards at Trappes, to the south-west of Paris.

On arriving over the target area, the crews found and identified it by a lake to the north-east and the red target indicators that had been dropped by six 'Oboe' equipped Mosquitos. Very soon large fires were to be seen burning in the marshalling yards. Over 1,200 tons of bombs fell on the target during the attack, causing extensive damage to the marshalling yards and rolling stock, which contained vital supplies waiting to be despatched. The operation was considered to have been very successful, for Trappes was put out of action for well over a month. Of the 18 aircraft detailed by 78 Squadron for this operation, one had failed to take off due to engine trouble but the other 17 carried out the raid successfully and all returned safely to base.

From the 8th to the 12th March the squadron was stood down but on 13th March orders were received from Group Headquarters for 78 Squadron to become part of a large force of bombers that would raid the railway yards at Le Mans. Of the 21 aircraft detailed for the operation, two failed to take off, one got bogged down in muddy ground and another had engine trouble. Once again the attack was a success, with severe damage being done to the marshalling yards and other installations. Many lines were cut, causing great upheaval to the German transport system in Northern France. Sadly, a number of French civilians lost their lives during the bombing. Though great care was taken to confine the bombing to the engine sheds and railway yards, some bombs inevitably caused damage to nearby civilian housing, causing many deaths. Only one aircraft failed to return to its base and this was a 78 Squadron Halifax III LM517 EY-Y. After taking off at 22.41 hours it had joined the main force making its way to the target area, where it was hit and badly damaged by intense flak, resulting in the deaths of four crew members.

Pilot W/O K. Withers RAAF | **W/Op** Sgt E. Buckland
F/E Sgt E. Currie | **A/G** Sgt A. Cantle-Jones | **A/G** Sgt D.W. McMillan DFM
All the above were killed and interred at Le Mans West Cemetery
Nav Sgt A.A. Jeffries, POW, Stalag 357 Kopernikus
B/A F/Sgt G. Tipping, POW, Stalag 357 Kopernikus

STUTTGART ONCE AGAIN BECAME the target for Bomber Command on the night of 15th/16th March 1944 and 78 Squadron detailed 23 aircraft for this attack, two of which failed to take off due to engine trouble and a further two returned early when fuel pumps to their overload tanks became unserviceable. Eventually 19 planes reached and bombed the target. At the debriefing, crews reported that the bombing had been scattered, although a large concentration of fires were seen burning furiously. All the aircraft returned safely to base.

78 Squadron's next operation was on the night of 18th/19th March when their Halifaxes became part of a force of 828 aircraft ordered to attack Frankfurt. Fourteen Halifaxes took off from RAF Breighton at 19.30 hours to rendezvous with the rest of the force, ready for the 500-mile journey, most of it over hostile territory heavily defended with guns of all calibres, not to mention the night fighters. Four of the squadron aircraft returned early, one with severe flak damage. Over 3,000 tons of bombs fell on city during this attack causing serious damage. It was reported that in excess of 55,000 people were made homeless, with widespread damage both to factories and nearby homes. The 78 Squadron aircraft all returned safely.

No operations were carried out between 19th and 21st March but on the night of the 22nd/23rd March, 23 of the squadron's aircraft took part in mixed sorties. Ten were detailed for a gardening raid on Kiel Bay and 13 were to rendezvous with a large force of bombers over the North Sea to carry out an attack on Frankfurt.

The ten aircraft on the gardening raid took off at 18.00 hours. Two returned to base early with their H2s sets u/s and brought their mines back with them. The rest went on to drop their mines accurately before returning to base. Of the 13 detailed to attack Frankfurt, two failed to take off and one returned with an unserviceable engine after jettisoning its bombs over the North Sea. One Halifax III was shot down by a Ju88 night fighter over the target area and crashed at Mohrweiler. Six of the crew were killed and laid to rest in the Reichswald Forest War Cemetery. The aircraft was Halifax III LW512 EY-Q.

Pilot Sgt S. Hampson | **Nav** Sgt F.G. Rees | **B/A** Sgt R.A. Renwick
W/Op Sgt P.F. Beard | **F/E** Sgt S.L. Toon | **A/G** Sgt T.A. Liddy
All the above were killed and interred at Reichswald Forest War Cemetery
A/G Sgt S.A. Waterhouse, POW, Stalag 357 Kopernikus

THERE WERE NO OPERATIONS or stand-by orders on 23rd March 1944, so crew training was carried out. Some attended lectures, while others carried out dinghy drill. Still more were sent on cross-country flights to familiarise themselves with the latest navigational aids. Being on stand-down did not mean merely hanging about, kicking your heels!

On the morning of 24th March aircrew members of 78 Squadron reported to their flight offices to be told they were on operations that night. Out on the dispersals, ground crews were already engaged in making the bombers ready for the coming raid. Petrol bowsers were pumping the required amount of fuel into each aircraft's tanks, while tractors driven by WAAFs busily pulled trailers loaded with bombs from the bomb dump, where they had already been fused and armed by the armourers ready for the night's operation.

While the pilot checked with the Flight Sergeant on the airworthiness of the aircraft, the rest of the crew carried out checks on the various positions that they would occupy during the flight. Gunners were always very fussy about the condition of their turrets, for a dead fly or similar speck on the Perspex could easily be mistaken for a prowling night fighter in the darkness. While this was going on, all communication with the outside world had been cut off, the only link being with Group Headquarters.

Later in the day the crews were called to the briefing room, where they all sat on long wooden forms, facing a map of Europe, which at present was covered by a curtain. After the roll call had been called they rose to their feet and the Station Commander entered the room, followed by a Wing Commander and his senior flight commanders. The doors were then closed by an RAF policeman, who stood outside on guard, then the curtain was drawn back to reveal that night's target.

It was Berlin. This drew an audible groan from all the crews in the room, for it was the target everyone dreaded. The city was surrounded by a huge concentration of searchlights and guns of all sizes, as well as night fighters.

At 18.30 hours the bombers began to move along the perimeter track at RAF Breighton and, one by one, took off into the darkening sky to rendezvous with a force of over 800 bombers drawn from Nos 1, 3, 4, 5, 6 and 8 Groups to take part in this operation. Of these, 84 aircraft would return early to their bases with problems ranging from instruments u/s to engines giving trouble, leaving 726 aircraft to carry out the attack.

The force crossed Denmark and into the Baltic, crossing the coast near Rostock, then turning east on a course that would take them to Berlin. Very soon the flak began to take its toll, then the night fighters joined in and before long several bombers had been shot down.

As they approached Berlin it was noticed that the wind had increased in strength. This had the effect of the bomber force arriving earlier than the planned ETA. Some aircraft were blown off course and many others overshot the target, but worse was to follow. Large numbers drifted off track and were picked up by deadly predictive flak when they unwittingly overflew heavily-defended areas. According to reports later issued by the Germans, 50 aircraft fell to the flak guns and the rest were victims of the night fighters. A total of 74 aircraft were lost, 284 air crew were killed and 137 became prisoners of war. Nine men succeeded in evading capture[1] and, thanks to the underground movements in the Netherlands, Belgium and France, they returned safely to this country. No 4 Group lost 15 Halifaxes during the raid and a further two crash-landed on returning to their base, killing both crews. Furthermore, 78 Squadron suffered the highest casualties that night, losing six aircraft. The first of these was Halifax III HX355 EY-D which was badly shot up over the target by a night fighter and abandoned in midair near Den Haag. The crew members all made a successful descent by parachute but were captured and became POWs. Their names were:

Pilot F/Lt E.W. Everett, POW, Stalag L1 Barth Vogelsang
Nav Sgt J.R. Stewart, POW, Stalag L1 Barth Vogelsang

---

[1] It should be noted that only those airmen who came to earth in the occupied territories on the way to and from targets in Germany were able to evade capture, thanks to the bravery of sympathetic citizens in their underground movements. Few, if any, who fell on German soil were able to escape.

B/A F/O J.K.M. Green, POW, No details available
W/Op Sgt G.E. Johnson, POW, Stalag 4B Muhlberg-Elbe
F/E Sgt K.H. Jones, POW, Stalag Luft 3 Sagan
A/G Sgt J.R. Graham, POW, Stalag L1 Barth Vogelsang
A/G P/O A.P. Sinden, POW, No details available

Halifax III LV903 EY-H was shot down over Berlin and there were no survivors. They were:

Pilot F/Lt D.F. Constable DFC. RAAF | 2n Plt F/Sgt G.T.A. Lovell
Nav Sgt C.M. Mcleod | B/A Sgt T. Ratcliffe | W/Op F/O H.A. Mace
F/E Sgt D.T. Cash | A/G Sgt E.T.W. Byford | A/G F/Sgt L. Schioler RCAF
All killed and interred at Berlin 1939-45 War Cemetery

Halifax III LW507 EY-K was shot down over Berlin. Two of the crew were killed and the rest taken prisoner. They were:

Pilot Sgt B.T. Smith, Killed, Berlin 1939-1945 War Cemetery
Nav Sgt L.W. Edwards, POW, Stalag 357 Kopernikus
B/A Sgt H. Middleton, POW, Stalag Luft 3 Sagan
W/Op Sgt S. Johnson, POW, Stalag 357 Kopernikus
F/E Sgt T. Willis, POW, Stalag 357 Kopernikus
A/G Sgt L. Daniels, Killed, Berlin 1939-1945 War Cemetery
A/G Sgt R.J. Finn RCAF, POW, Stalag 357 Kopernikus

After returning from Germany with serious damage Halifax III LW510 EY crashed at Cranfield, Bedfordshire, killing all seven crew members. Four were buried at the Cambridge City Cemetery, the rest in their home towns:

Pilot F/O M.A. Wimberley, Killed, Cranfield, Bedfordshire
Nav F/Sgt W.H. Shields, Killed, Cranfield, Bedfordshire
B/A F/O R.S. Kelly RAAF, Killed, Cranfield, Bedfordshire
W/Op Sgt L.J. Edge, Killed, Cranfield, Bedfordshire
F/E Sgt H.J. Neal, Killed, Anfield Cemetery, Liverpool
A/G Sgt D.H.G. Brignell, Killed, Cranfield, Bedfordshire
A/G Sgt H.R. Nelson, Killed, Anfield Cemetery, Liverpool

After completing its bombing run, Halifax III LW518 EY-A was hit by flak and crashed at Fahlhorst, killing all on board. They were interred at Fahlhorst Cemetery but later reburied at the Berlin 1939-45 War Cemetery.

Pilot F/Sgt H.K. Barden | Nav F/O A. Lees | B/A F/Sgt N.S. Davidson
W/Op F/Sgt V.W. Spencer | F/E Sgt F. Curtis
A/G Sgt J.A. Lincoln | A/G Sgt P.D. Cheal
All killed, interred at Berlin 1939-45 War Cemetery

Halifax III LW589 EY-G was shot down by a night fighter while on the homeward flight. It crashed at Les Hautes Rivieres in the Ardennes region of France, killing all on board. They were buried at Les Hautes Rivieres Communal Cemetery. They were:

Pilot F/Sgt H. Jackson | **Nav** Sgt J. Dear | **B/A** Sgt J. Smith
W/Op Sgt H.D. Patchett | **F/E** Sgt P.J.S. Crawford
A/G Sgt R.W. McNeil | **A/G** Sgt W.G. Baker
All killed and interred at Les Hautes Rivieres Cemetery, France

THE SIX EMPTY HARDSTANDINGS at the dispersal areas on the morning after the Berlin raid must have caused great sadness among those serving at RAF Breighton but they would be given no time to dwell upon the loss of their colleagues. By midday six new aircraft were on the dispersals and replacement crews from the OTU were settling into their new quarters.

The following night 26th/27th March, 78 Squadron detailed 16 aircraft for an attack on Essen, which was being mounted by aircraft from Nos 3, 4, 5 and 6 Groups. Two returned early to Breighton due to engine faults but 14 went on to bomb the primary targets, the marshalling yards at Aulnoye and the Krupp works in Essen. The raid was very successful and inflicted serious damage. On their way to the target the bombers were able to avoid the night fighters by making a sudden change of course a few minutes after crossing the Dutch coast, which left the nightfighters too far away to intercept them, but twelve aircraft were lost during the attack on Essen. One of these belonged to 78 Squadron; Halifax III LK749 EY-J was shot down by a night fighter while returning from the target area and crashed 11 km from Philippeville, Belgium, killing all on board.

Pilot F/Sgt F. Lovatt | **Nav** P/O C.A. Weeks | **B/A** F/O F. Henderson
W/Op Sgt E.W. Roberts | **F/E** Sgt W.J.R. Smith
A/G Sgt G. Schofield | **A/G** Sgt D.O. Cottrell
All killed and interred at Hotton War Cemetery, Belgium

A FEW NIGHTS LATER on 30th March the squadron lost another three aircraft which were part of a force of 795 that set out to bomb Nurnberg. With such large numbers of unescorted heavy bombers, it was inevitable that with each raid, more and more of them would become victims of night fighters and the flak that surrounded important targets. During this raid it would become all too clear to the higher echelons within the Air Ministry how strong the German night fighter force had become since early 1943.

The forecast of high cloud that had been given during the briefing did not materialise and this left the bombers totally exposed in clear skies and bright moonlight. The night fighters could not fail to see the condensation trails they left behind them. The German fighter controller had assembled his force directly ahead of the bombers and when their paths converged, the fighters intercepted and literally decimated the bomber force. The terrible toll of men and aircraft that took place that night would go down in history as one of the greatest air battles of World War II.

The first aircraft to be lost by 4 Group was a 78 Squadron Halifax LK762 EY- when it was shot down by a night fighter approximately 10 miles north-east of the 'Ida' Beacon. The carnage continued all the way to the target and by the time the bombers had reached Nurnberg, more than twenty aircraft had been lost. Close on 2,000 tons of bombs were dropped on the target during the attack. This figure would have been much higher but for the number of aircraft that returned early with various problems. Those aircraft that did get through inflicted heavy damage, but this did not justify the number of aircraft that were lost. In all 105 bombers failed to return, 531 air crew were killed, 9 seriously wounded and 157 became prisoners of war. Eleven men managed to evade capture. Of the 16 Halifaxes that had taken off from RAF Breighton to take part in this raid, four returned early with various faults, nine eventually bombed the target and three were lost.

Halifax III LK762 EY-Z was the first to be shot down on the way to Nurnberg, killing four of the crew, who were buried at Rheinberg War Cemetery.

Pilot Sgt R. Horton, Killed, Rheinberg War Cemetery
Nav Sgt J. Ord, Killed, Rheinberg War Cemetery
B/A F/O R.D. Holland, POW, Stalag L1 Barth Vogelsang
W/Op Sgt B.V. Byatt, Killed, Rheinberg War Cemetery
F/E Sgt J.H. Connolley, POW, Stalag 357 Kopernikus
A/G Sgt J.W. Love, Killed, Rheinberg War Cemetery
A/G Sgt F.H. Wilson, POW, Stalag 357 Kopernikus

Halifax III HX241 EY-P was also shot down whilst making its way to the target. It crashed at Allendorf with the loss of all on board, who were buried locally and later re-interred at the Hannover War Cemetery, including the American pilot. The crew was:

Pilot F/Lt H. McC. Hudson RCAF | **Nav** F/O A.G. Taylor DFC
B/A P/O W. Uyen RCAF | **W/Op** Sgt H. Monks | **F/E** Sgt H. Hillis
A/G F/Sgt L. Nugent | **A/G** Sgt J.W. Morris
All killed and interred at Hannover War Cemetery

Halifax III LV899 EY-Q is thought to have been the victim of a night fighter while on its return journey. It crashed near Charlville-Mezieres in France, killing all on board, who were buried nearby at Maubert-Fontaine Communal Cemetery. They were:

Pilot WO2 F.W. Topping RCAF | **Nav** F/O W.L. Cruse
B/A F/Sgt G.D. Torbet RCAF | **W/Op** Sgt W.J. Batchouski
F/E Sgt W.A. Littlewood | **A/G** Sgt T. Lanaghan | **A/G** Sgt J.G. Vaughan RCAF
All killed and interred at Maubert-Fontaine Cemetery, France

THUS ENDED THE DEEP penetration raids into Germany and for those who had survived the strain of the past two and a half years, the end had not come too soon. Many were at breaking point, although this was something they would never admit at the time. Indeed, they were not allowed to admit it for fear of the stigma of the dreaded accusation of 'lacking moral fibre' or LMF for short, that horrible pejorative term invented by the top brass at the air Ministry to stigmatise and punish any aircrew members who snapped under the strain of the near suicidal missions they were ordered to carry out, night after night, until their luck ran out.

When the war was over and the figures were calculated it was realised that bomber command aircrew stood less than a 50-50 chance of survival. Many of those who did survive had their nerves shot to pieces. Nowadays they would be recognised as suffering from post-traumatic stress but no such terms existed at the time and no help was available other than the camaraderie they all shared, for nobody except themselves knew what it had really been like.

~ Chapter 9 ~

D-Day & the Invasion of Europe

WITH THE DATE OF THE invasion of Europe approaching, Bomber Command now began to concentrate their operations on the destruction of railway marshalling yards in Northern France, for these were filled with vast stocks of guns, tanks and ammunition, ready to be sent to any part of the coast in the event of the anticipated invasion by the Allied forces. The lives of thousands of men could depend upon the bomber crews destroying these marshalling yards.

During a raid on Tergnier in northern France, which took place on 10th/11th April 1944, aircraft from 78 Squadron became part of a 156-strong force that mounted an attack on the rail yards located there. Ten Pathfinder Mosquitos led the attack and the bombing that followed was accurate, causing severe damage to the yards. German night fighters were very active throughout the raid and 10 Halifaxes were lost. The 18 aircraft that had been despatched from RAF Breighton for this operation all reached and bombed the target, which had been identified by red and green target indicators, and dropped their bombs from a height of 15,000 feet. Many bomb bursts were observed and the raid was considered to have been effective. One aircraft failed to return to Breighton after the raid.

Halifax III LV877 EY-S crashed at Pierrecourt (Seine-Maritime) killing six members of the crew, who were buried in Poix-de-la-Somme churchyard.

Pilot F/Sgt L. Tait | **Nav** F/Sgt V.H. Hawkins | **B/A** WO2 C.L. Wetherby RCAF
F/E Sgt W.N. Smith | **A/G** Sgt R.R. Rudd RAAF | **A/G** Sgt R. Graham
All the above killed and interred at Poix-de-la-Somme Churchyard, France
W/Op Sgt W. Keenan, POW, Stalag 357 Kopernikus

78 SQUADRON DID NOT carry out any further operations until 18th April when once again the target was the marshalling yards at Tergnier. As on 10th April, 18 aircraft took part in the attack from a height of around 15,000 feet, the target having been identified by the Pathfinders with red and green target indicators. Many bomb bursts were seen in the target area and the attack was considered most effective. All the aircraft returned to base safely.

Two nights later 21 Halifaxes were despatched from Breighton with orders to carry out an attack on the railway marshalling yards at Ottignies. On arriving over the target area they found it had been well marked by red and green target indicators dropped by the Pathfinder Mosquitos which had accompanied the 4 Group aircraft as usual. The railway lines could be clearly seen from the light of the flares and the crews pressed home the attack, which was considered successful. No losses were sustained.

The night of 22nd/23rd April saw 21 Halifaxes from RAF Breighton join aircraft from squadrons in Nos 1, 3, 4, 5, 6 and 8 Groups in mounting an attack on the heavy industrial area of Dusseldorf. For some crew members it was a reminder of the early days of 1943, when night after night hundreds of bombers had taken off from their bases to bomb 'Happy Valley', as the Ruhr was ironically known, and none of them looked forward to the reception they would receive on reaching the heavily-defended target area.

Only 18 of the 78 Squadron aircraft reached and bombed the target, which had been identified by Pathfinder aircraft with the usual red and green target indicators. By the time 78 Squadron arrived it was already well alight, with large fires burning out of control in several parts of the area, started by bombers from other squadrons that had arrived earlier. Bombing took place from a height of 20,000 feet and crews reported seeing large explosions and smoke rising to 10,000 feet. One of the 78 Squadron Halifaxes was forced to return early with a sick navigator on board and another had to abandon the sortie due to failure of a port engine. One aircraft had failed to take off due to the starboard engine being unserviceable. Otherwise, no losses were sustained.

On the morning of 24th April orders were received from 4 Group Headquarters for an attack on Karlsruhe. Among the bombers that made up the force taking part in this operation were 22 Halifaxes from 78 Squadron, along with aircraft from Nos 1, 3, 4, 5 and 6 Groups. They made their rendezvous off the Yorkshire coast they set course for Germany. As usual they met an intense wall of flak as they crossed the Dutch coast, to which several of the bombers succumbed. Of the 22 aircraft that left RAF Breighton, 21 reached and attacked the target, bombing from heights varying from 17,500 to 20,000 feet. Crews reported seeing a large concentration of fires in the target area. Night fighters claimed at least ten of the bombers but the anti-aircraft gunners also claimed their share of the aircraft lost in the raid. One of the 78 Squadron Halifaxes returned early due to vibration in the rear turret and two aircraft failed to return.

Halifax III LW515 EY-A crashed at Le Culot, 14 Km SSE of Leuven, Belgium, killing all on board, who were initially buried in a local cemetery but were later transferred to Heverlee War Cemetery. They were:

Pilot F/O T. Speller | **Nav** F/O H.J. Kadwill | **B/A** F/Lt A. Dalrymple
W/Op Sgt F.R. Nicholls | **F/E** Sgt A.G. Haywood | **A/G** Sgt A. Line
A/G F/Sgt C. Greer
All killed and interred at Heverlee War Cemetery, Belgium

Halifax III LV958 EY-O was abandoned at 20,000 feet following the loss of power from both port engines. It crashed near the railway line some 10km ESE of Morhange in France. Only two crew members survived. The dead were buried at Benestroff Communal Cemetery. The crew was:

Pilot F/O J. McCartney | **W/Op** Sgt J.E. Waltham
F/E Sgt H. Gibbs | **A/G** Sgt T. Borque RCAF | **A/G** Sgt J. Skeat
All the above were killed and interred at Benestroff War Cemetery
Nav F/Sgt N.W. Brown, POW, Stalag 357 Kopernikus
B/A F/O M.M. Holgate, POW, No details available

ON THE MORNING OF 26th April, orders were received by 78 Squadron to carry out a raid on the railway marshalling yards at the French town of Villeneuve-St-Georges. 18 of the squadron's aircraft took off from Breighton at 2200hrs and when they arrived in the target area, they found it had been marked by red and green target indicators dropped by the Pathfinders. Very soon high explosive and incendiary bombs were raining down, causing widespread damage to warehouses and ammunition trains standing in .the sidings. One of the 78 Squadron aircraft Halifax LV873 EY-Q was hit by flak and crashed in the southern outskirts of Paris at Choisy-le-Roi, about 8 km NNW of the target. There were no survivors. The crew were buried at Clichy New Communal Cemetery. They were:

Pilot F/Sgt J.H. Wilkinson | **Nav** F/O A.A. Bell | **B/A** P/O D.P. Garroway
W/Op F/Sgt F.R. Sampson | **F/E** Sgt J.C. Fell
A/G F/O W.K. Raby RCAF | **A/G** Sgt L.R. Dyment RCAF
All were killed and interred at Clichy-le-Roi Cemetery, France

AT THE END OF April 1944 the Officer Commanding 78 Squadron, Wing Commander G.K. Lawrence, was appointed to the rank of acting Group Captain. On his posting to Headquarters Bomber Command, his place was taken by Squadron Leader A. Markland, who was appointed to the rank of acting Wing Commander at 78 Squadron.

Flight Lieutenant F. Furlay was appointed to the rank of acting Squadron Leader to Command 'C' Flight and Flying Officer G.J. Parsons appointed to the rank of acting Flight Lieutenant, Captain of Aircraft. Acting Flight Lieutenant F. Taylor was awarded a DFC (Immediate).

May 1st saw an attack mounted on the railway yards at Malines, in Belgium. 17 aircraft had been detailed for this operation and they all reached and bombed the target which had been identified by the Pathfinders, with red and green spot illuminating markers. When the crews were being debriefed on their return to base, several of them reported the bomb bursts being scattered and it was stated that it had been a rather unsatisfactory attack. All the aircraft returned safely to base.

Fire destroyed Halifax III LV795 EY- on the airfield at RAF Breighton on 8th May. Later that day, 16 aircraft were detailed for an attack on marshalling yards and engine sheds at Berneval. Of the 16 Halifaxes that took off, 14 reached and bombed the target that had been marked by a cluster of target indicators dropped by Pathfinders. Bombing took place from 8,000 feet. Two of the Halifaxes returned to base early due to engine failure. After jettisoning their bombs over the sea, they landed safely. All the other Squadron aircraft returned safely after the raid.

The following night, the squadron received orders to repeat the attack on Berneval and 16 aircraft were despatched, though only fifteen reached and carried out the attack, which did not produce the effect that had been expected. One of the aircraft carried out three attempts to bomb before finally jettisoning its bombs in the sea. Severe damage was done to the marshalling yards and this in turn caused long delays to urgent war materiel being moved to where it was needed. Sadly, some bombs fell on the houses of French railway workers, causing deaths and injuries to civilians who were our allies, but since these houses were located so close to the railway yards, the likelihood of this happening must have been realised by those who planned the raid. All the squadron aircraft returned safely to base.

The following night the large marshalling yards and locomotive depot at Lens, just outside Paris, came in for attention from several squadrons of No 4 Group, including 78 Squadron. The attack was carried out from a height of only 8,000 feet and inflicted heavy damage, preventing urgent supplies from being moved. Once again, all the 78 Squadron aircraft returned safely to base.

The attacks on railway marshalling yards and locomotive repair depots continued, with Trouville coming in for an attack by the Halifaxes of 78 Squadron on the night of 11th/12th May. Of the 13 aircraft that set out, only 11 reached and bombed the target due to a 'met' report which had failed to forecast high winds. Most crews bombed on the red target indicators marking the dropping zone, but reported the bombing was scattered, though it did improve as the attack developed. Two of the Halifaxes failed to reach the target area on time and did not drop their bombs, these were jettisoned in the sea before returning to base. All the 78 Squadron aircraft returned safely.

Following this operation 78 Squadron were stood down for a week. This gave the ground crews extra time to carry out major servicing and repair of the squadron's aircraft, not that any of them failed to be airworthy when they were needed for an operation, for the ground crews worked out on the dispersals in all weather conditions, sometimes working round the clock to make certain their aircraft were maintained on top-line.

ON THE MORNING OF the 19th May, orders were received from Group headquarters for 78 Squadron to join aircraft from other squadrons in a group in a raid on marshalling yards in Boulogne. They reached and attacked the target, which had been accurately identified by Pathfinder aircraft with red and white target indicators. Bombing took place from heights of 13,000 to 14,000 feet. Crews reported seeing several large fires burning out of control and many bomb bursts were observed. The bombing was considered to have been concentrated and the attack was pronounced a success. A further eight aircraft took off from RAF Breighton that night to carry out a gardening raid. Seven of them planted their mines in the allotted areas, but one was forced to abort the sortie and return with its mines, due to failure of the H2s set. No aircraft were lost that night.

Seven aircraft were detailed to take part in a gardening raid in Kiel Bay on the night of 21st/22nd May, but due to failure of its H2s set, 1 aircraft failed to take off. The remaining six Halifaxes dropped their mines in the target area from a height of 14,000 feet before returning safely to base.

Bomber Command were kept busy carrying out attacks on the French railway marshalling yards. On 22nd May they attacked Orleans, to the South-west of Paris and 78 Squadron contributed 22 aircraft to this operation. Along with other 4 Group squadrons, they bombed the target from a height of 10,000 feet. It had been marked with red and green target indicators and the concentrated bombing that followed inflicted heavy damage to the marshalling yards. Crews reported seeing large fires burning in the sidings. The operation was considered very satisfactory. Two aircraft returned early with engine problems but no aircraft losses were sustained that night.

Gardening operations took place during the nights of 22nd/23rd and 26th/27th May, with mines being laid in areas off the French coast and the Frisian Islands. The aircraft all returned safely to base.

During the night of 24th/25th May, aircraft from Nos 3, 4, 6 and 8 Groups carried out an attack on the railway yards at Aachen. Taking part were 18 Halifaxes from 78 Squadron. The bombers had no way of avoiding the heavy flak and night fighters that defended the route to the target and consequently, several of them were lost. There were further losses over the target area and still more as the bomber force aircraft made their way back to their bases. As they were passing over Antwerp, they found the port was under attack by Lancasters and Mosquitos. Flares being used to assist the bombing during this raid also illuminated the aircraft returning from Aachen, making them easy targets for the night fighters. The raid on Aachen cost Bomber Command 27 aircraft and 135 air crew killed. One man was seriously injured and 49 became prisoners of war. Six men succeeded in evading capture.

78 Squadron lost one aircraft in this raid, it was shot down by a night fighter near Bergse Maas in Noord Brabant, Netherlands. There were no survivors. It was Halifax III LV905 EY-W.[1]

Pilot P/O E.B. Wilson | **Nav** F/O S.C. Peterson RCAF
B/A F/O N.A. Marston DFC | **W/Op** F/Sgt J. Henderson
F/E Sgt W.J. White | **A/G** Sgt G.H. Butler | **A/G** Sgt J.T.L. Leblanc RCAF
All were killed and interred at Jonkerbos War Cemetery, Netherlands

A gardening operation was carried out by eight 78 Squadron Halifaxes during the night of 26th/27th May, off the Dutch and Belgian coasts. The target areas being identified by their H2s sets. Visibility was good, but no parachutes were reported as being been seen to open. All the aircraft returned safely to base.

Aircraft from Nos 1, 4 and 6 Groups took part in an attack on a military camp at Bourg-Leopold during the night of 27th/28th May 1944. When the bombers arrived over the target area, they found it accurately marked by the Pathfinder aircraft with yellow, green and white target indicators. They commenced their attack from a height of 18,000 feet, and the raid was a success, but 11 aircraft were lost, one was a 78 Squadron Halifax. One aircraft had failed to take off from Breighton due to failure of the starboard outer engine. Halifax III LW519 EY- was attacked by a night fighter before

---

[1] See panel on opposite page, based on an article written in 2011 by Sgt Tony Hibberd when SNCO I/C 78 Sqn Operations (and Voluntary 78 Sqn History Officer).

A Lost 78 Squadron Halifax and its Crew Recovered

At 2255 on 24th May 1944, 78 Squadron Halifax III, LV905/EY-W "Willie" departed from RAF Breighton and, along with 431 other aircraft from Bomber Command, set course for an attack on railway marshalling yards at Aachen, Germany.

The Halifax was on its return flight when it was attacked and shot down by a Luftwaffe Me110 night fighter. It crashed in flames into a peat marsh on the edge of the tiny village of Hank, in the Netherlands. All seven crew members were killed. The aircraft broke up on impact and two of the crew were thrown clear. One was Sgt Butler, the other was unidentified. Both were buried locally soon after the crash. The front section of the aircraft quickly sank 30 feet into the peat marsh, where it, and the other five members of the crew, remained for over 60 years.

Of the 182 Whitley and Halifax aircraft lost by 78 Squadron during WWII, 41 of them came down over the Netherlands and the local people have a great affection for the RAF in general and 78 Sqn in particular. In 2003 locals from Werkendam formed the *Salvage Halifax 1944 Foundation*. They raised 250,000 Dutch Guilders, enabling the Royal Netherlands Air Force (RNLAF) to excavate the aircraft. In 2005, 80% of the aircraft was recovered, along with the remains of all five missing crew members. This enabled the identity of the 'unknown' crew member buried many years previously to be established. The bodies of the two men buried locally were exhumed and all seven former comrades were formally reburied with full military honours in the Jonkerbos War Cemetery, Nijmegen on 27th September 2006.

Later the same day, a memorial consisting of a propeller from the aircraft was unveiled near the crash site and the RNLAF Aircraft Recovery Unit offered to donate another of the propellers from LV905/EY-W "Willie" to 78 Squadron as a goodwill gesture, to enable a similar memorial to be erected at RAF Benson.

On 15th October 2010 a Merlin helicopter departed Benson for the RNLAF Aircraft Recovery Unit near Rotterdam where the propeller unit was carefully loaded.

Next day the Merlin flew to the village of Hank, where LV905/EY-W had crashed. The crash site was clearly visible from the air, as the Dutch had lit seven fires in memory of the seven crew. On arrival the Merlin crew were met by the local Mayor and members of the *Salvage Halifax 1944 Foundation* committee.

At the memorial a wreath was laid and a two-minute silence observed. The Mayor thanked present-day members of 78 Squadron for attending and stated that it remains the duty of the people of the Netherlands never to forget the sacrifices made by Allied forces, and in particular the Royal Air Force. At the crash site an account of the aircraft's last moments was read aloud and the emotion and appreciation shown by the Dutch community towards the RAF was described as 'truly humbling' by the RAF contingent present. On departure the RAF Merlin helicopter trailed both the Dutch National Flag and the RAF Ensign, to the evident delight of all assembled below.

In April 2011 a monument to the fallen aircrew of 78 Squadron created from the salvaged propeller was unveiled at RAF Benson (see photo below).

reaching the target, causing heavy damage to the aircraft and seriously wounding three members of the crew. It went out of control and the bomb aimer, Sergeant D.B. Bell baled out on finding the intercom was out of order. Fortunately, the pilot managed to regain control of the aircraft and brought it back safely, landing at Woodbridge, where it was declared beyond repair. The injured crew members were taken to the East Suffolk and Ipswich Hospital. Sergeant Bell, who had baled out, did not survive and was buried at Oostvoorne Protestant Cemetery.

Pilot F/Sgt K.L. Long, Escaped uninjured
Nav F/O T. Chiverton, injured, taken to E Suffolk & Ipswich Hospital
B/A Sgt D.B. Bell, Killed, Oostvoorne Protestant Cemetery
W/Op , Sgt L. Brown, injured, taken to E Suffolk & Ipswich Hospital
F/E , Sgt D.B. Dew, injured, taken to E Suffolk & Ipswich Hospital
A/G Sgt J. Law, uninjured | **A/G** Sgt T. Owen, uninjured

On the same night 78 Squadron detailed four aircraft to carry out a gardening operation. The mines were dropped in their allocated areas and all the Halifaxes returned safely to base.

May ended with an attack on Trappes taking place, when 19 aircraft took part in a raid on the marshalling yards. Following the last visit by 78 Squadron on 6th March it had been left in a seriously damaged condition, but since that time the Germans had repaired the damage wrought by Bomber Command and once again it was filled with rolling stock containing tanks, guns, ammunition and other materials, ready to be despatched at a moments notice. When the bombers arrived they found that target had been identified with red and green markers, and they immediately began the attack. Bombs were observed falling on the target. The operation was a success and once again, all the aircraft returned to Breighton safely.

During May the aircraft of 78 Squadron spent 876.30 hours on operational flying and a further 352 hours on training flights.

On 2nd June 1944 78 Squadron detailed 20 aircraft for two operations that were to take place that night. At 2300 hours, 10 Halifaxes took off to rendezvous with 95 aircraft from other squadrons in the Group to attack the railway marshalling yards at Trappes once more. This time, however, things would be different. The clear weather and moonlit conditions prevailing at the time suited the night fighters and they were to make the best of the situation. As the bombers approached the target area, the sky lit up and the crews saw the target quickly become clearer as flares and red and green target indicators dropped by the Pathfinders exploded into action. Bombing took place from 10,000 feet, and all around them, crews could see aircraft unloading their deadly loads of high explosives. It was a most impressive sight but they were not given time to savour it, for moments later, the night fighters pounced on them and shattered bombers began falling out of the sky. What should have been an effective attack had now become a the loss of 15 aircraft for 4 Group, Bomber Command, with 158 Squadron taking the brunt of the casualties. 78 Squadron were more fortunate, for all their aircraft returned safely to base.

The Squadron's second operation that night was a raid on the French port of Brest, in which 10 aircraft took part. Heavy damage was done to several ships, and the dock installations. All the aircraft returned safely to base.

At 02.00 hours on the night of 5th/6th June 1944, 24 aircraft took off from Breighton to attack the area of Mont Fleury. Though the crews were not aware of it at that time, part of this attack was to herald the start to the invasion of Europe from the West. The target area was identified by the use of red and green target indicators and the bombing was carried out from 10,000 feet. Though visibility was poor with 10/10th cloud, the bombing was considered to have been accurate. A gun battery on 'Gold' Beach in Normandy, which threatened to prevent vital supplies from reaching the hard pressed invading Allied troops, was attacked by 78 Squadron aircraft. Two bombers failed to I.D. the primary target and their bombs were jettisoned, one aircraft failed to take off due to oiling up when the engine was run up.

78 Squadron detailed 26 Halifaxes for operations on the morning of 6th June. The target was St Lo, which was roughly twenty miles behind the beach-head. The attack was carried out from only 3,000 feet, with bombs being dropped on red and white target indicators. Fires had already been started by a wave of bombers that had preceded them. Visibility was moderate with 5-10/10ths cloud, making it difficult for the crews to see the results of their efforts. All the aircraft returned safely.

The following night 7th/8th June, 4 Group aircraft carried out an attack on Juvisy and 78 Squadron despatched 16 aircraft for the operation. This raid was to be on the German lines covering the Allied beachhead. 11 aircraft dropped their bombs from between 2-3,000 feet. The dropping area being identified by Red and Green target indicators, also on the instructions of the Master Bomber. The bombing was considered to be concentrated, though two aircraft did not bomb, as they were unable to identify the markers, while another was attacked by a night fighter while on its bombing run. The navigator was killed and the bomb aimer wounded. A further aircraft was attacked whilst over the target, the rear gunner being killed in the ensuing fight.

Four 78 Squadron aircraft were reported as missing after the operation.

Halifax III LV868 EY- was badly mauled after carrying out a successful attack on the target. The pilot, F/Lt D. Davies succeeded in getting the badly damaged Halifax back to West Malling, in Kent, where he crash-landed it. Sergeant C.W. Lillico was mortally wounded during the attack and later died from his injuries. He was buried in his home town of Alnwick, Northumberland. The crew was:

Pilot F/Lt D. Davies | **Nav** P/O V. Spence
B/A P/O J. McNabney RCAF | **W/Op** F/Sgt W. Parton
F/E P/O A. Cadman | **A/G** Sgt J. Firth
All of the above survived a crash landing uninjured
A/G Sgt C.W. Lillico, wounded, died later in hospital

The second aircraft lost was Halifax III MZ568 EY-E which took off at 22.52 hours from Breighton. It was reported to have exploded in mid-air after being hit by flak over France. Scattered debris was found between Corbeil-Essones and Courances, a village some 10 km away. The body of Flying Officer Gold RCAF was interred in the Corbeil-Essones Communal Cemetery. F/Lt Bisset was the squadron's signals leader. The crew was:

Pilot P/O J.A. Cole RCAF | **Nav** F/O L. Gold. RCAF
B/A Sgt G.N. Cribbin | **W/Op** F/Lt T.N.W. Bisset
F/E Sgt D. Balmforth | **A/G** Sgt H. Tattler | **A/G** Sgt T. Newman
All were killed and buried at Courances Cemetery, France

Halifax III MZ577 EY-O crashed 4 km South of Lieusaint after being badly damaged during the bombing attack. The 5 crew members who died are buried in Villeneuves-St-Georges Old Community Cemetery, with the exception of Lieutenant Evans USAAF who rests in the US Military Cemetery at Epinal, France. Sergeant R. Wann was taken prisoner but was repatriated on board the RMS *Arundel Castle*. The crew was:

Pilot F/Sgt M. McClear RCAF, Killed, Villeneuves Cemy
Nav Lt C.O. Evans USAAF, Killed, US Military Cemetery, Epinal
B/A Sgt S.F.H. Kelley RCAF, Killed, Villeneuves Cemy
W/Op Sgt R.O. Connor, Killed, Villeneuves Cemy
F/E Sgt R. Wann. RCAF, POW, Repatriated 6/2/1945
A/G WO2 E.D. Woods RCAF, Killed, Villeneuves Cemy
A/G F/Sgt J.W. Angus, POW, Stalag Luft 3 Sagan

Halifax III MZ636 EY-T was shot down and crashed in the vicinity of Bretigny-sur-Orge (Essone) approx 6 km NE of Arpajon. There were no survivors. The remains of all the crew members were buried in the Bretigny-sur-Orge Communal Cemetery. They were:

Pilot F/Lt G.A. Marrows | **Nav** F/O D.J. Bryant | **B/A** F/Sgt .R. Scott
W/Op J.P. Whelan RAAF | **F/E** Sgt S.T. Tanser
A/G Sgt J.H. Sheehan | **A/G** Sgt F.W. Holroyd
All were killed and interred at Bretigny-sur-Orge Communal Cemetery

THAT SAME NIGHT EIGHT more of the squadron's aircraft were detailed for a gardening operation off Brest. Seven took off, but only six planted their mines. One did not take off due to an unserviceable engine. The second one aborted when the undercarriage would not lock after take off. The mines were jettisoned on Spaldington bombing range, before the aircraft returned to Breighton.

Bomber Command operations continued by day and night to support the Allied forces fighting tenaciously to hold onto the bridgehead they had fought so hard to form. 4 Group aircraft carried out raids on all the major marshalling yards handling enemy war materials destined for the Normandy battle area. 78 Squadron took part in an operation on 9th June, when 13 aircraft attacked Laval airfield. Bombing took place from a height of 2-3,000 feet, and bombs were seen to drop squarely on the target that had been marked by bright yellow target indicators. This attack was followed by a raid on Amien, on the night of 12th/13th June, when the Halifaxes of 78 Squadron carried out an attack on the Railway centre. The bombing was reported to be very concentrated and successful, and a large number of fires could be seen wherever the crews looked, but the price for their success was costly, for three aircraft were lost that night.

There had been no word from them since they had taken off at 22.00 hours. The first was Halifax III LV820 EY-F which crashed at Bosc-Mesnil (Seine-Maritime) 4 km ESE of St Saens. Six of the crew were buried in Poix-de-la-Somme Churchyard, France. No trace of F/O Albon was found and his name is listed on the Runnymede Memorial. The crew was:

Pilot F/O H.T. Hills | **Nav** F/O K.C.M. Hayman | **W/Op** Sgt W. M Biehl
F/E Sgt R.J. Campbell MiD | **A/G** Sgt M.F. Dilkes | **A/G** Sgt S.G.R. Barham
All the above were buried at Poix-de-la-Somme Churchyard, France.
B/A F/O E. Albon listed on Runnymede Memorial

Halifax III LV915 EY-H took off at 22.18 hours from Breighton and after carrying out a successful bombing attack on Amiens was shot down by flak, killing all on board. The remains of the crew members were buried in Poix-de-la-Somme Churchyard, France. They were:

Pilot F/O J.F. Whylie RCAF | **Nav** F/O J.S. Ritchie RCAF
B/A F/O G.J. Lancaster RCAF | **W/Op** Sgt D.I. Davies | **F/E** Sgt W. Duncan
A/G Sgt W. Couper | **A/G** Sgt J.E. Byers
All were killed and buried at Poix-de-la-Somme Churchyard, France

The third aircraft lost in this operation was Halifax III MZ631 EY-Y. After taking off from Breighton at 22.18 hours this aircraft took part in the operation to bomb the railway centre at Amiens and was afterwards shot down, crashing at Lonqueil (Seine-Maritime), killing the entire crew. They were buried in the village churchyard, approximately 12 km from Dieppe. The crew was:

Pilot F/Sgt S.A. Rae RNZAF | **Nav** F/O H. Sager RCAF
B/A Sgt F.G. Tomlinson | **W/Op** Sgt H.G. Colwell | **F/E** Sgt R.E. Miles
A/G Sgt F.E. Spinks | **A/G** Sgt T. Gilmartin
All were killed and buried at Lonqueil churchyard, France

AT 23.30 hours on the night of 14th/15th June, 16 Halifaxes took off from Breighton to carry out an attack on the railway marshalling yards at Douai. On reaching the target area the 78 Squadron crews saw fires that had been started by the first wave of bombers burning furiously. They dropped their bombs from 8,000 feet and this added to the general confusion below. Several explosions were reported before the last aircraft turned for home. 78 Squadron lost one aircraft in this operation, it was shot down and crashed at Bersee (Nord), 18 Km SSE of Lille, France, killing the entire crew. Their bodies were interred at Bersee Communal Cemetery.

Pilot F/Lt E.W.J. Murray | **Nav** F/Sgt L.W.A. Pierce | **B/A** F/O N.E. Cooper
W/Op Sgt W.H. Freer | **F/E** Sgt A. McIlroy
A/G Sgt J.H.B. Killingbach | **A/G** Sgt C.G. Wilson
All were killed and buried at Bersee Cemetery, Lille, France

CHAPTER 10

'V' Weapon Launch Sites & Other Targets

I T WAS AT THIS POINT in the war that the Germans unveiled their latest weapon, the V1 flying bomb. This was an unmanned aircraft propelled by a rocket motor with a range of around one hundred miles. The offensive began on June 13th 1944, when radar stations on England's south coast picked up four unidentified aircraft. After passing over the Kent and Sussex countryside, they suddenly dived into the ground and exploded. This was the start of an offensive designed to terrify the civilian population of Great Britain into submission.

These attacks were not altogether unexpected. For some time French underground agents had been sending reports from northern France and together with photographic evidence received from Reconnaissance squadrons during the Autumn of 1943 and Spring 1944, there was clear evidence that launching sites for some kind of rocket propelled weapon were in a well advanced state. Medium bombers from RAF and USAAF squadrons carried out raids on the launching sites, causing a great deal of damage, and this forced the Germans to find other sites that were better concealed. Farms and other large buildings were very quickly commandeered, as were many of the orchards in that part of France, for they provided excellent camouflage for the launch sites. In May the heavy bomber squadrons were ordered to carry out attacks on these launch sites.

On the night of the 15th/16th June, 16 aircraft were despatched from Breighton to carry out a raid on the French town of Fouliard. They reached and bombed the target from a height of 8,000 feet. Huge fires were caused and considerable damage was reported. All the aircraft returned safely to base. That same night, four aircraft carried out a gardening operation. The mines were dropped in position, with the aircraft using their H2s sets to find the dropping zone.

A force of 14 aircraft took off from Breighton on the night of 18th/19th June to mount an attack on Domleger, although only 13 carried out the attack. One returned early due to the navigator misplacing his instruments. The same night four aircraft carried out a gardening raid, from which, all the aircraft returned safely.

On the night of 22nd/23rd June, 24 aircraft were detailed for 'Ops', with Laon being the target, but only 21 reached the target area, one returned early when the starboard inner engine failed. Two Halifaxes collided on the outward journey, but they carried on and bombed the target, landing at Manston on return to the UK. The attack was well concentrated and considered to be very successful. After the bombers had returned to base, two were found to be missing.

Halifax III LK840 EY-J had been shot down by a night fighter and crashed near Quinquempoix (Oise), 6km north of St-just-en-Chaussee. Three of the crew survived but the remainder lost their lives and were buried at Quinquempoix Communal Cemetery. The crew was:

Pilot F/O D.L. Irwin RCAF, Killed, Quinquempoix Communal Cemetery
Nav F/O H.A. Fuhr RCAF, Killed, Quinquempoix Communal Cemetery
B/A Sgt W.S. Sharratt, POW, Stalag Luft 3 Sagan.
W/Op F/O B. Shepstone, Killed, Quinquempoix Communal Cemetery
F/E Sgt A. Gill, POW, Camp details not known.
A/G , Sgt W.C. Brown, Evaded capture
A/G Sgt T.R. Owen, Killed, Quinquempoix Communal Cemetery

Halifax III MZ692 EY-P was shot down over the target on what is believed to have been the crew's first operational sortie. The crew members all baled out and parachuted to safety; five were taken prisoner but two managed to evade capture:

Pilot P/O R.N. Mills RAAF, POW, Stalag Luft 3 Sagan
Nav F/Sgt K.C. Mills RAAF, POW, Stalag Luft 3 Sagan
B/A F/Sgt I.R.C. Innes RAAF, Evaded capture
W/Op F/Sgt E.L. Johnston RAAF, POW, StalagLuft 3 Sagan
F/E Sgt C.H. Wright, POW, Stalag Luft 7 Bankau-Kruelberg
A/G F/Sgt J.P. Gwillan RAAF, POW, Stalag Luft 3 Sagan
A/G F/Sgt D.R. Foden RAAF, Evaded capture

THE FIRST DAYLIGHT OPERATION undertaken by 78 Squadron took place on 24th June 1944. Their target was the V1 launch site at Noyelles-en-Chaussee, about 20 km east of Arras. Bombing took place from a height of 16,000 feet and was considered by the crews to have been well concentrated and effective. This was later borne out when photographs taken during the raid were developed. One aircraft returned early due to failure of the starboard outer engine. Around this time, some of the squadrons were being called upon to carry out two operations within a 24-hour period.

The V1 launch site at Montorqueil was the target for Sunday 25th June. One hundred Halifaxes from 4 Group took part in the attack on the site,

23 of them being 78 Squadron aircraft. The target had already been identified by the Pathfinders, with red target indicators and the crews reported excellent results, with the target completely blanketed with bomb bursts. One aircraft was forced to return early with hydraulic failure. When the aircraft returned to their bases, they encountered bad visibility, which meant some of them had to be diverted to other airfields until the weather improved. Fortunately, all the 78 Squadron aircraft landed safely.

With the end of June approaching, 4 Group aircraft operated by day and night, attacking the launch sites, yet the flying bombs continued to arrive over London, killing hundreds of civilians and causing damage to thousands of homes. In the area surrounding Watten and Wizernes, another fiendish weapon was about to be launched against the British Capital. It was the V2 Rocket. This missile was much larger and it carried a more powerful charge of high explosive, but there was a more sinister side to it. Unlike the V1, which had a noisy motor that gave people warning that it was on the way, the V2 did not give any warning, just a sudden explosion, followed moments later by the chaos of debris everywhere, with people lying dead and badly injured. It was one of the most evil weapons yet devised by German scientists.

A force of 103 Halifaxes from No 4 Group carried out a concerted attack on the V2 launch site at Wizernes near Boulogne on the morning of 26th June, but due to the immense strength of the concrete bunkers which not only housed the launching pad but also the area where these rockets were assembled, the attack failed to make any impression. A few days later 617 Squadron, led by Wing Commander Leonard Cheshire, successfully destroyed it with six-ton 'Tallboy' bombs that their Lancasters carried.

The last days of June saw a concentrated attack by Halifaxes and Lancasters of the RAF, along with Fortresses and Liberators of the USAAF, on the launch areas, by day and night. Every site received a thorough pounding from hundreds of bombers, with all the launching and supply sites that were situated in the area between Dieppe and Amiens receiving the major force of the attack. These attacks continued until July 7th, giving General Montgomery the opportunity to make certain the Allied forces were ready to make an all out drive to reach the River Seine and the city of Caen.

The aircraft of 78 Squadron carried out several attacks on Flying Bomb launch and supply sites, starting on July 1st when 16 aircraft attacked St Martin-le-Hortier (a V2 site). A second attack, this time by 23 aircraft, took place the following day and on 4th July the site was attacked yet again, this time by 19 aircraft. It became the turn of Croixdale to be bombed by aircraft of Nos 1, 4, and 6 Groups on 6th July, to which 78 Squadron contributed 16 aircraft, which all returned safely after carrying out their mission.

Late in the evening of 7th July 1944 a combined force of nearly 500 heavy bombers attacked the heavily fortified villages that surrounded Caen, making certain their bombs were dropped well behind the German lines, so that Allied troop positions would be safe whilst the attack took place. The operation was very successful, considering the highly concentrated bombing that was carried out. However, the attack itself did not have the desired result, since the bombs had fallen in areas that were not occupied by any of the large German troop concentrations in the area. The city of Caen was very badly damaged, particularly the northern parts, which were reduced to rubble. From all these attacks, the 78 Squadron aircraft that were involved returned safely.

Aircraft of 4 Group mounted an attack on the Benapre V1 launch site on 9th July. As usual, the Pathfinders identified the target with their target indicators, ready for the bombers that followed close behind. The operation was a success but 78 Squadron lost one Halifax shortly after leaving Breighton, when the port outer engine failed. The bomb load was jettisoned into the sea and the crew were preparing to return to base when the port inner engine faltered and died and as a consequence they were forced to ditch some three miles off the coast at 12:27 hrs. Fortunately, all the crew were picked up by an ASR launch within the hour and were none the worse for their ordeal. The aircraft was Halifax III LV799 EY-C:

Pilot F/O E.W. Andrew | **Nav** F/O E.W.McElroy RCAF
B/A F/O C.G.Parker RCAF | **W/Op** WO2 W.Long. RCAF | **F/E** Sgt G.Price
A/G F/O B.T.Rogers RCAF | **A/G** P/O T.Bridgeman RCAF
All escaped unhurt after ditching in the North Sea

It was the first loss by 78 Squadron since the attack on Laon on 22nd June.

The night of the 12th/13th July saw an attack carried out on the V1 launch site at Thiverney by aircraft of 4 Group. 78 Squadron despatched 20 Halifaxes on this raid and they all returned safely. On the same night, other 78 Squadron aircraft carried out a gardening raid around the island of Heligoland. This operation was also carried out without any losses being reported.

A flying bomb storage depot at Nucort was the target for aircraft of 4 Group during the night of 15th/16th July. Sixteen aircraft were detailed for the raid by 78 Squadron and at 22.00 hours the heavily laden bombers began trundling around the perimeter track to reach the runway. Soon they were thundering along and as the end of the runway approached at enormous speed, the huge, heavily-laden aircraft slowly lifted into the sky. On arriving over the target area they found that the Pathfinders had carried out their work with great accuracy. They dropped their bombs squarely on the target and turned for home, leaving behind a shattered storage site, proof that a successful attack had taken place. All aircraft returned safely.

Bomber Command Headquarters issued orders for an attack to be mounted in support of Allied troops advancing south-west of Caen. The operation commenced early on the morning of 18th July and 78 Squadron Halifaxes began taking off at 03.30 hours and arrived over the target to find the area for bombing was marked by yellow target indicators. They dropped their bombs from a height of 6-8,000 feet, completely blanketing the whole area with bomb bursts. For this attack 28 aircraft had been despatched from Breighton, the highest number ever to be operated by the Squadron in a single mission, and they all returned safely to base, having taken part in the heaviest and most concentrated attack ever undertaken by the Allied Air Forces. As the RAF bombers were leaving the scene, the USAAF aircraft were starting their bombing attack.

The Following night 18th/19th July, 78 Squadron detailed 27 aircraft for a raid on the V1 launch site at Acquet. During the raid one of the Halifaxes was shot down, crashing at Neufmoulin (Somme), about 6 km NE of Abbevile with the loss of all those on board. The remains of the crew members were buried in a collective grave at Neufmoulin Communal Cemetery, France. The aircraft was Halifax III NA513 EY-O:

Pilot W/O G.H. Stratford | **Nav** F/O I.D.H. Clarson | **B/A** F/O W.T. Harding
W/Op F/O M.P. Moreton | **F/E** F/O R.H. Duncanson
A/G Sgt G. Allenby | **A/G** Sgt D.R. Brown
All were killed and buried at Neufmoulin Communal Cemetery, France

WHEN THE CREWS CHECKED the 'Battle Orders' on the morning of 20th July it was to find that 'Ops' were on again that night. Going out to the dispersals, they found a hive of activity, with petrol bowsers making certain each aircraft received the necessary amount of fuel for the coming night's operation, and tractors towing long trains of dollies laden with bombs. There was no time for standing around to talk. Each pilot had a word with the Flight Sergeant in charge of the ground crew before having a look around his aircraft to see for himself that everything was in order, while members of his crew carried out checks on the equipment in each of their own positions within the aircraft. When they were all satisfied that everything was in order, they made their way over to the various messes for lunch, later gathering in the briefing room, where they learned that the target that night was to be the Welheim oil refinery at Bottrop in the Ruhr Valley. It was some time since 78 Squadron had last attacked this area, and when the briefing had been completed, they made their way over to the parachute section to collect their parachutes and Mae Wests before going into the crew room to empty their pockets of personal possessions, so that there would be nothing of value to a German interrogator, in the event of them being shot down. Donning their equipment, they filed out to the transports that were waiting to take them out to the dispersals.

Within a short time the Halifaxes were making their way along the perimeter track one behind the other, until they reached the runway. As each aircraft received clearance for take-off, the captain eased the throttles through the gate with the flight engineer's hand following, ready to ensure they were locked full open. Moments later, with their engines on full boost, the huge bomber would thunder down the runway and, slowly but surely, claw its way into the air. One behind the other, 28 Halifaxes took off and made their way to a point off the Yorkshire coast where they would rendezvous with other aircraft from Nos 4 and 6 Groups, before commencing the long journey to the cauldron of searchlights, flak and night fighters that awaited them in 'Happy Valley'.

Halifax III LV901 EY- took off at 22.54 hours from Breighton and with aircraft from Nos 4 and 6 Groups, made its way to the target area. Following the raid, all the 78 Squadron aircraft returned safely, but as LV901 was taxying back to its dispersal, its undercarriage collapsed. The Halifax was damaged beyond repair, though none of the crew were injured, they were:

Pilot F/O J.E. Carson | **Nav** Sgt E.P. Mendoza | **B/A** Sgt J.W. Shelley
W/Op Sgt T. Llewellyn | **F/E** P. Murphy | **A/G** Sgt I. Williams | **A/G** Sgt E. Welsman

Two nights later, on 23rd/24th July, the aircraft of 78 Squadron visited the port of Keil, their target being the U-Boat building yards. With the Battle of the Atlantic practically won by the Royal Navy, Admiral Doenitz was demanding more of the new larger submarines being built in these yards, which had a longer range and could attack shipping off the eastern seaboard of America, where ships were allowed to sail without escorts, making them easy targets for the U-Boats. Approaching the target area, the crews saw the target indicators dropped by the Pathfinders to mark the target zone and, with complete disregard for the heavy curtain of flak, they continued on their bomb runs, causing devastating damage to many of the factory buildings. No 4 Group lost one aircraft during the operation, a 102 Squadron Halifax based at Pocklington. All the 78 Squadron aircraft returned safely to base.

The third in the series of attacks on the Ruhr took place the following night of 24th/25th July, when aircraft belonging to 78 Squadron joined those from Nos 1, 3, 4, 5, 6 and 8 Groups to attack Stuttgart's Bad Cansatt, the main industrial area. As they crossed the Dutch coast, the predictable wall of searchlights and intense flak greeted the bombers and several of them became victims. Though the operation was pronounced successful, 23 bombers were lost in the attack but on this occasion none of them were 78 Squadron aircraft, which all returned safely to base, though most of them had suffered flak damage to some degree, providing the ground crews at RAF Breighton with a good deal of work to be undertaken in order to make them airworthy for the next operation.

After spending a week bombing the Ruhr, RAF Bomber Command returned to the business of attacking the V1 Flying bomb storage and launching sites. During the night of 25th/26th July, an attack was carried out on the launching sites at Foret du Croc and Ferfay. Fortunately there were no losses on this operation.

The following night of 28th/29th July 1944, the aircrews of 78 Squadron were ordered to direct their attentions on the large V1 Flying Bomb launching and storage site at Foret de Nieppe. For this operation 16 of the squadron's aircraft had been detailed to take part and they duly pressed home the attack. The operation was successful but one aircraft failed to return. After attacking the target Halifax III MZ340 EY-X was hit by flak and crashed at Ramskapelle (West Vlaanderen), near Nieuwpoort, Belgium. Of the seven crew members five survived the ordeal and were taken prisoner but two lost their lives:

Pilot F/Lt W.G. Hoffman RCAF, Killed, Ramskapelle, Belgium
Nav F/O W.I. Bell, POW, details not known.
B/A F/O R.E. Collier, POW, details not known.
W/Op P/O R.H. Winter, Killed, Ramskapelle. Belgium
F/E P/O K.W.L. Burns, POW, details not known
A/G Sgt G.R.G. Marley, POW, Stalag Luft 7 Bankau-Kreulberg
A/G Sgt R.C. Laing RCAF, POW, Stalag Luft 7 Bankau-Kreulberg

DURING THE MONTH OF July 1944, 30 operations had been carried out by aircraft of 78 Squadron. Operational flying hours were: By Night 867 hours; By Day 453 hours.

DURING THE RUN UP to the D-Day landings in Normandy on 6th June, Bomber Command had carried out repeated attacks on strategic targets which were designed to hamper vital supplies getting to points where German troops were massed, awaiting a possible invasion by the Allies. These raids had been very successful and Air Chief Marshal Sir Arthur Harris was the first to acknowledge the efforts made by both aircrews and ground staff. Operations continued after D-Day, when the bombers gave their full support to the troops on the ground by attacking the heavily fortified city of Caen. In addition to this, they carried out many attacks on the V1 Flying bomb launch and supply sites, despite having to face concentrations of anti-aircraft guns which protected the targets.

At 11.40 hours on 1st August 78 Squadron despatched 16 Halifax aircraft to attack the rocket installations at Bois-de-Cassan. The target was bombed from a height of 15-16,000 feet, with a number of the bombs being dropped in the centre of a large cloud of smoke. It was a concentrated attack, in the course of which several aircraft suffered flak damage, but nevertheless they all returned safely to base.

Later that day Foret-du-Nieppe became the target for the aircrews of 78 Squadron, with 10 aircraft taking off at 18.20 hours. The target was attacked from 15,000 feet, after being identified by yellow target indicators. The Master Bomber was reported as being indistinct over the radio. Once again, all the aircraft returned safely to base.

These attacks were set to continue every day. On the afternoon of 3rd August, 26 Halifaxes bombed Bois-de-Cassan and Foret-de-Nieppe, when severe damage was inflicted on the V1 launch and storage sites. On 5th August, 23 Halifaxes visited the sites again. Each time the damage was reported to be heavy, but still the rockets continued to be launched from these and many other sites along the coastal region of France, from Dieppe to the west of Calais.

On 10th August Halifaxes of 78 Squadron joined aircraft from other squadrons in 4 Group to carry out a raid on the railway junction at Dijon, causing a severe delay to urgent supplies for the beleaguered German Army which was fighting hard to stem the advance of the Allied armies.

During the next two days Chappelle Notre Dame and Bruinswick were also bombed and on 14th August 78 Squadron Halifaxes became part of a force of 800 bombers that set out to attack the German strongpoints which were holding up the Allied advance on Falaise. With great precision he aircrews of No 4 Group carried out their part in the attack by bombing German held positions within two thousand yards of the Canadian lines.

This was followed by a raid on Tirlemont and Eindhoven early on the morning of 15th August by a force of 200 Halifaxes from No 4 Group with 20 of these aircraft being contributed by 78 Squadron. The target was Tirlemont airfield and when the attack was over bomb craters covered the runways, making it impossible for aircraft to use them.

A gardening raid was carried out on Keil Bay during the night of 14th/15th August by twelve of the 78 Squadron Halifaxes. They dropped their mines with the aid of their H2s sets and returned safely to base. The next day 14 Halifaxes carried out a raid on the French port of Brest, paying particular attention to the dry docks that were in constant use by German heavy naval units in need of urgent repairs. Due to broken cloud, it was difficult to observe the full results of the bombing, but when they turned for home, the 78 Squadron crews were satisfied that it would be some time before the French port would be of any further use to the Germans.

On the night of the 18th/19th August a force of over 200 Halifaxes belonging to No 4 Group, led by Mosquitos and Lancasters of the PFF, carried out a raid on a synthetic oil plant at Sterkrade. 78 Squadron despatched 19 aircraft to take part in this operation. They took off at 21.00 hours and although they had heavy flak to contend with, no night fighters appeared to interfere with the bombing. The operation was a complete success and all the aircraft returned safely to the UK.

A gardening raid earlier in the month had been had been carried out with no losses but this was not to be repeated on the night of 25th/26th August when six Halifaxes took at 23.00 hours from Breighton to drop mines off the French port of La Rochelle. They successfully completed the drop and turned for home but near Cheltenham one of the aircraft developed a fault and crashed into a quarry, killing all the members of its predominantly Canadian crew. It was Halifax III MZ311 EY-

Pilot F/Lt M. Howes RCAF | **Nav** F/O E. Freeman RCAF
B/A F/O C. McCartney RCAF | **W/Op** Sgt E. Harris | **F/E** Sgt J. McCardle
A/G F/O J. Glenn RCAF | **A/G** F/Sgt R. Hamilton RCAF
All killed in a crash landing at Cheltenham, England

A V2 LAUNCH SITE at Watten near Boulogne came in for attack by 4 Group aircraft on 26th August. Among those taking part in the raid were twenty-one Halifaxes from RAF Breighton. It was a very successful raid and another German launch site was put out of action. No aircraft were lost.

Two days later 4 Group Headquarters issued orders for a daylight raid to be mounted by 216 Halifaxes on the Rheinpreussen AG synthetic oil refinery at Homberg-Meefbeck, on the west bank of the Rhine, preceded by Mosquitos and Lancasters of the Pathfinders. They were also provided with a long range, fighter escort for this operation. A concentrated attack was carried out on the target, and though the flak was intense, no German fighters appeared and no aircraft were report missing after the raid.[1]

By early September German radar stations had been over-run by Allied troops, which made life a lot safer for the bomber crews, for though fighter production was at an all time high, with over 450 night fighters being built in August, increasing to over 500 during September, the Germans were suffering from a crucial shortage of fuel to operate them. During the months that followed, engagements by night fighters became even more rare, though the flak remained as heavy as ever, and many aircraft continued to be lost during attacks on the well defended, areas.

During the first week in September 78 Squadron took part in two big operations. The first was a raid on Lumbres, in which 24 of their aircraft joined other squadrons to destroy a Flying Bomb storage site. Bombing took place from a height of 18,000 feet on instructions from the Master Bomber, who was flying above the attack force. Weather conditions at the time allowed the target to be clearly seen, and the bombing was reported to be well concentrated and accurate.

Two days later an attack took place on an airfield at Soesterberg and 17 of the Halifaxes that took part in the raid were from RAF Breighton. The crews reported seeing many hits on the runways, and aircraft parked in the dispersal areas. In spite of intense flak, no losses were reported.

Stubborn resistance by the German garrison that was holding out at Le Harve forced the Allies to bypass the port and wait for Bomber Command to bomb the Germans until they surrendered. After a series of raids in the first week of September, which failed to produce any sign of them giving up, an attack by close on 1,000 aircraft took place on 10th September, 245 of them belonging to 4 Group, of which 26 were 78 Squadron Halifaxes. The operation was a complete success and the next day, 11th September, the German garrison surrendered.

During the night of 11th/12th September, 11 aircraft took off from Breighton to carry out a gardening raid over the Kattegat in Norway. With all the ports in France now denied to the Germans, it was the only route available for U-Boats returning to port after their forays into the Atlantic. It also provided the only link with the German forces occupying Norway. Altogether 44 mines were sown and all the aircraft returned safely.

---

[1] By this time the Luftwaffe was becoming seriously depleted and losses of Bomber Command aircraft were consequently considerably reduced.

The 12th September saw an attack on the synthetic oil plant at Scholven-Buer by over 100 aircraft of 4 Group. Weather conditions over the target area were excellent, allowing the target to be picked out quite easily. Very soon a pall of thick black smoke could be seen rising from oil storage tanks. The raid was a complete success and no losses were reported.

On the morning of 13th September a briefing took place at which only eight of the 78 Squadron crews were present. When the target was announced the crews began to feel rather apprehensive, for it was to be Munster and this would involve a daylight trip deep into northern Germany, with the possibility of meeting Luftwaffe fighters en route. In the event, no enemy aircraft were encountered. But they knew a heavy barrage would await them on reaching the target area. Nevertheless, they pressed home the attack, sending ton after ton of high explosive and incendiary bombs onto the target, causing large fires. The operation was a total success, with all the aircraft returning home safely.

Another operation took place that night and this time 16 aircraft took off from Breighton to become part of a force of 102 Halifaxes from 4 Group that attacked the synthetic oil plant at Nordsteen. Due to haze covering the target area, the crews were unable to see the markers set down by the Pathfinder force and had to bomb on instructions from the Master Bomber. One of the 78 Squadron Halifaxes MZ787 EY- had started its bomb run when it was hit by flak which wounded the bomb aimer. The flight engineer quickly opened the bomb doors and jettisoned the bombs on target. When the bombers turned for home, a large area of the plant was left burning fiercely. MZ787 returned safely to base, and the wounded bomb aimer was removed to hospital.

An attack on Kiel during the night of 15th/16th September by 22 aircraft of 78 Squadron resulted in the loss of Halifax III LV869 EY-G which took off at 22.25 hours but was lost without trace somewhere en route and presumably ditched into the North Sea. The names of the crew are commemorated on the Runnymede Memorial.

Pilot F/Lt N.M. Harding | **Nav** F/O K.J. Nethercott | **B/A** F/O M.M. Maguire
W/Op Sgt C.S. Quelch | **F/E** Sgt G. Pesticcio
A/G Sgt A.J. Coburn | **A/G** Sgt G.A.M. Simpson
All were lost and their names listed on the Runnymede Memorial

DURING THE NEXT FEW days operations were carried out over Boulogne and Calais with good results from both raids being obtained.

Wing Commander A. Markland DFC, DFM was awarded the DSO in September. It appeared in the *London Gazette* on 19th September 1944.

During the night of 23rd/24th September, a raid was carried out on Nuess by aircraft of 4 Group and 24 Halifaxes from RAF Breighton took part in the raid. Heavy damage was done to the target but one oof 78 Squadron's aircraft was lost during the attack. It crashed near the town of Weert (Limburg). Three members of the seven man crew survived the encounter but four lost their lives. Three of them were buried at Molenpoort Roman Catholic Cemetery but Sgt Nutbrown lies in Weert War Cemetery. Their aircraft was Halifax III MZ763 EY-S

> **Pilot** F/O J.S.R. Swanson, Killed, Molenpoort Catholic Cemetery
> **Nav** F/Sgt A.T. Barnes, POW, Stalag Luft 7 Bankau-Kruelberg
> **B/A** Sgt P.F. Robert, Evaded Capture
> **W/Op** Sgt A. Campbell, Killed, Molenpoort Catholic Cemetery
> **F/E** Sgt A. Nutbrown, Killed, Weert War Cemetery
> **A/G** F/O W.T. Grew, Killed, Molenpoort Catholic Cemetery
> **A/G** Sgt J.S. Bennett, Evaded Capture

In company with other aircraft from 4 Group, 23 Halifaxes took off from Breighton in the afternoon of 25th September to attack targets in Calais. On arrival the crews found it covered by 10/10th cloud, with the result, the Master bomber ordered all aircraft back to their bases with their bombs. One crew, however, did not get the message and went on to bomb the target. All aircraft returned safely.

The following morning, 78 Squadron were sent back to attack Calais. This time, they found it had been identified with Pathfinders target indicators. The bombing was well concentrated and a large explosion was seen at 10.05 hours. Following the successful attack, the Halifaxes all returned safely to Breighton.

In October 1944, Squadron Leader J. Kentish (Pilot), was awarded an immediate DFC, following two tours of operations. Flight Lieutenant E. Andrew was also awarded an immediate DFC, following one tour of operations, which included a successful ditching at the start of the tour.

A gardening raid codenamed 'Silverthorn' was carried out by 11 Aircraft of 78 Squadron on 4th October, when a total of 44 mines were sown. They all returned safely to base.

A major operation by 240 Halifax aircraft of 4 Group took place on 6th October. Their targets were the two synthetic oil plants at Gelsenkirchen (Buer Scholern and Sterkrade Holten). With these oil plants so vital to the Germans, there were plenty of fighters to be seen, waiting for the slightest opportunity to pick off an unsuspecting bomber. 78 Squadron despatched 20 Halifaxes to take part in the operation, which began their bomb runs upon reaching the target area. The bomb aimers, having been directed by the red target indicators dropped by the Pathfinders, watched their bombs exploding and setting fire to the oil plants, and very soon oily black smoke could be seen billowing up into the sky, and they knew the oil production would be seriously disrupted for many weeks to come.

A high price was to be exacted for the success of this operation, however. As they turned to leave the target area, two of the Halifaxes collided, killing both crews. Both these aircraft belonged to 78 Squadron. They crashed on the island of Overflakkes. There were no survivors.

The first aircraft was Halifax III LL588 EY-O

Pilot F/O R.L. Stanley | **Nav** Sgt C. Hapgood | **B/A** Sgt J. McKillop
W/Op Sgt A. Moss | **F/E** Sgt G. Kemp | **A/G** H. Tilburn
The above were all interred at op Zoom Cemetery, Bergen
A/G Sgt M. Lockett, Den Rommel Cemetery

The second aircraft also crashed at Overflakkes. Seven members of its eight-man crew were buried at Bergen op Zoom Cemetery. The body of Sergeant R. Hough was never found; his name is commemorated on the Runnymede Memorial. The aircraft was Halifax III MZ310 EY-U

Pilot F/O C. Crawford | **2nd Plt** F/O D.S. McGregor RCAF
Nav Sgt T. Anderton | **B/A** F/Sgt C. Clement | **W/Op** F/Sgt J. Charley RAAF
F/E Sgt A. Reilly | **A/G** Sgt J. Divens
The above were all interred at op Zoom Cemetery, Bergen
A/G Sgt R. Hough listed on the Runnymede Memorial

The third 78 Squadron aircraft lost that night was Halifax III LW511 EY-Z, which was hit by flak and crashed at Gahlen, near the town of Schermbeck, with the loss of all those on board. They were:

Pilot W/O J. Bradburn | **Nav** F/Sgt R.J. Holland | **B/A** Sgt R. Crerar
W/Op Sgt R. West | **F/E** Sgt D. Menzies
A/G F/Sgt E. Borkofsky RCAF | **A/G** Sgt A.C.L. Todd
All were interred at Reichswald Forest War Cemetery, Germany

A further six aircraft belonging to the Squadron had taken off from Breighton that night to take part in a gardening operation (codename 'Rosemary'). The weather was good and 20 mines were laid with the aid of H2s. All the planes returned safely.

At 11.30 hours on the morning of 7th October, 21 Halifaxes of 78 Squadron took off from RAF Breighton to become part of a force consisting of 238 aircraft. The target on this occasion was the German town of Kleve, on the German/Dutch border. The reason for the attack was that heavily-armed

German units stationed here posed a threat to the advancing 21ˢᵗ Army Group and Bomber Command had been asked to assist in opening the way forward. The bombing was well concentrated and a large amount of damage was reported.

78 Squadron lost one aircraft in the attack. It was shot down by flak and the crew were all killed. Their names are recorded on a special memorial at the Reichswald Forest War Cemetery, as the precise location of their graves is unknown. For this reason their names are also listed on the Runnymede Memorial. Their aircraft was Halifax III LV796 EY-K:

Pilot P/O J. Gillespie | **Nav** F/O F. Hill | **B/A** F/O E. Turnbull | **W/Op** Sgt C. Miller
F/E Sgt E. Knight | **A/G** Sgt H. Porter | **A/G** Sgt G. Sharrocks
All killed and interred Reichswald Forest War Cemetery

A FORCE OF 375 Halifaxes from 4 Group, led by Pathfinders, set out on the night of 9ᵗʰ October; their target was the German town of Bochum. With thick cloud affecting visibility, the Pathfinders had to rely on H2s to identify the target before they could drop the red target indicators ready for the bombers following close behind. Within a short time, well over 1,500 tons of high explosive and incendiary bombs were raining down on the Ruhr town. Although the results of the attack could not be seen due to thick cloud, photographs taken later showed severe damage had been inflicted. Eight aircraft taking part in the raid failed to return but none of these belonged to 78 Squadron, whose aircraft all returned safely to base.

A directive issued by Bomber Command Headquarters on 13ᵗʰ October, ordered an all-out bombing raid on the city of Duisburg on the 14ᵗʰ and 15th October 1944. Over a thousand aircraft, including 474 from Nos 4 and 6 Groups in Yorkshire, took part in the largest daylight raids made by the RAF since the heavy bomber raids of 1943.

The flak defences in the Ruhr had always been dreaded by every air crew with Duisburg being no exception, but attacks carried out on 14ᵗʰ and 15ᵗʰ October indicated that the city's air defences were now depleted. Nevertheless, a total of 17 aircraft were lost. On this occasion no losses were sustained by 78 Squadron.

Aircraft of 4 Group raided Wilhelmshaven on the night of 15ᵗʰ/16ᵗʰ October, with 12 Halifaxes from RAF Breighton participating. The visibility was very poor and bombing was scattered. All the aircraft returned safely. On the same night, a gardening raid (codename 'Yew') was carried out by six Halifaxes of 78 Squadron, off the coast of Denmark. The mines were dropped from a height of 15,000 feet and all the aircraft returned safely.

The 23rd and 24th October saw more than 8,000 tons of bombs dropped on the city of Essen, which had been bombed many times since 1941 because it was the home of the Krupps armaments works, which supplied most of the guns used by the German Navy. More than a thousand aircraft had taken part in the first attack. Halifaxes and Lancasters had dropped a total of 4,538 tons of high explosives and incendiary bombs on the target. This was followed by a further 3,684 tons of bombs the following day. These two successive attacks caused widespread destruction throughout the city and left scores of buildings in ruins. When the second attack was over, the Krupps works had been so badly damaged that production was completely halted. The city that had once been the centre of arms production would never again produce arms for Nazi Germany.

78 Squadron lost one aircraft, Halifax III LV872 EY- in the raid. After attacking the target and successfully making their way back to the UK, a serious fire had broken out in the port inner engine, which resulted in the aircraft being abandoned near Woodbridge in Suffolk. The crew all survived their ordeal largely unscathed:

Pilot F/O C. Wenzel RCAF, Escaped uninjured
Nav F/O T. Young RCAF, Escaped uninjured
B/A F/Sgt M. Mcfarlane RCAF, Injured but safe
W/Op Sgt F. Sonowski RCAF, Escaped uninjured
F/E Sgt H. Oldham, Injured but safe
A/G F/Sgt E. Green RCAF, Injured but safe
A/G F/Sgt C. Goodman RCAF, Injured but safe

WESTKAPELLE BECAME THE TARGET for the aircraft of 78 Squadron on 28th and 29th October. The first raid took place on the morning of the 28th, when 11 Halifaxes bombed the heavy artillery positions located there. There was no difficulty in seeing the green target indicators that had been dropped by Mosquitos of the Pathfinder Force. The bombing was accurate and concentrated and all the Halifaxes returned safely to base. The following day, Westkapelle again became the target. After such a pounding, many of the crews could not understand how the island's defences managed to fight back so doggedly. This was to be the last attack on the island, for the port of Antwerp was now open to Allied naval and ground forces.

Two days later it was back to night operations for 78 Squadron, when they were briefed to take part in an attack on Cologne. Twenty-one of the squadron's Halifaxes were detailed for the raid. On arriving over the target, they found it had been identified by red Wanganui flares by the Pathfinders. Bombing was carried out from 18,000 feet with extensive damage being inflicted on the factory buildings and houses below. The aircraft returned to base and within hours a second attack on the same target was mounted by the squadron, and this time 13 Halifaxes were involved in the raid which inflicted further damage to a city that had endured more than its fair share of bombings since the 'thousand bomber raids' had started earlier in the war.

November 1944 commenced with an attack on Dusseldorf by nearly 1,000 Lancasters, Halifaxes and Mosquitos. The weather was fair, which allowed the target to be clearly seen, though there was a slight ground haze. Red indicator flares identified the target and the bomb runs began at 19.00 hours, delivering a thorough and well concentrated attack. However, with heavy flak and night fighters being deployed, it was obvious that there would be significant casualties on this operation, and when the last aircraft had returned to base Bomber Command was found to have lost 27 aircraft in the raid, although on this occasion none of the losses were borne by 78 Squadron, all of whose aircraft returned in one piece. However, a new danger to the bombers was about to be introduced by the German Air Force. Built by Messerschmitt, it was known as the Me262. Several crews reported having seen it whilst taking part in the Dusseldorf raid and this would prove to be true during the next few days.

Bochum became the target for Nos 1, 4, 6 and 8 Groups on the night of 4th November, when a force of over 700 Lancasters, Halifaxes and Mosquitos took off from their bases in Yorkshire and Lincolnshire. Red and green indicators lit up the target and bombing commenced from 17,500 feet delivering their deadly payload of 3,322 tons of high explosive and incendiary bombs, causing widespread damage to the town. The crews reported seeing many fires burning out of control. One aircraft belonging to 78 Squadron was lost in the attack and this was Halifax III LK838 EY-E. Of its seven man crew only one survived and became a prisoner of war. All the others were killed but only one body was ever found and duly buried in Venray War Cemetery. The remaining crew members names are commemorated on the Runnymede Memorial. They were:

Pilot F/O E.A. Love RCAF, Venray War Cemetery
Nav Sgt C.D. Evans, Runnymede Memorial
B/A F/O K. Brookes RCAF, Runnymede Memorial
W/Op F/Sgt K. Collins RCAF, Runnymede Memorial
F/E Sgt G. Harding, Runnymede Memorial
A/G F/Sgt A. Roach RCAF, POW, Stalag 6J Dorstein Westphalia
A/G F/Sgt M. Jodrell RCAF, Runnymede Memorial

Gelsenkirchen became the target for 17 Halifaxes of 78 Squadron on 6th November 1944, when they became part of a force of over a thousand bombers that set out to destroy the marshalling yards and warehouses where vital supplies for the German Army were stored. On arriving over the target, which had been identified by the large built up area that it covered, the bombers commenced their bomb runs. The average bomb load for each of the Halifaxes was one 2,000 high explosive 'cookie' and 4,000 lb of incendiary bombs, and very soon these began to rain down on the target. Extensive damage was done to the rolling stock standing in the marshalling yards and surrounding buildings and when the bombers turned for home they left behind large fires and palls of smoke rising high into the sky. Five aircraft were lost in the raid but on this occasion all the 78 Squadron aircraft returned safely.

Following the Gelsenkirchen raid, 78 Squadron were given a ten day break from operations before taking part in an attack on Julich on 16th November, in which the other 4 Group squadrons would be involved. On the appointed day 21 Halifaxes trundled down the runway at RAF Breighton and with their engines on full boost they slowly climbed away to join all the other aircraft taking part in the operation. On reaching the target area, they found it had been identified and marked by the PFF crews, and they dropped their bombs from a height of 12,000 feet, causing fires to rage over the whole of the town. Three aircraft were lost in the raid but none of them belonged to 78 Squadron.

On the night of 18th/19th November 78 Squadron despatched 14 aircraft to carry out a raid on Munster. Bad weather was experienced on the outward journey and when they arrived over the target area the crews found it covered in 10/10ths cloud. However, Pathfinder aircraft had already outlined the target zone with sky markers ready for the bombers following close behind, to drop their bombs. With cloud obscuring the target the bombers were unable to see any results as they turned for home. After dropping its bombs, one of the 78 Squadron aircraft developed brake pressure problems and consequently the pilot was forced to divert to RAF Carnaby on return to the UK, where the damaged aircraft crash landed. The crew all managed to escape unhurt. The aircraft was Halifax III MZ849 EY-

Pilot F/O C. Wenzel RCAF | **Nav** F/O T. Young RCAF | **B/A** Sgt T. Greenslade
W/Op Sgt F. Sonowski RCAF | **F/E** Sgt B. Dixonet
A/G Sgt E. Bell | **A/G** Sgt J. Mcmanus
Crash landed on return to UK but all escaped uninjured

Following an attack on Sterkrade by Halifaxes of 78 Squadron during the night of 21st/22nd November 1944, Halifax III MZ810 EY-T returned to base and requested permission to land but due to a change in wind direction the pilot, Flight Lieutenant M.S. Buchanan DFC RAAF, was instructed to circle the airfield while the duty runway was altered. A report received minutes later stated that the Halifax had crashed into a tree on the Spaldington range, roughly two miles from the airfield, where it had immediately burst into flames, killing the crew. They were:

Pilot F/Lt M.S. Buchanan DFC. RAAF | **Nav** F/Lt W.J. Robertson RCAF
B/A F/O L.A. Welsh RCAF | **W/Op** F/O J.H. Rice | **F/E** Sgt R.J. Baron
A/G P/O J. McCannon | **A/G** Sgt J.V. Reddington
All killed in a crash landing after returning to the UK

The three Commonwealth Officers were buried in Harrogate (Stonefall) Cemetery. The others were taken to their respective home towns in the United Kingdom for burial. The body of Pilot Officer McCannon was taken home to the Republic of Ireland.

The bombing of Essen, which took place on the 29th and Duisburg on the 30th November were badly affected by the heavy cloud existing at that time of the year. It proved troublesome for both Pathfinders and bomber crews, and meant a great deal of dependence had to be placed on the H2s sets. Bombing was carried out on the glow of the red TIs. The light from several explosions lit up the clouds, raising the crews hopes that their bombs were causing some damage below.

The town of Hagen was bombed by aircraft from Nos 4 and 6 Groups, on the the night of 2nd/3rd December. 24 Halifaxes from 78 Squadron took part in this raid which not only caused damage to factories, but also to the morale of the civilian population, which was taking a terrible pounding night after night. Three nights later Nos 4 and 6 Groups aircraft again joined forces to attack the important marshalling yards and communication centres at Soest. Clear visibility enabled the crews to observe the results of their work, and at the debriefing session on returning to base, several crews reported seeing two large explosions in the target area.

The following day the city of Osnabruck was visited by the aircraft of 78 Squadron. They commenced their attack at 21.00 hours, dropping their bombs on the glow from red TIs dropped by Pathfinder aircraft. A force of 21 Halifaxes left RAF Breighton and they all returned safely.

Due to bad weather, all operations were halted until the 12th December, when eight aircraft were despatched from RAF Breighton to bomb Essen. Once again thick cloud prevented the crews from being able to observe the results of the bombing. The target was identified by red and green sky markers, on which the bombs were dropped. There was a single aircraft casualty from this operation, a 105 Squadron Mosquito, which was shot down, killing the two-man crew on board.

78 Squadron despatched nine Halifaxes at 23.30 hours on the night of 14th/15th December to carry out a gardening raid off the Dutch-German coastal area. The target was identified with the help of their H2s sets. 36 mines were dropped and all the aircraft returned safely to base.

During the remainder of December, raids were carried out on targets in Duisberg, Bingen and Coblenz, considerable damage being reported following each attack. The year ended with an attack by aircraft of 4 Group on Cologne, in which 21 aircraft from 78 Squadron took part. Two aircraft were lost in this raid but neither of them belonged to 78 Squadron.

There were no operations from RAF Breighton on January 1st 1945 due to mist and fog patches with occasional sleet preventing aircraft taking off safely. The following day 24 aircraft were detailed for operations and the target was to be Ludwigshaven. One Halifax failed to reach the target area due to its port engine becoming unserviceable. Visibility over the target was fair and the remaining 23 aircraft pressed home the attack. Target marking by the Pathfinders was good and bombing was carried out from a height of 18-20,000 feet. The results of this raid were considered to have been very effective.

Following two days of being stood down, 78 Squadron received orders from Group Headquarters to take part in a raid on Hannover on the night of 5th/6th January. At RAF Breighton 21 aircraft were detailed for the operation, which also involved squadrons from Nos 1, 3, 4, 5, 6 and 8 Groups. Unfortunately, only 18 of the Breighton aircraft reached the target, three were forced to return to base with engine failure. Bombing was carried out from 18-19,000 feet, and although damage to the industrial area was very heavy, the intensive flak barrage caused heavy losses for Bomber Command. A total of 32 aircraft were lost, 108 air crew were killed, 4 were injured and 67 were made prisoners of war. Three men evaded their captors. All the 78 Squadron aircraft returned safely to base.

The next night 24 aircraft took off from Breighton to join aircraft from Nos 1, 4, 6 and 8 Groups in an attack on an important rail junction at Hanau. 10/10th cloud was encountered over the target, and the crews were forced to drop their bombs on the glow of marker flares dropped by Pathfinder aircraft. All the 78 Squadron aircraft returned safely to base, but one Halifax had suffered extensive damage to the main-plane, caused by the heavy flak over the target.

As soon as each aircraft landed, the ground crew carried out a thorough inspection, looking for any damage caused by flak or night fighters. Though it was now becoming obvious that the war in Europe was rapidly coming to an end, the Germans continued to put up a tremendous defence against the aircraft of Bomber Command as they returned, night after night, to bomb what little remained of the arms producing areas of which Germany was once so proud.

A gardening raid which took place on 12th January seems to have been something of a failure. Of the five Halifaxes that took off from Breighton, two were forced to bring their mines back due to faulty release gear and one failed to reach the target area due to the failure of the H2s set.

The large railway marshalling yards at Saarbrucken were attacked by aircraft from Nos 4 and 6 Groups, on the 14th January. A force of 18 aircraft from 78 Squadron took off to partake in the raid. The visibility was good and they bombed on red and green target indicators dropped by the Pathfinders from a height of 17-19,000 feet. A large concentration of bombs were seen to burst around the aiming point and masses of smoke was seen rising from the marshalling yards. One of the 78 Squadron Halifaxes abandoned the mission due to the starboard inner engine becoming unserviceable and a second aircraft failed to complete the attack due to the hydraulics being u/s. On return it landed at Carnaby. All the remaining 78 Squadron aircraft returned safely to base.

The Luftwaffe fuel storage depot at Dulmen became the target the next night. On this occasion only four aircraft from 78 Squadron took part. On reaching the target area they found there was good visibility and the target had been well marked by the Pathfinders. Bombing was accurate and took place from a height of 19,000 feet. A large explosion was observed at 23.20 hours and smoke rose high in the air. One aircraft was reported to have been lost in the operation but all the 78 Squadron Halifaxes returned safely to base. A further three aircraft took part in a gardening raid that same night and after dropping their mines in the selected area, they also returned safely.

On the 16th January, 4 Group Headquarters ordered an attack to be carried out on Magdeburg, in which 23 Halifaxes from 78 Squadron had been detailed to partake. Of these 22 reached the target, bombing from a height of 18-20,000 feet, on red and green target indicators that had been dropped by Lancasters of the Pathfinder Force. Tremendous fires and several explosions were seen. The operation was considered very effective and successful. One aircraft was forced to return early with its starboard engine unserviceable. There were no other casualties.

No further operations took place during the next eleven days due to freezing weather conditions, but on the night of 28th/29th January the 4 Group squadrons launched an attack on Stuttgart, with 78 Squadron contributing 16 aircraft. The force reached the target to find it covered by 10/10ths cloud. Bombing took place from 18,500 – 19,500 feet on red and yellow sky markers. The cloud prevented an accurate assessment of any results, but large fires were seen to light up the clouds and three large explosions were reported to have been observed at 23.34; 23.35; and 23.37 hours. Though all the aircraft returned safely, there were three incidents. One Halifax returned with two 1000 lb bombs and 7 incendiary clusters still on board, due to the bomb doors failing to open. One Halifax landed at RAF Benson due to a shortage of fuel and a second aircraft landed at Carnaby[1] due to a loss of brake pressure.

February 1st saw an attack carried out on Mainz and 21 aircraft from 78 Squadron took off from RAF Breighton to take part in this raid. Of these, 19 attacked the primary target from a height of 18 – 20,000 feet directed by red and green sky markers and Gee. Many large fires were observed and the raid was considered to be well concentrated and successful. Halifax MZ764 EY- returned early with its starboard inner engine u/s. Halifax NA495 EY- also returned with one of its port engines u/s. On landing, this aircraft overshot the runway and bogged down. No injuries were reported among the crew.

Orders were issued by Group Headquarters on the morning of 2nd February for an attack to be carried out on the oil plant at Wanne-Eickel. Along with all the other squadrons in 4 Group, 78 Squadron detailed 20 Halifaxes for the raid. (In the event, two of these failed to take off due to engine trouble). Only 16 of the remaining 18 aircraft are known to have reached the target, which was covered by 10/10th Strato-Cumulus cloud, with tops at 6.000 feet. Due to this cloud cover the majority of crews bombed on the red glow of the markers reflecting on the clouds, or as directed by Gee. Several explosions were reported in the target area and some were quite large between 23.26 and 23.34 hours. Any accurate assessment of damage was not possible. Though night fighter activity was negligible, two aircraft were badly damaged by flak. One of 78 Squadron's

---

[1] RAF Carnaby was one of several emergency airfields for bombers returning from operations with battle damage.

aircraft aborted the mission due to its bomb aimer being taken ill, this was Halifax MZ762 EY- which returned to base otherwise unharmed.

One of the Squadron's aircraft failed to return. This was Halifax III NA167 EY-F which crashed on its way back from the target. Four members of its crew were killed, three were buried at the Reichswald Forest War Cemetery, but the body of air gunner F/Sgt E.H. Fletcher was never found and is is commemorated on the Runnymede Memorial.

Pilot F/O J.L. Gutzewitz RNZAF | **W/Op** F/Sgt F.V. Robinson | **A/G** Sgt F. Cowell
interred at Reichswald Forest War Cemetery
A/G Sgt E.H. Fletcher, *listed on Runnymede Memorial*
Nav P/O L.B. Stuart RNZAF | **B/A** P/O L.P. O'Brien RNZAF and
F/E F/Sgt W.J. Paterson all became POWs, no details available

DURING A GARDENING RAID on the Heligoland Bight the next night, three aircraft from 78 Squadron dropped their mines as ordered, without encountering any opposition from night fighters. Light flak was reported from the direction of Spickerooge. Visibility was fair with 5 – 8/10th cloud which allowed the crews to observe the mines being dropped. All three aircraft returned home safely.

On the night of 4th/5th February 19 aircraft took off from RAF Breighton to take part in an attack on Bonn. One of them, Halifax III Z 619 EY-I failed to bomb due to its bomb doors failing to open. Visibility over the target was poor, with 9/10th cloud. The Pathfinder aircraft were six minutes late arriving and several crews bombed on Gee co-ordinates. Marking by the Pathfinders started at 20.47 hours and crews bombed on red and green target indicators through cloud. Adding to the confusion, red flares with yellow stars were seen, probably dummies, which probably accounted for the bombing being scattered. A number of fires were seen through cloud patches and their glow was visible for 70-100 miles on the return journey. All the aircraft returned safely, though one landed at RAF Carnaby, having sustained some damage.

After a two night break 14 aircraft from 78 Squadron were detailed for a raid on Goch, which can only be described as a shambles. Two aircraft returned early due to engine trouble and only five of the remaining 12 dropped their bombs on mixed salvos of red and green target indicators provided by the Pathfinders and two crews reported seeing large explosions in the target area. The Master Bomber was first heard to give instructions to bomb below cloud and lastly to abandon the mission. The remaining aircraft obeyed this latter command and turned for home.

On the same night six of the squadron's aircraft carried out a gardening raid at Keil Fjord. Five dropped their mines at the locations they had been given as targets, but one Halifax suffered a defect with its H2s set and was unable to make an accurate run, so its crew dropped their mines at an alternative location. Some fighter activity was reported over Denmark on the return journey, but all the aircraft returned safely.

At 02.30 hours on the morning of 9th February 78 Squadron despatched 16 Halifaxes to join aircraft from other 4 Group squadrons in an attack on the oil plants at Wanne Eickel. The attack took place in conditions of 4–6/10th cloud. The red and green target indicators identifying the target were seen by all the crews and bombing was accurate with explosions being observed at 06.23 and 06.25 hours. Columns of black smoke and fires in the target area were reported. The flak was fairly heavy, but there was no fighter activity. Halifax III NA176 EY-K piloted by F/O Hatherell returned early due to the mid upper gunner being sick. All the aircraft returned safely.

The 12th February 1945 saw a change of command in No 4 Group, when Air Vice-Marshal C.R. Carr, who had commanded the Group since 26th July 1941, was replaced by Sir John Whitley (Later Air Marshal Sir John Whitley KBE, CB, DSO, AFC). He lost no time in planning his first operation as Group Commander, by ordering a strong force to carry out an attack on the Braunkohle-Benzine synthetic oil plant at Bohlen, near Leipzig. Unfortunately, this operation was unsuccessful due to bad weather in the target area. 78 Squadron had despatched 23 aircraft but only 21 managed to reach the target, which was covered by 8/10th cloud. Most of the crews succeeded in identifying the target by the green target indicators, and the glow of fires that could be seen through the clouds. Some crews reported seeing red TIs, but the PFF marking was the worst seen for some time, with flares scattered over a wide area. On top of this, decoy fires in the target area added to the confusion.

A number of large explosions were observed, one at 22.07 hours produced masses of dark red flames. Of the 368 aircraft which took part, mostly Halifaxes, only one failed to return, though a second bomber was written off when it crashed at its home base of Holme-on-Spalding Moor. The two 78 Squadron aircraft that were forced to abandon the raid were Halifax III MX392 which landed at Carnaby 23 minutes after taking off, with its starboard outer engine unserviceable and Halifax III MZ495 EY- which abandoned the mission over enemy territory, due to loss of power. It landed at Manston safely. It was thought that the results of the operation would prove disappointing. Several aircraft suffered problems on the return journey, but they all reached their bases safely.

Two days later 78 Squadron was ordered to carry out an attack on Chemnitz on the night of 14th/15th February and 16 aircraft were detailed for the raid. It was carried out in conditions of 8–10/10ths cloud, the cloud tops being 8,000 feet. The target indicators could not be seen so aircraft bombed on the glow of incendiary bombs and Wanganui and white illuminating flares. While over the target, one Halifax, piloted by P/O Phillips was attacked four times by a Ju88 and one port engine was put out of action. Both gunners returned fire and on the third attack the enemy's port wing was seen to be glowing. The Ju88 broke off the attack on the fourth pass with its port wing on fire and the Halifax crew claimed it as possibly destroyed. Another aircraft was attacked on its homeward journey by an ME262. The Halifax returned fire and the enemy aircraft was seen to burst into flames and explode on the ground.

One aircraft aborted the raid over enemy territory due to its intercom being u/s. All the Squadron's aircraft returned safely to the UK but four of them didn't make it back to their home base; two landed at Tuddenham, one at Woodbridge and one at Manston. The latter aircraft was Halifax III MZ791 EY-T.[1] On the outbound flight its navigation aids had failed and at 21.21 hours an alternative target was bombed from 13,000 feet. On return it landed at RAF Manston in Kent. There were no injuries but the Halifax was beyond repair and eventually struck off charge on 5th July.

Pilot F/Lt J. Davidson | **Nav** P/O E. Tidman | **B/A** F/Sgt K.C.Cutting
W/Op Sgt W.C.Black RAAF | **F/E** Sgt W.Robertson
A/G Sgt S.Gladdery | **A/G** Sgt W.J.Gall

FOUR 78 SQUADRON HALIFAXES had been detailed for a gardening raid (codename 'Sweet Pea') that night. Three of them dropped their mines as ordered with the aid of their H2s sets. Heavy flak was encountered in the Holbeek area and one of the aircraft was believed to have been hit.

Though its exact fate was never established, Halifax III MZ499 EY-X failed to return and was presumed lost over the North Sea. The names of its crew are commemorated on the Runnymede Memorial.

Pilot F/Lt H.S. Cumming | **Nav** P/O J.S. Thompson
B/A P/O S.A.W. Tressider | **W/Op** F/Sgt E.P. Yates | **F/E** P/O J.S. Rice
A/G F/Sgt I. Williams | **A/G** P/O M. Schwartz RCAF

---

[1] MZ791 was one of a batch of 44 Halifax Mk III bombers delivered to Nos 4 and 6 Groups in Yorkshire, between 23rd June- 14th July 1944.

ORDERS WERE RECEIVED FROM 4 Group Headquarters for a raid on Wessel to take place on the night of 17th/18th February and 19 aircraft were duly despatched from RAF Breighton by 78 Squadron. They took off in bad weather and this persisted all the way to the target where, on the instructions of the Master Bomber, the raid was abandoned. However, one aircraft failed to hear the order and bombed on Gee co-ordinates. All the aircraft returned safely to this country but due to bad weather at Breighton only four aircraft managed to land there, the rest of the squadron diverted to other bases. 10 landed at Tuddenham; one at Carnaby; two at Mildenhall; one at North Pickenham; and one at Manston. With so many of the aircraft landing at various bases around the country, it was late the following day before the last 78 squadron aircraft arrived back at its home base.

The night of 20th/21st February saw an attack carried out on the Reisholz district of Dusseldorf, with 78 Squadron detailing 15 aircraft to take part in the raid. Over the target 10/10ths cloud was encountered, preventing the crews from seeing the red target indicators clearly and they were forced to bomb on the red glow that lit up the clouds. Though this was paler than the TIs, it did not tempt any of the crews away from the primary target. A number of the crews reported that on their homeward journey the red glow in the target area could be seen increasing and decreasing from time to time. Several minor explosions had also been observed. Night fighters were active while the bombers were on the way to and from the target area, and several combats were reported, with a number of aircraft being shot down as a result. Slight to moderate flak, which had been predicted during the briefing, was also encountered, bursting at around 16 – 17,000 feet in barrage form. Searchlights were active but largely ineffective due to the cloud. One Halifax crew reported having a combat with a Ju88 and a Me410, which lasted for 13 minutes, with strikes being claimed on both enemy aircraft by the Halifax gunners. Though seven RAF aircraft were seen to be shot down, all the 78 Squadron Halifaxes returned safely to base.

The 4 Group squadrons carried out several operations during the days that followed but each time the heavy cloud base made it very difficult for the Pathfinders to find and mark the targets. Dusseldorf and Worms were attacked on 21st and 22nd February, with Essen being singled out for a daylight attack by 16 aircraft from 78 Squadron on 23rd February. The raid took place in conditions of 10/10ths Strata-Cumulus with a very tenuous base at 13,000 feet and tops of 21–22,000 feet. Sky marking was by Green smoke markers, but only 5 aircraft were able to bomb on them owing to the density of the cloud. The remainder of the aircraft bombed on Gee co-ordinates or H2s or both. No results were seen and no incidents reported. Flak was negligible and no night fighter activity was reported. All the aircraft returned safely to base.

On 24th February 15 aircraft were detailed to carry out an attack on Kamen during the hours of daylight. They took off at 13.00 hours from RAF Breighton, their ETA over the target being 16.45 hours. Once again the bombing had to be carried out in conditions of 10/10th cloud with tops of 5,000 feet. No target indicators could be seen, so all the aircraft bombed on Gee co-ordinates or on H2s on the instructions of the Master Bomber, with the exception of Halifax 'H' which bombed on D.R. as its Gee and H2s were unserviceable. No results were observed. A small amount of heavy flak was encountered in the target area and was repeated by the Dortmund defences as the aircraft were returning returning to their bases. No fighters were encountered and all the aircraft returned safely to base.

Following a stand-down of two days, 23 aircraft from 78 Squadron were detailed to take part in a raid on Mainz. The bombers arrived over the target at 16.30 hours in conditions of 10/10ths cloud with tops of 9-10,000 feet. All aircraft bombed on green smoke puffs as directed. Two crews reported a considerable amount of brownish smoke billowing up from the target area, but otherwise, no results were observed owing to the cloud. Flak in the target area was light to moderate and no enemy fighters were seen, but crews were impressed with the RAF fighter cover, which was excellent. The Breighton aircraft all returned safely.

There were no operations on the 28th February 1945.

The first operation in March was on Cologne, and once again it was a daylight raid. 78 Squadron Halifaxes arrived at 10.00 hours, to find conditions for bombing were perfect with 4/10th cloud allowing good vertical and horizontal visibility. The Rhine and built up area, several marshalling yards with road and rail bridges across the Rhine visible. Most crews heard the Master Bomber's instructions to bomb on 'Pickwick' allowing for an after-shoot of 200 yards. The main concentration of bombing was in the built up area of Cologne, especially around the aiming point. All that part of the town was covered with smoke, which was drifting southwards, and the most northerly of the Rhine bridges appeared to be down. A heavy concentration of bombs fell around the Cathedral, which was thought to have received a direct hit, though this was disproved after the war ended. In the opinion of those crews that took part in the raid, the attack was successful. Two of the aircraft were damaged, but all the 78 Squadron Halifaxes returned safely to base.

Bomber crews found they could now afford to relax a little while flying over enemy territory for the Luftwaffe were now suffering from a crippling shortage of fuel. During the night of 3rd/4th March 19 aircraft belonging to 78 Squadron became part of a force of 201 Halifaxes from 4 Group that set out to attack the synthetic oil plant at Kamen. On reaching the target area without being challenged, they found it had a 5/10th cloud layer and visibility that was good to moderate. All aircraft identified the target which was marked by red TIs that could be seen through the cloud. Explosions were reported at 22.02; 22.04; and 22.05: The explosion at 22.04 lasted about 15 seconds. Destruction was on such a scale that production at the factory was completely halted. Flak defences were moderate and fighter flares were seen on the run in to the target but there were no reports of bombers being attacked.

However, unknown to the bomber force, the Luftwaffe were about to inflict a surprise attack on the bomber airfields in Yorkshire and Lincolnshire. As the Halifaxes and Lancasters returned from raiding Germany, scores of Ju88s and He219s came from behind and mixed with the unsuspecting bombers as they were approaching their airfields in preparation to land. The Germans code-named it 'Operation Gisela'. They began firing cannons and machine guns at the unsuspecting bombers with their navigation lights making them easy targets, and they dropped their bombs on the brightly lit up runways. No 4 Group lost 11 aircraft on that fateful night, though no 78 Squadron aircraft were lost. One 78 Squadron Halifax was diverted to Abingdon and one landed at Wymeswold because its Gee was u/s and it was short of fuel.

A gardening raid was carried out in the Heligoland Bight on the night of 4th/5th March by Halifax aircraft of 78 Squadron. They dropped their mines on target with the aid of H2s fixes. Flak was light and the aircraft returned safely.

Following the bad weather at the start of the year, Bomber Command were now re-commencing their attack on Germany. During the night of 5th/6th March, 21 aircraft took off from RAF Breighton at 17.00 hours to partake in an attack on Chemnitz, but 5 of them were forced to return early due to various problems. On reaching the target area at 21.45 hours, the 16 remaining Halifaxes found 10/10th cloud covering the target area. The Master Bomber was heard instructing crews to bomb on the red glow of the sky markers with green stars, when these went out, the centre of the white glow was reflected on the clouds, otherwise no results were seen. All the 78 Squadron aircraft returned safely, though one was diverted to

Manston due to tracer damage, this was Halifax III MZ659 EY- which landed safely with no injuries to the crew being reported.

Aircraft of Nos 4 and 6 Groups took part in an attack on the oil refinery at Hemmingstadt during the night of 7th/8th March. Visibility was poor in spite of there being only 3-5/10th cloud when the aircraft reached the target area at 22.00 hours. Marking of the target was confusing and it appears that the illuminating white flares and the green target indicators were very scattered. A large orange flash was seen in the target area at 22.01, leaving several small fires burning. A lot of brown/black smoke was seen rising up to 12,000 feet, coming from the neighbourhood of the target indicators, but no other results were seen. Flak was negligible and there was some fighter activity. One of the 78 Squadron Halifaxes suffered heavy damage after being attacked by a Ju 88 night fighter, but it made a safe return to its base at Breighton, and there are no reports of any injuries to the crew.

The next night Hamburg became the target for the aircraft of 4 Group and 78 Squadron contributed 17 of its Halifaxes. On their arrival at the target area, they found the visibility was good with only slight cloud. The target had been identified by green target indicators, that were well concentrated. A series of explosions in the target area was reported from 21.31 to 21.42, with a particularly spectacular explosion, orange in colour, with sheets of flame 500 – 1000 feet high at 21.35 hours. The bombing was reported to have been concentrated. Flak was intense on the outskirts of the target area and night fighter activity was moderate. 4 Group lost three aircraft on this operation, but all the 78 Squadron aircraft returned safely.

During the next two days there were no 'Ops' for the Squadron but on the afternoon of the 11th March Bomber Command launched the heaviest attack of the war so far so far when 1,079 aircraft took to the skies to bomb Essen. At 15.10 hours 78 Squadron despatched 22 of its Halifaxes and very soon the huge armada was on its way to inflict a devastating amount of damage. The attack took place in conditions of 10/10th cloud and the crews were instructed by the Master Bomber to bomb on the blue smoke puffs. Very soon a large pall of smoke was seen coming up through the clouds, some crews claimed it reached a height of 9 – 10,000 feet. It covered an area of two miles in diameter and later turned to a brown colour. Though the flak was slight to heavy in the target area, there was no sign of fighter activity reported. When the last of the bombers had departed, this once huge engineering centre was now nothing but a mass of ruined buildings from which it would take many years to recover. Bomber Command lost only four aircraft in this operation. One of the 78 Squadron aircraft was slightly damaged by flak, but they all returned safely to Breighton.

A further operation was launched the next day. This time the number of aircraft taking part was over eleven hundred and the target was Dortmund. 78 Squadron contributed 21 Halifaxes to the raid and they took off at 13.00 hours from RAF Breighton, to join up with the rest of this huge force of bombers making its way toward the target area. Once again the crews were forced to bomb on blue or green smoke puffs due to cloud cover, but thanks to the accurate marking by the Pathfinder Force, the target was dealt a massive blow when close on 5,000 tons of bombs rained down on the centre of Dortmund. Columns of grey and black smoke billowed up through the clouds, followed by a large explosion in the target area at 16.55 hours. This created a pall of smoke that was still visible after crossing our lines on the homeward journey. Flak was light with no enemy fighters reported. This was to be the last time that Dortmund was bombed; like Essen, it was now little more than a pile of rubble.

The destruction of arms and oil producing areas went on with Wuppertal becoming the next target when 4 and 6 Groups combined to carry out a raid on the afternoon of 13th March 1945. A force of 22 Halifaxes took off from RAF Breighton. The attack took place in conditions of 6 – 8/10ths cloud. Bombing was well concentrated and all the aircraft returned safely to their bases.

During the next three days, aircraft from 78 Squadron joined those from other squadrons in Nos 4 and 6 Groups, bombing Hamburg, Bottrop and Hagen, causing heavy damage to the target areas. But the enemy were not yet entirely beaten, for aircraft losses amounted to 17 bombers, although none of these belonged to 78 Squadron.

After a break of two days, 4 Group carried out an attack on Witten in West Germany and 78 Squadron contributed 20 Halifaxes to this raid. They found the weather over the target was clear, with just a slight ground haze. The Pathfinders were late arriving, but the marking was good. The bombing was well concentrated with many fires seen blazing in the target area, and when a large orange explosion lit up the sky at 04.19 hours, it was identified as coming from the area of the steelworks south-west of the aiming point. Masses of black smoke was observed rising from there which could still be seen for over a hundred miles after leaving the area. There were no night fighters to contend with and the flak was moderate. Nevertheless, several aircraft were shot down, with two of them being seen to disintegrate completely in mid air. One of the 78 Squadron aircraft was fortunate to make it back to base, after suffering the loss of its starboard outer engine when hit by flak over the target area.

A raid on the Recklenhausen railway yards on 20th March was a failure. The Pathfinders were late arriving and the Master Bomber instructed the crews to bomb on the best navigational aids or visibility. Due to intensive jamming by the Germans, many crews were prevented from bombing accurately, causing the attack to become very scattered. It appears from photographs taken afterwards that only two aircraft were anywhere near the target. Following the attack, the main force came back on a reciprocal course, owing to them following the leading aircraft. In doing so, they encountered more flak than they otherwise would have done. Once again, 78 Squadron were fortunate to have all their aircraft return safely.

An attack on Dulmen two days later somewhat made up for the abortive raid on 20th March. On this occasion 18 aircraft had taken off from RAF Breighton and on reaching the target area they found patchy cirrus cloud above 20,000 feet giving moderate to good visibility. The Master Bomber stated that the target indicators were accurately placed, but were partly obliterated by smoke. A large number of bombs were seen to burst in the midst of dense black and brown smoke and when the aircraft left the target area, it was covered in a dense pall of smoke.

No 4 Group Halifaxes mounted a bombing raid on Sterkrade on the 24th March and among the aircraft taking part were a number of Halifaxes of 78 Squadron. The target had been well identified by the Pathfinders using red target indicators, with the bombing that followed being well concentrated and accurate. Two very bright red explosions in the target area were seen at 13.16 hours, one in the centre of the target and the other about two hundred yards south. The second one was followed by a huge sheet of yellow flame followed by billows of black smoke, and a large factory was seen to disintegrate. As the aircraft were leaving the area, the whole of the marshalling yard was covered in smoke. The flak was light, and no fighters were reported to have been seen by the crews taking part in the raid. All the 78 Squadron aircraft returned safely, though one landed at RAF Carnaby and one at RAF Manston with serious flak damage.

The last operation during March 1945 saw 22 aircraft from 78 Squadron detailed to attack Osnabruck. In the event only 19 planes took off, the other three being non-starters. The bombing was accurate with heavy damage inflicted and the raid was considered to have been successful. On its return one of the squadron's Halifaxes landed at RAF Carnaby due to flak damage.

THE FIRST OPERATION IN April took place in the evening of the 4th when 327 aircraft from Nos 4, 6 and 8 Groups took part in an attack on one of Germany's last remaining oil plants, the Rhenania AG plant at Harburg. For this raid 78 Squadron detailed 21 aircraft, although in the event only 18 carried out the attack in conditions of well broken cloud. Good visibility helped the crews to identify the target, which had been marked with mixed red and green target indicators. Crews also identified the target by the southern Elbe and docks. Several explosions were reported, one being exceptionally large to the extent that it lit up the whole area of attack. The raid was considered to have been most successful. Six night fighters were reported to have been seen in the target area, but no combats were reported. The flak was fairly intense, with light searchlight activity.

78 Squadron lost one of its aircraft in this operation, which exploded with great force after being hit by flak. As a result, debris and the bodies of the crew were scattered over a large area and consequently burials took place at cemeteries as far apart as Hamburg, Hannover and Becklingen. The aircraft in question was Halifax III MZ460 EY-R

Pilot F/Lt R.E. Cox | **Nav** F/Lt A.J. Lewsley | **B/A** P/O A.K. Taylor
W/Op P/O B.M.E. McLeod RAAF | **F/E** Sgt J.S. Johnston
A/G P/O J.G. Burns | **A/G** F/O M.H. Pattison
All killed and buried at various cemeteries in Germany

THE SUBMARINE YARDS AT Hamburg came in for attention from the aircraft of No 4 Group on the night of 8th/9th April. A force of 20 Halifaxes took off at 20.00 hours from RAF Breighton and on arrival over the target area, they found it had been marked by the Pathfinders with red and green flares. The instructions from the Master Bomber were confusing, which may account for the scattered bombing. Smoke and fires were seen under the light cloud. Flak was moderate, but enemy fighter activity was considerable. On the homeward journey, several bombers were attacked by night fighters, but after return fire by the bombers, the fighters broke off the engagement, though one was seen to crash in flames.

A number of aircraft suffered serious damage from the fighter attacks, but managed to return safely to base. On it's return one of the 78 Squadron aircraft crashed on high ground near Bridlington in Yorkshire, killing three crew members. The two Canadians were buried at Harrogate (Stonefall) Cemetery, while Sgt Steele RAF was interred at Shoreham-by-sea cemetery. The aircraft was Halifax III MZ361 EY-D

Pilot F/Lt V.L. Jackson, Injured but safe

Nav W/O T.W. Fry RCAF, Killed, Harrogate (Stonefall) Cemetery
B/A F/Sgt J.M. Pougnet RCAF, Killed, Harrogate (Stonefall) Cemetery
W/Op Sgt M.H. Steele, Killed, Shoreham-by-Sea Cemetery
F/E Sgt C.K. Gray, Injured but safe
A/G F/O F.G. Jones, Injured but safe
A/G F/Sgt J. Sims, Injured but safe

A GARDENING RAID BY 78 Squadron Halifaxes took place on Flensburg Fjord took place the same night. Seven aircraft took off at 22.30 hours and all laid their mines as ordered. The weather was fine with good visibility. No defences were encountered and all the aircraft returned safely. On the return journey Halifax III MZ995 developed problems and two of the crew baled out over the North Sea. They were the rear gunner P/O B. Hoddinott RCAF, who was picked up by a trawler, and flight engineer P/O F.W. Birks, whose body was washed up later at Cromer on the Norfolk coast. The aircraft landed safely at RAF Breighton.

On 10th April 1945, in accordance with instructions from Headquarters Bomber Command, 78 Squadron was reduced from three to two flights. To effect this reduction 'C' Flight was disbanded and eight crews from this flight were posted to North Creake for allocation between Nos 171 and 199 Bomber Squadrons. These eight crews proceeded to North Creake on 18th April 1945 and the remaining crews were divided between 'A' and 'B' Flights.

Between the 16th and 24th April, 78 Squadron were re-equipped with Halifax Mk VI aircraft. The first of these new aircraft were taken over by the squadron from No.44 Base and re-arming was completed on the 24th April.

A maximum effort was ordered by Bomber Command Headquarters on the morning of 18 April 1945, when Heligoland became the target. 617 Lancasters and 332 Halifaxes made up the force that raided the German naval base. When the raid was over, Heligoland had been completely destroyed.

Seven days later at 09.40 hours on the 25th April 1945, 15 aircraft from 78 Squadron were ordered to prepare for a daylight bombing raid on Wangerooge (the most easterly of the Frisian Islands). They were to become part of a force of 482 aircraft from Nos 4, 6 and 8 Groups that would attack the stronghold that controlled the approaches to Bremen and Wilhelmshaven. The crews identified the target by means of red and green target indicators and visual means. The bombing was reported to be concentrated with one large explosion taking place at approximately 17.03 hours. The Master Bomber was heard to stop the bombing after seeing some of the bombs landing on the foreshore. Moderate amounts of heavy flak was encountered from the defences on this island, and also from Langerooge and Spinkerooge. A total of 308 Halifaxes, 158 Lancasters and 9 Mosquitos made up the force that attacked this target. Bomber Command lost 7 aircraft: Two Halifaxes from Holme-on-Spalding Moor (No 76 Squadron); One Halifax from Elvington (No 347 Squadron); Two Halifaxes from Linton-on-Ouse (Nos 408 and 426 Squadrons) and two Lancasters from Croft (No 431 Squadron). All the 78 Squadron aircraft returned safely to base on this occasion. One crew reported seeing a jet-propelled aircraft of some kind being chased by two Spitfires, otherwise no air activity was reported. No further operations took place during April.

The End of Hostilities

BETWEEN 1ST AND 6TH May no further operations took place and on the 7th May 1945 78 Squadron transferred from Bomber Command to Transport Command, marking the end of the squadron's remarkable contribution to the victorious outcome for the Allied forces in World War II.

On 7th May 1945, 78 Squadron (in common with most of the units in 4 Group and with Headquarters No 4 Group) ceased its long association with Bomber Command. The appended copy Headquarters Transport Command LM/507/Org.3. States:

> "With effect from 7th May 1945 Headquarters No 4 (Bomber) Group to be renamed, Headquarters No 4 (Transport) Group."

DURING JUNE 1945 A number of German cross-country training flights took place. On 30th June the first two Dakota aircraft were allotted to the squadron and collected from RAF Down Ampney, Gloucestershire. No other flying took place.

On 5th July the conversion of crews to Dakotas was started and by the end of the month they commenced formation flying.

In September 1945 78 Squadron were despatched to Middle East Command and based at Almaza. The squadron was brought under the control of 282 Wing and its long association with 4 Group ended.

The Squadron's Headquarters at RAF Station Breighton closed down on 17th September 1945 and re-opened at Almaza on 20th September. The move was carried out without incident except for one unfortunate accident to aircraft KP235, piloted by Flying Offcer G.E. Venables, which crashed at Istres in Southern France on the morning of 5th September. All the crew and eleven passengers were killed and the remaining nine passengers seriously injured. Two of these subsequently died.

78 Squadron commenced operating in its new role in the Middle East at Almaza on 13th September 1945.

The Squadron Postwar

Since that time, 78 Squadron been disbanded and reformed on four occasions. The first time it was disbanded was at Fayid on 30th September 1951. It was then reformed at Khormaksar on 15th April 1956. It was disbanded once more on 21st December 1971 at Sharjah in the Middle East, to be reformed yet again from Nos 1310 and 1564 Flights at Mount Pleasant, in the Falkland Islands on 1st May 1986.

From 1988 to 2007, 78 Squadron was the only RAF squadron permanently based in the Falkland Islands. Four Panavia Tornado F3s which provide air defence were operated by No.1435 Flight, while No. 1312 Flight operated a Vickers VC10 and one Lockheed Hercules C3.

In December 2007, No. 78 Squadron reverted to its previous identity of No. 1564 Flight and a new 78 Squadron stood-up at RAF Benson as part of the Joint Helicopter Command on 28 January 2008, flying the Agusta Westland Merlin HC3 and six new Merlin HC3A helicopters purchased from Denmark. The squadron shared the total fleet of 28 RAF Merlin helicopters with No. 28 (AC) Squadron, also based at RAF Benson.

Following the transfer of the squadron's Merlins to 845 Naval Air Squadron of the Fleet Air Arm, 78 Squadron was disbanded on 30th September 2014 and has remained inactive since.

On 24 March 2020, the squadron was awarded a battle honour, recognising its role in the War in Iraq between 2003 and 2011.

Honourable Mentions

The Ground Crews

AT THIS POINT, I feel it would not be right for the story to end without mentioning the contribution made by the ground crews. Known colloquially at the time as 'erks' these other ranks of the RAF far outnumbered their aircrew counterparts. They were the RAF tradesmen, trained for a wide variety of roles connected with the maintenance of the aircraft and their contribution was no less important than those who actually flew the aircraft. Throughout the war these unsung heroes carried out their work at the dispersal areas in all weathers, knowing that the success of the attacks and the lives of the aircrews depended on the work they carried out. At first light, after the aircraft had returned from an operation, the fitters and riggers would go over the aircraft from nose to tail. The wings and fuselage were checked for holes caused by flak and machine gun fire. The bomb racks were checked and all the electrical gear examined. While this was being done, mechanics would be checking the engines, and instruments and armourers would be checking the weaponry, along with many other maintenance tasks that needed to be carried out before the aircraft was allowed back into the air. By means of all this effort some aircraft were kept flying for many operational sorties whilst others, sadly, were shot down on their very first mission.

The Waafs

ALONG WITH THE GROUND crews must be included and salute to the ladies of the Women's Auxiliary Air Force, the WAAFs, who in their capacities as clerks, cooks, drivers, telephonists, instrument repairers, parachute packers, radar operators, dental orderlies and even aircraft maintenance mechanics, did so much to help the RAF squadrons, often working very long hours when the job called for it. Many of these girls married members of the aircrews, in the full knowledge that their husbands might not survive their tour of operations. All too often these young women became widows within weeks, or even days, of getting married. Nevertheless, they continued with their allotted tasks and their contribution is not to be underestimated. The Royal Air Force has every right to be proud of them.

The Pathfinder Force

IT WOULD BE REMISS of me not to mention the Pathfinder Force, No 8 Group Bomber Command, before finishing this story. From the time of its inception in August 1942, until the end of the war in 1945, its Commander was the late Group Captain, later to become Air Commodore and finally Air Vice-Marshal D.C.T. Bennett CB, CBE, DSO.

When the Battle of the Ruhr commenced on the night of 5/6th March 1943, the Headquarters of No.8 Group was at Wyton, Huntingdonshire, and the Group consisted of No.7 Squadron based at Oakington, having 23 Stirlings; No.35 Squadron at Graveley, having 24 Halifaxes; No.83 Squadron at Wyton having 18 Lancasters; No 156 Squadron at Warboys with 18 Lancasters and No 109 Squadron based at Wyton equipped with 22 Mosquitos. A total of 105 aircraft.

The Pathfinder Force took part in every major operation from August 1942, until the end of the War in Europe in 1945 and their contribution was immeasurable. Until the idea of marking targets with coloured flares was thought of, RAF bombing had been very inaccurate. In order to drop their flares the Pathfinder aircraft went in ahead of the main bomber stream and ran the gauntlet of intense flak and night fighter activity in the process. Many good men were lost as a consequence.

Escape, Evasion & Underground Resistance

ALTHOUGH THE VAST MAJORITY of airmen who managed to parachute safely to earth or who survived the crash landings in enemy occupied territory were subsequently captured and became prisoners of war, some Air Crew members managed to evade capture and eventually return to the United Kingdom, thanks to the invaluable assistance they received from 'Comète' (the French Underground Movement) and other pipelines in Belgium and the Netherlands.

Five of such evaders belonged to 78 Squadron. They were: Flight Sergeant I.R.C. Innes RAAF and Flight Sergeant D.R. Foden RAAF. Both were crew members of Halifax III MZ692 EY-P, which was shot down on the night of 23rd June 1944; Sergeant W.C. Brown, a crew member of Halifax III LK840 EY-J, shot down during the same operation; Sergeant J.S. Bennett and Sergeant P.F. Roberts, crew members of Halifax MZ763 EY-S, shot down during a raid on Neuss on the night of 23/24 September 1944. These men returned to England with enough stories to fill an entire book in themselves.

But they were only able to return home thanks to the selfless and courageous activities of ordinary civilians who had become part of the underground movements in occupied Europe. These admirable people put their own lives, and those of their families, in grave danger by helping their allies, but they did so just the same. This called for courage of the highest order. They knew that if they were caught by the Gestapo they would, in all likelihood, be tortured and murdered, and this fate indeed befell many of them. Some were taken to Gestapo Headquarters to be questioned, subjected to all kinds of torture in an attempt to make them betray their colleagues and afterwards either shot or sent to a concentration camp. But this did not deter others from carrying on with the work of harbouring stranded airmen and helping them to return to England, re-join their squadrons and carry on with the fight against the Nazis.

This, surely, is the very definition of heroism.

RAF Breighton

THE SMALL VILLAGE OF Breighton is situated in rural surroundings near the river Derwent in the East Riding of Yorkshire, 20 miles east of Leeds. The airfield lies half a mile to the north west of the village and the site is to this day surrounded by flat, open farmland to the east in the direction of the Humber estuary and the North Sea.

Construction work began in 1941 and three intersecting concrete runways were laid, the main being 1,600 yards and the two subsidiaries both 1,100 yards. Unique for a Bomber Command station was their common intersection, necessitated by the restricted size of the airfield due to the land falling away towards the River Derwent on the west side and a stream to the south. Twenty-four hardstandings were positioned around the perimeter track and were all of the large pan type. Three of these were repurposed when three large hangars were erected, a T2 and a B1 north of the runway near Gunby village and another T2-type hangar on the south side of the airfield. (One of the T2 hangars is still there.)

The technical site was to the south-west. Bomb stores were off the south-east side. Two communal a sick quarters and nine domestic sites provided for a maximum 1,223 male and 191 female personnel.

The Station was officially opened in January 1942 as a satellite station for Holme-on-Spalding-Moor under the control of No.1 Group, RAF Bomber Command. Its first occupants were 460 Squadron RAAF, which had been formed a few weeks earlier, who arrived from RAF Molesworth with their Vickers Wellington bombers. This squadron first operated on the night of March 12, 1942, when five aircraft were despatched to join a raid on Emden.

In the course of the next six months 460 Squadron RAAF participated in 61 operations, losing 29 Wellingtons, which was the highest percentage loss of all Bomber Command Wellington squadrons. Later that year they re-equipped with the Avro Lancaster and its forerunner the Avro Manchester. This squadron fought with distinction from Breighton until May 1943, when they moved south to RAF Binbrook in Lincolnshire.

In June 1943 the airfield was transferred to 4 Group Bomber Command and became home to 78 Squadron RAF, equipped with Handley Page Halifax four-engine bombers. Work was undertaken to extend all three runways; the main to 1,950 yards and 1,400 yards for both the subsidiaries.

In extending the perimeter track to the runway ends, several hardstandings were lost and although more pans were built the airfield had only 34 in total after these alterations were completed.

After the arrival of 78 Squadron operations began almost immediately and continued until May 1945, when RAF Breighton switched from Bomber Command to Transport Command with 78 Squadron flying Halifax VIs and, latterly, Douglas Dakotas. In September 1945 the Squadron moved to Egypt and RAF Breighton was placed on 'Care and Maintenance'.

In 1959 RAF Breighton was brought out of mothballs and became a Thor Intercontinental Missile Base with the formation of 240 Squadron. Assigned to defend and protect these weapons was 112 (Fighter) Squadron armed with 32 Bloodhound surface-to-air missiles.

Unmarried personnel were billeted at nearby RAF Church Fenton and there were married quarters in Acomb, York. RAF Breighton was one of a cluster of sites in Yorkshire to house this deadly nuclear deterrent, the others being RAF Driffield, RAF Carnaby, RAF Catfoss and RAF Full Sutton.

The airfield was vacated by the RAF in the mid 1960s and has since been repurposed as an industrial estate and storage are and is the home of a variety of businesses. Part of the old airfield is still used for flying although, the main runways are not used for this purpose; a grass runway has been constructed on the south side of the site, and is used by a private flying club owned and operated by the Real Aircraft Company.

Afterthoughts

WHEN THE WAR ENDED in 1945 those who had served in 78 Squadron had every right to be proud of their achievements. It had been a long and hard-fought campaign and many good men had been lost along the way. They would never be forgotten. Among the squadron's ranks had been men from every county in England, Wales and Scotland, from Northern Ireland and the Irish Republic, from Canada, Australia, New Zealand, South Africa, the USA, Poland, Czechoslovakia, Argentina and other far-flung places in the world whose sympathies lay with the Allied cause.

This had been a hard-fought total war in which many had laid down their lives. The tactics had been uncompromising, the fighting brutal in the extreme, a death struggle between the nihilism of the Nazi regime and the liberal values of the free world.

But liberal values alone were not enough to defeat the Nazis. History well remembers prewar British Prime Minister Neville Chamberlain waving his useless piece of paper signed by Adolf Hitler that allegedly promised 'peace in our time'. Hitler had no intention of keeping that promise, of course, as even Chamberlain himself must have known at the time. His intentions were honourable enough. He desperately wanted to avoid another European war, and with good reason. He and his generation remembered only too vividly the hideous slaughter of the trench warfare on the Western Front during the Great War, which had ended only 20 years previously. Surely there must be some way to avoid entering into another similar conflict?

But Germany had fallen into the hands of a madman with delusions of grandeur who could not be reasoned with. Hitler had dreams of European and then world domination which he intended to achieve through the use of force and which could only be thwarted by the use of superior force. This became abundantly clear when the German invasion of Europe began in 1939. Too late the pacifists and appeasers realised that Nazi Germany was not a nation that could be trusted to honour its side of any bargain or agreement, only militarily force was going to stop them.

In the end the cost of doing so was almost beyond comprehension. For five years the industrial capacity of all major nations was given over almost entirely to the production of weapons and other materials required to wage war. Millions of bullets and bombs of every kind, hundreds of thousands of military vehicles, ships and aircraft required in turn millions of tons of steel and coal to manufacture them and millions of gallons of oil to propel them, most of which literally went up in smoke during the course of the conflict.

Revisionists would later try to decry the tactics of Bomber Command, maintaining that the aerial bombardment of cities and their civilian populations was morally unacceptable, an unforgivable war crime, which made the Allies no better than their despised enemy. But their moralising ignores the fact that the Nazis were an intractable enemy. They were not going to be persuaded by reasoned argument to lay down their weapons of war or to give up their plans for military conquest. There was only one way to stop them; they had to be beaten on their own terms by superior military might. Only then would they admit defeat. The events related in this book are evidence enough that this was the case. The Germans fought with great tenacity until the very last. They were not easily defeated.

And the men of No.78 Squadron RAF played their part in this defeat and played it magnificently. Far too many of them had to give their lives in the process but their sacrifice was not in vain. The evil Empire of the Nazis was defeated and the thousand year Reich they had envisaged never came to pass. The peoples of the world could breathe a collective sigh of relief. They had been spared the yoke of slavery that Nazi domination would surely have brought with it.

As the dust settled and the smoke of war dissipated, the survivors could concentrate on rebuilding their broken world and turning it into something better than before. And they had the brave young men 78 Squadron and their many counterparts in the Allied Armed Forces to thank for that opportunity.

A MONUMENT COMMEMORATING THE Commonwealth and Allied Air Forces stands on Plymouth Hoe. A plaque on the memorial records the losses suffered by all the Commands during the 1939–1945 conflict. This figure amounts to 110,006. Bomber Command aircrews suffered a particularly high casualty rate: of a total of 125,000 aircrew deployed, 57,205 were killed (a 46 percent death rate), a further 8,403 were wounded in action and 9,838 became prisoners of war. Therefore, a total of 75,446 airmen (60 percent of all operational airmen) were either killed, wounded or taken prisoner.

Statistics

No. 78 Squadron RAF

Motto: **Nemo Non Paratus** (Nobody Unprepared)
Squadron Codes: **YY** (prior to Munich Crisis), **EY** (thereafter)

OPERATIONAL RECORD

THE TOTAL NUMBER OF operational sorties flown by aircraft of 78 Squadron during World War II amounted to 6,337, which consisted of 6,017 bombing sorties and 320 minelaying sorties. The total tonnage of bombs dropped, including mines, was 17,000 tons (7,000 tons of which were dropped between D-Day 6th June and 30th April 1945, more than a third of the total.) The squadron attacked a total of 167 different targets in a total of 502 attacks. Approximately 1,064 mines had been laid.

The squadron had destroyed 31 enemy aircraft. This figure does not include 35 that are known to have been damaged and a further eleven that were probably destroyed. During the period 1941-1945, 48 combats took place for which no claims have been made. Enemy aircraft destroyed consisted of: ten JU88s, two ME110s, one He113, two Fw190s, three Me109s, three Me410s, one Me210, four Me163s and 5 unidentified aircraft.

Total operational flying hours amounted to 35,000 hours.

The mileage covered by MT vehicles was some 3,973,000 miles

Total aircraft losses incurred by 78 Squadron throughout the war, including those lost in non-operational incidents, amounted to 182 aircraft (57 Whitleys and 123 Halifaxes)

78 Squadron flew most the most sorties in 4 Group (although only 4 sorties more than 10 Squadron.) They suffered the most aircraft losses and highest percentage losses of any Halifax squadron (along with 102 Squadron) and the third highest losses in Bomber Command (sharing this distinction with 44 and 102 Squadrons). They are believed to have dropped the greatest tonnage of bombs in 4 Group.

BATTLE HONOURS

On 11th February 1965, a standard was presented to 78 Squadron by Lt Gen Sir Charles Harrington, adorned with the following battle honours:

Home Defence 1916–1918. Fortress Europe 1940–1944. Ruhr 1940–1945.
Invasion Ports 1940. Biscay Ports 1940–1943. Berlin 1940–1944.
Channel & North Sea 1942–1945. Normandy 1944.
France & Germany 1944–1945.

RAIDS FLOWN

Whitley Mk V: 163 bombing raids
Halifax MkII, III and VI: 323 bombing; 32 minelaying; 7 leaflet

SORTIES AND LOSSES

Whitley Mk V: 1,217 sorties,
55 aircraft lost on operations, 2 on non-operations

Halifax Mk II, III and VI: 5,120 sorties in total

Halifax Mk II 60 lost on operations, 1 on non-operations

Halifax Mk III 63 lost on operations,
1 on non-operations, 1 in ground incident

Halifax Mk VI no losses

Totals: 6,337 sorties ~ 182 aircraft lost

The squadron lost 910 men killed in action
and 272 became prisoners of war

Harrietsham, Aug 1916 – April 1917
Telscombe Cliffs (Newhaven), April 1917 – Sept 1918
Hornchurch, Sept 1918 – Sept 1919
Disbanded Sutton's Farm, September 1919
Re-formed Boscombe Down, June 1935 – Feb 1937
Dishforth, Feb 1937 – Oct 1939
Linton-on-Ouse, Oct 1939 – June 1940
Dishforth, June 1940 – April 1941
Middleton-St-George, April 1941 – Oct 1941
Croft, Oct 1941 – June 1942
Middleton-St-George, June 1942 – Sept 1942
Linton-on-Ouse, Sept 1942 – June 1943
Breighton, June 1943 – Sept 1945
Transferred to 216 Group Middle East Command, 4th September 1945
Almaza, Sept 1945 – Sept 1946
Kabrit, Sept 1946 – Feb 1951
Fayid, Feb 1951 – Sept 1951
Disbanded on 30th September 1951
Re-formed at Khormaksar 15th April 1956
Moved to Sharjah on 13th October 1967
Disbanded on 21st December 1971
Re-formed at Mount Pleasant, Falkland Islands 1st May 1986
Disbanded in Falklands December 2007
Re-formed at RAF Benson as a helicopter squadron of Joint Helicopter
Command on 28 January 2008.
Disbanded on 30th September 2014.
On 24 March 2020, the squadron was awarded a battle honour,
recognising its role in the War in Iraq between 2003 and 2011.

1916–1917 Royal Aircraft Factory BE.2c and BE.2e
1916–1918 Royal Aircraft Factory BE.12 and BE.12a
1917-1917 Royal Aircraft Factory SE.5a
1917–1918 Sopwith 1½ Strutter
1917-1917 Royal Aircraft Factory FE.2d
1917–1918 Royal Aircraft Factory BE.12b
1918–1919 Sopwith Camel
1918–1919 Sopwith Snipe
1936–1937 Handley Page Heyford III
1937–1939 Armstrong Whitworth Whitley I
1939–1940 Armstrong Whitworth Whitley IVA
1939–1942 Armstrong Whitworth Whitley V
1942–1944 Handley Page Halifax II
1944–1945 Handley Page Halifax III
1945-1945 Handley Page Halifax IV
1945–1950 Douglas Dakota
1950–1954 Vickers Valetta C1
1956–1959 Scottish Aviation Pioneer CC1
1958–1965 Scottish Aviation Twin Pioneer CC1
1965–1971 Westland Wessex HC2
1986–2006 Boeing Chinook HC1, HC2
1986–2007 Westland Sea King HAR3
2007–2014 AgustaWestland Merlin HC3/HC3A

AIRCRAFT SERIAL NUMBERS

Heyford II: K4868
Heyford III: K5193
Whitley I: K7196
Whitley IV: K9017
Whitley IVA: K9050
Whitley V: T4029 'Q' : Z6640 'R' :
Halifax II: W1015 'V'
Halifax III: MZ361 'D'; LV869 'G':
Halifax VI: RG667
Dakota: KP233
World War I Serial numbers not available:
Post World War II serial numbers are likewise not available.

A LARGE NUMBER OF 78 Squadron aircrew ended up as prisoners of war after being shot down over enemy occupied territory. After interrogation they were interned in a variety of POW camps, some designated for officers only and some for other ranks. The names of 272 individuals are listed below in alphabetical order along with the number of the aircraft in which they were flying when shot down and the date of their final sortie. As far as we know it is a comprehensive list.

F/O P.D. Ablett	Halifax DT768	16/07/43	Stalag L3 Sagan/Belaria
W/O L. Adams RCAF	Halifax JB873	14/05/43	Stalag 357 Kopernikus
W/O H.J. Adams	Halifax DT775	11/04/43	Stalag 357 Kopernikus
F/Sgt W.H. Allelly	Halifax W7926	24/05/43	Stalag 357 Kopernikus
W/O J.W. Angus	Halifax MZ577	08/06/44	Stalag L3 Sagan/Belaria
F/Sgt W. Ashley	Halifax JB973	04/05/43	Stalag L3 Sagan/Belaria
F/Sgt J.F. Baker	Halifax LW262	04/10/43	Stalag L3 Sagan/Belaria
F/Lt E.W. Barnes	Halifax JB903	04/05/43	Stalag L3 Sagan/Belaria
F/Sgt A.T. Barnes	Halifax MZ763	24/09/44	Stalag L7 Bankau-Kreulberg
F/Lt A.C. Beales	Halifax LW229	06/09/43	Stalag L3 Sagan/Belaria
F/Lt W.H. Bear	Halifax JD160	24/05/43	Stalag L3 Sagan/Belaria
F/Sgt A. Beatson	Halifax JB873	14/05/43	Stalag L1 Barth Vogelsang
W/O L.A. Beckett	Whitley P4950	29/12/40	Stalag 357 Kopernikus
F/Sgt J.A. Bell	Halifax HR659	17/04/43	Stalag 357 Kopernikus
F/O W.I. Bell	Halifax MZ340	28/07/44	No Camp details known
F/Sgt H.H. Bennett	Halifax LW291	21/12/44	Stalag 357 Kopernikus
F/Sgt E.K. Blackweall	Halifax JB903	04/05/43	Stalag 357 Kopernikus
F/Sgt W. Boddy	Halifax JN974	04/12/43	No Camp details known
P/O E.H. Bodman	Halifax W1115	12/08/42	Stalag L3 Sagan/Belaria
F/O D.F. Booth	Halifax LW320	21/12/43	Stalag L3 Sagan/Belaria
F/O A. Boothby	Halifax LW320	21/12/43	Stalag L3 Sagan/Belaria
S/Ldr B.J. Bourchier RCAF	Halifax DT780	04/04/43	Stalag L3 Sagan/Belaria
Sgt M. Bradbury	Halifax LW509	25/02/44	Stalag 357 Kopernikus
W/O2 T.S. Brandon RCAF	Halifax W7782	09/09/42	Stalag 344 Lamsdorf
F/Lt G.C. Brown	Whitley P5026	29/11/40	Stalag L3 Sagan/Belaria
W/O R.A. Brown	Halifax W1067	26/06/42	Stalag L6 Heydekrug
F/Sgt N.W. Brown	Halifax LV958	25/04/44	Stalag 357 Kopernikus
F/Sgt J.A.G. Buchanan	Halifax JD475	06/09/43	Stalag 4B Muhlberg-Elbe
P/O K.W.L. Burns	Halifax MZ340	28/07/44	No Camp details known
F/Sgt R.H. Caldwell	Halifax JD475	06/09/43	Stalag 4B Muhlberg-Elbe
W/O S. Calkwell	Whitley T4156	20/11/40	Stalag 357 Kopernikus

F/Lt B.A. Campbell RCAF	Halifax JB903	04/05/43	Stalag L3 Sagan/Belaria
F/Sgt G.M. Campbell	Halifax JD108	14/07/43	Stalag L1 Barth Vogelsang
F/Lt J.A. Cant	Whitley Z6283	17/08/41	Stalag L3 Sagan/Belaria
F/O E.R. Carrington	Halifax JD330	26/07/43	Stalag L3 Sagan/Belaria
F/Sgt J.C. Cash	Halifax JN974	04/12/43	Stalag 357 Kopernikus
S/Ldr J.H.B. Chapple	Halifax JB903	04/05/43	Stalag L3 Sagan/Belaria
P/O R. Chisholm	Halifax JD328	01/09/43	Stalag 4B Muhlberg-Elbe
F/Sgt D.R. Chiswell RCAF	Halifax HR687	06/03/43	Stalag 344 Lamsdorf
F/Sgt F. Churchyard RCAF	Halifax W7926	24/05/43	Stalag 357 Kopernikus
F/Sgt M. Clark	Halifax DT775	11/04/43	Stalag 357 Kopernikus
W/O G.E. Clay	Halifax DT777	14/05/43	Stalag L1 Barth Vogelsang
P/O J. Clingly	Halifax LW301	23/10/43	Stalag 4B Muhlberg-Elbe
F/Sgt F.A. Coates	Halifax DT777	14/05/43	Stalag L1 Barth Vogelsang
F/O R.E. Collier	Halifax MZ340	28/07/44	No Camp details known
F/Sgt A. Collins	Halifax LW794	26/02/44	No Camp details known
F/Sgt L.W. Colman	Halifax LW236	09/10/43	Stalag 4B Muhlberg-Elbe
Sgt J.H. Connoley	Halifax LK762	31/03/44	Stalag 357 Kopernikus
F/O K.E. Cooper RCAF	Halifax LW273	24/09/43	Stalag L3 Sagan/Belaria
W/O2 H. Corbishley RCAF	Halifax W1115	12/08/42	Stalag 344 Lamsdorf
P/O D. Crompton	Halifax JD414	28/08/43	Stalag L3 Sagan/Belaria
F/Sgt R.F. Cumming	Halifax W7926	24/05/43	Stalag 357 Kopernikus
F/Sgt J. Cunningham	Halifax BB236	02/10/42	Stalag 344 Lamsdorf
F/O P. Daulby	Halifax JB928	26/06/43	Stalag L3 Sagan/Belaria
F/Sgt R.T. Davies	Halifax JD330	26/07/43	Stalag 4B Muhlberg-Elbe
F/Sgt R.A. Davies	Halifax LW229	06/09/43	Stalag 4B Muhlberg-Elbe
P/O R.C.W. Dennis	Halifax HR659	17/04/43	Stalag L3 Sagan/Belaria
F/Lt J.R. Denny	Whitley P5026	29/11/40	Stalag L3 Sagan/Belaria
F/Sgt R. DesJardins RCAF	Halifax DT777	17/04/43	Stalag 357 Kopernikus
W/O J.R. Dickinson	Halifax W1061	12/08/42	Stalag L6 Heydekrug
W/O D.B. Donaldson	Halifax W1067	26/06/42	Stalag L6 Heydekrug
F/O R. Donnan	Halifax JD160	24/05/43	Stalag L3 Sagan/Belaria
F/Sgt E.A. Drury	Halifax W7937	04/04/43	Stalag L6 Heydekrug
F/Sgt W.A. Dunleavy RCAF	Halifax JD406	28/08/43	No Camp details known
F/Sgt C.M. Edgehill	Halifax JD454	07/09/43	Stalag 4B Muhlberg-Elbe
Sgt L/W. Edwards	Halifax LW507	25/03/44	Stalag 357 Kopernikus
F/Lt E.W. Everett	Halifax HX355	23/03/44	Stalag L1 Barth Vogelsang
W/O J.E. Everson	Whitley P5026	29/11/40	Stalag 357 Kopernikus
F/Sgt J. Fagan	Halifax JD148	28/07/43	Stalag 4B Muhlberg-Elbe
Sergeant E.W. Farr	Halifax BB236	02/10/42	Stalag L6 Heydekrug
F/Sgt T. Ferguson	Halifax JD148	28/07/43	Stalag 4B Muhlberg-Elbe
F/Sgt R.J. Finn RCAF	Halifax LW507	25/03/44	Stalag 357 Kopernikus
F/Lt W.G.F. Fisher	Halifax HR659	17/04/43	Stalag L3 Sagan/Belaria
F/Sgt A.R. Flexman	Halifax LW794	26/02/44	Stalag 357 Kopernikus

W/O E.G.S.H. Freeman	Whitley Z9151	07/11/41	Stalag 357 Kopernikus
Sgt J.T. Frost	Halifax JN974	04/12/43	No Camp details known
W/O H. Gamble	Halifax JB973	04/05/43	Stalag L3 Sagan/Belaria
W/O J. Geary	Whitley Z6283	17/08/41	Stalag 357 Kopernikus
F/Lt L.G. Geddes RCAF	Halifax W7698	02/06/42	Stalag 344 Lamsdorf
W/O H.E. Gell	Halifax JB924	14/05/43	Stalag 357 Kopernikus
F/Lt R.E.H. George	Whitley T4156	20/11/40	Stalag L3 Sagan/Belaria
F/Lt G. Gibson	Halifax W1067	26/06/42	Stalag L3 Sagan/Belaria
F/Lt D.J. Gibson	Halifax DT768	16/07/43	Stalag L3 Sagan/Belaria
F/Sgt C. Gibson	Halifax LW226	24/09/43	Stalag L6 Heydekrug
F/Sgt A.D. Gillespie	Halifax JB928	26/06/43	Stalag L6 Heydekrug
F/Sgt T.D. Gower	Halifax LW301	23/10/43	Stalag L1 Barth Vogelsang
Sgt J.R. Graham	Halifax HX355	23/03/44	Stalag L1 Barth Vogelsang
F/O J.K.M. Green	Halifax HX355	23/03/44	No Camp details known
W/O A. Greenacre	Halifax W1180	06/08/42	Stalag 344 Lamsdorf
F/Sgt A.J. Guy	Halifax JB928	26/06/43	Stalag 357 Kopernikus
WO J.P. Gwillam RAAF	Halifax MX692	23/06/44	Stalag L3 Sagan/Belaria
W/O T. Hall	Whitley Z9151	07/11/41	Stalag 357 Kopernikus
F/O H.C.S. Hamley	Halifax LW229	06/09/43	Stalag L3 Sagan/Belaria
F/Lt J.E. Hanna	Halifax W7662	04/05/42	Stalag L3 Sagan/Belaria
W/O E.F. Harries	Halifax JD160	24/05/43	Stalag 357 Kopernikus
F/O S. Hauxwell	Halifax W7931	27/03/43	Stalag L3 Sagan/Belaria
F/Sgt S.N. Heavisides	Halifax JD377	01/09/43	Stalag 4B Muhlberg-Elbe
F/Sgt D.S. Hemelik	Halifax LW301	23/10/43	Stalag 4B Muhlberg-Elbe
Sgt J.R. Heslop	Halifax JB973	04/05/43	Stalag L3 Sagan/Belaria
Sgt W. Heubner USAAF	Halifax JN974	04/12/43	No Camp details known
F/Sgt H. Hiley	Halifax LW313	04/12/43	Stalag L3 Sagan/Belaria
F/Sgt R. Hillary	Halifax JB903	04/05/43	Stalag 357 Kopernikus
W/O A.W. Hoare	Halifax DT773	17/04/43	Stalag 357 Kopernikus
F/Lt G.M. Hobbs	Halifax W1275	03/10/42	Stalag L3 Sagan/Belaria
F/Sgt F.G. Hockin	Halifax JB973	04/05/43	Stalag L3 Sagan/Belaria
F/O E.C. Hocking RNZAF	Halifax LW794	26/02/44	Stalag 357 Kopernikus
W/O E.T.H. Hodge	Halifax W7782	09/09/42	Stalag 357 Kopernikus
F/Sgt W.F. Hodgson	Halifax W7937	04/04/43	Stalag 357 Kopernikus
F/O M.M. Holgate	Halifax LV958	25/04/44	No Camp details known
F/O R.D. Holland	Halifax HX241	31/03/44	Stalag L1 Barth Vogelsang
W/O B.W.T. Horn	Halifax W7926	24/05/43	Stalag 357 Kopernikus
W/O D.H. Howard	Halifax DT780	04/04/43	Stalag 357 Kopernikus
W/O2 J.K. Howes RCAF	Halifax W1061	12/08/42	Stalag L4 Sagan/Belaria
Sgt K. Hughes	Halifax LW313	04/12/43	Stalag 4B Muhlberg-Elbe
W/O R.R.H. Hulleat	Halifax W7931	27/03/43	Stalag 357 Kopernikus
W/O J.H. Hunt	Halifax W1036	02/10/42	Stalag 344 Lamsdorf
F/Sgt C. Hunt	Halifax JD453	31/08/43	No Camp details known

W/O S.V.F. Hurrell	Halifax DT775	11/04/43	Stalag 357 Kopernikus
F/Sgt A.J. Hutchinson	Halifax JB928	26/06/43	Stalag 357 Kopernikus
F/Lt P. Hyden	Halifax DT775	11/04/43	Stalag L3 Sagan/Belaria
W/O W. Ingles	Halifax DT780	04/04/43	Stalag 357 Kopernikus
W/O G. Irving	Halifax W7926	24/05/43	Stalag L6 Heydekrug
F/Sgt C.F. Jaggard	Halifax JD453	31/08/43	Stalag 4B Muhlberg-Elbe
F/Lt J.H. Jamieson RCAF	Halifax W7937	04/04/43	Stalag L3 Sagan/Belaria
F/Sgt B. Janke RAAF	Halifax LW794	26/02/44	Stalag 357 Kopernikus
W/O E.L. Johnson RAAF	Halifax MX692	23/06/44	Stalag L3 Sagan/Belaria
W/O2 G.R. Johnson RCAF	Halifax W7931	27/03/43	Stalag 357 Kopernikus
F/Sgt J.E. Johnson	Halifax HX355	23/03/44	Stalag 4B Muhlberg-Elbe
Sgt S. Johnson	Halifax LW507	25/03/44	Stalag 357 Kopernikus
F/Lt P.J. Jones	Halifax R9364	02/06/42	Stalag L3 Sagan/Belaria
Sgt G. Jones	Halifax HR874	06/09/43	Stalag 4B Muhlberg-Elbe
W/O K.H. Jones	Halifax HX355	23/03/44	Stalag L3 Sagan/Belaria
W/O2 L.C. Jupp RCAF	Halifax W1061	12/08/42	Stalag 357 Kopernikus
P/O M.M. Kaye	Halifax LW232	23/09/43	Stalag L3 Sagan/Belaria
F/Lt R.W. Keen	Halifax W7931	27/03/43	Stalag L3 Sagan/Belaria
F/Sgt W. Keenan	Halifax LK762	31/03/44	Stalag 357 Kopernikus
W/O2 R.G. Kendall RCAF	Halifax W1245	12/08/42	Stalag 344 Lamsdorf
F/Sgt G.A. Kennaby	Halifax LW313	04/12/43	Stalag 4B Muhlberg-Elbe
W/O E. Kerr	Whitley Z6283	17/08/41	Stalag 357 Kopernikus
F/Lt B.V. Kerwin	Whitley P5026	29/11/40	Stalag L3 Sagan/Belaria
W/O2 T.L. Kidd RCAF	Halifax W1275	03/10/42	Stalag 344 Lamsdorf
W/O D. Kimber	Halifax W1115	12/08/42	Stalag 344 Lamsdorf
F/Lt H.J. King	Halifax JB903	04/05/43	Stalag L3 Sagan/Belaria
W/O J.W. Knight	Whitley T4156	20/11/40	Stalag 357 Kopernikus
F/Sgt E.J. Lacey	Halifax DT780	04/04/43	Stalag 357 Kopernikus
P/O R.C. Laing RCAF	Halifax MZ340	28/07/44	Stalag L7 Bankau-Kreulberg
F/Sgt D. Lamb	Halifax JD248	24/08/43	Stalag 4B Muhlberg-Elbe
F/O P. Langsford RNZAF	Halifax DT773	17/04/43	Stalag 357 Kopernikus
F/O D. Laver	Halifax LW509	25/02/44	Stalag L3 Sagan/Belaria
F/Sgt A.C. Layshon	Halifax HR687	06/03/43	No Camp details known
F/Sgt W.A. Lea	Halifax LV816	20/02/44	Stalag 357 Kopernikus
F/Sgt J. Lee	Halifax JB855	23/05/43	Stalag L7 Bankau Kreulberg
F/Sgt B.A. Lee	Halifax DT768	16/07/43	Stalag 357 Kopernikus
W/O D.F.J. Lemon	Halifax W1115	12/08/42	Stalag 344 Lamsdorf
W/O F.E. Lemon	Halifax W7931	27/03/43	Stalag 357 Kopernikus
F/Sgt G. Leverett	Halifax DT777	14/05/43	Stalag 357 Kopernikus
S/Ldr G.D. Leyland	Halifax W7698	02/06/42	Stalag L3 Sagan/Belaria
F/Lt J.B.T. Loudon	Whitley P4950	29/12/40	Stalag L3 Sagan/Belaria
F/Sgt A. Loveland	Halifax HR687	06/03/43	No Camp details known
F/O D.W. Lusty	Halifax JB928	26/06/43	Stalag L3 Sagan/Belaria

F/Lt H.A. Mace	Halifax LV903	25/03/44	Stalag L1 Barth Vogelsang
Sgt J.O. Mander RCAF	Halifax JD160	24/05/43	Stalag 357 Kopernikus
F/Sgt K.E. Markillie	Halifax W1036	02/10/42	Stalag 344 Lamsdorf
Sgt G.R.G. Marley	Halifax MZ340	28/07/44	Stalag L7 Bankau-Kreulberg
Sgt L.D.E. Marriot	Halifax DT777	14/05/43	Stalag 357 Kopernikus
F/Sgt H.W. Marshall	Halifax JD330	26/07/43	Stalag 4B Muhlberg-Elbe
F/Sgt J. Marshall	Halifax JD377	01/09/43	Stalag 4B Muhlberg-Elbe
W/O J.W. Massie	Whitley P5026	29/11/40	Stalag 357 Kopernikus
F/Lt J. McDonald	Halifax JD108	14/07/43	Stalag L3 Sagan/Belaria
F/O C.M. McLeod	Halifax LV903	25/03/44	Stalag 357 Kopernikus
W/O A.M. McMillan	Whitley P4950	29/12/40	Stalag 357 Kopernikus
F/Lt C.E. Melin RAAF	Halifax LW509	25/02/44	Stalag L3 Sagan/Belaria
F/Sgt K.W. Mercer	Halifax HR687	06/03/43	Stalag 344 Lamsdorf
F/Sgt H. Middleton	Halifax LW507	25/03/44	Stalag 357 Kopernikus
F/Sgt C. Miles	Halifax JD475	06/09/43	Stalag 4B Muhlberg-Elbe
F/Sgt K.R. Miller RCAF	Halifax LW301	23/10/43	Stalag 4B Muhlberg-Elbe
W/O1 T.B. Miller GM RCAF	Halifax R9364	02/06/42	Stalag L3 Sagan/Belaria
P/O R.N. Mills RAAF	Halifax MX692	23/06/44	Stalag L3 Sagan/Belaria
P/O K.C. Mills RAAF	Halifax MX692	23/06/44	Stalag L3 Sagan/Belaria
F/Sgt A.C.P. Minnitt	Halifax JB873	14/05/43	Stalag L4 Sagan/Belaria
F/Sgt L.C. Minshaw	Halifax HR659	17/04/43	Stalag 357 Kopernikus
W/O E.G.S. Monk	Halifax W1115	12/08/42	Stalag 344 Lamsdorf
F/Lt R.C. Mordaunt	Whitley T4156	20/11/40	Stalag L3 Sagan/Belaria
W/O2 G.E. Morrison RCAF	Halifax W1036	02/10/42	Stalag 344 Lamsdorf
F/Sgt H. Mott	Halifax HR874	06/09/43	Stalag 4B Muhlberg-Elbe
F/Sgt S.J. Muldoon	Halifax HR874	06/09/43	Stalag 4B Muhlberg-Elbe
F/Sgt L. Nugent	Halifax HX241	31/03/44	Stalag 357 Kopernikus
W/O J.F. O'Reilly	Halifax DT777	14/05/43	Stalag L1 Barth Vogelsang
F/Lt A.N. Orr	Halifax DT773	17/04/43	Stalag L3 Sagan/Belaria
F/Sgt N.F. Page	Halifax LW315	09/10/43	Stalag 4B Muhlberg-Elbe
W/O T. Paterson	Whitley Z9151	07/11/41	Stalag 357 Kopernikus
W/O E.W. Penn	Whitley Z9151	07/11/41	Stalag 357 Kopernikus
F/Lt W.T. Perriment	Halifax JD454	07/09/43	Stalag L3 Sagan/Belaria
W/O2 W.J.H. Perry RCAF	Halifax DT777	14/05/43	Stalag L4 Sagan/Belaria
F/Sgt J.W. Pople	Halifax JB873	14/05/43	Stalag L4 Sagan/Belaria
F/O G.W. Preston	Halifax JD476	28/09/43	Stalag 357 Kopernikus
F/Sgt C.J. Price	Halifax DT775	11/04/43	Stalag 357 Kopernikus
F/Sgt O.V. Proctor	Halifax HR687	06/03/43	Stalag 344 Lamsdorf
W/O C.G. Pugsley	Halifax W7698	02/06/42	Stalag 357 Kopernikus
F/Sgt H.S.H. Quinn	Halifax JD328	01/09/43	Stalag 4B Muhlberg-Elbe
Sgt K.R. Rabbage	Halifax LW271	21/12/43	No Camp details known
F/Sgt S.G. Reed	Halifax DT775	11/04/43	Stalag 357 Kopernikus
F/O C.F. Richens	Halifax LW509	25/02/44	Stalag L3 Sagan/Belaria

F/O J. Rigby	Halifax LW320	21/12/43	Stalag L3 Sagan/Belaria
F/Sgt J. Rimmer	Halifax LW273	24/09/43	Dulag Luft Wetzlar
F/Sgt A.J. Roach	Halifax LK838	05/11/44	No Camp details known
Sgt T. Roberts RCAF	Halifax JB928	26/06/43	Stalag 4B Muhlberg-Elbe
F/Sgt J.E. Roberts	Halifax JD148	28/07/43	Stalag 4B Muhlberg-Elbe
Sgt W. Robertson RCAF	Halifax JD455	09/10/43	Stalag 4B Muhlberg-Elbe
F/O V.A. Robins DFC	Halifax JD310	24/08/43	Stalag L3 Sagan/Belaria
F/O A.R. Robinson	Halifax JD377	01/09/43	Stalag 4B Muhlberg-Elbe
F/O C. Rowlands RNZAF	Halifax JD377	01/09/43	Stalag 4B Muhlberg-Elbe
F/Lt J.V. Saunders RCAF	Whitley Z9151	07/11/41	Stalag L3 Sagan/Belaria
Sgt R.L. Scheisher	Halifax LW226	24/09/43	No Camp details known
P/O N. Schnier RCAF	Halifax JD328	01/09/43	Stalag 4B Muhlberg-Elbe
P/O F.N. Scott RCAF	Halifax LW226	24/09/43	Stalag L3 Sagan/Belaria
W/O2 G.E. Sendall RCAF	Halifax W7937	04/04/43	Stalag 357 Kopernikus
F/Sgt W. Sharratt	Halifax LK840	23/06/44	Stalag L3 Sagan/Belaria
F/Lt R. Shipley	Halifax W1180	06/08/42	Stalag L3 Sagan/Belaria
F/Sgt N. Simpson	Halifax JD453	31/08/43	Stalag 4B Muhlberg-Elbe
P/O A.P. Sinden	Halifax HX355	23/03/44	No Camp details known
F/Sgt K.A. Skidmore RAAF	Halifax JD329	31/07/43	Stalag 4B Muhlberg-Elbe
F/Sgt T.T. Slater	Halifax DT773	17/04/43	Stalag 357 Kopernikus
Sgt S. Smith	Halifax JN974	04/12/43	No Camp details known
F/O K.F. Smith	Halifax LW509	25/02/44	Stalag L3 Sagan/Belaria
F/Sgt J. Sowter	Halifax JD148	28/07/43	Stalag 4B Muhlberg-Elbe
F/Sgt D.R. Spencer	Halifax JD328	01/09/43	Stalag 357 Kopernikus
W/O A.G. Springthorpe	Halifax W1067	26/06/42	Stalag 357 Kopernikus
F/O H.J. Standfast	Halifax JD855	23/06/43	Stalag L3 Sagan/Belaria
F/Sgt L.L. Stas	Halifax DT780	04/04/43	Stalag 357 Kopernikus
F/O C.A. Steven	Halifax HR659	17/04/43	Stalag L3 Sagan/Belaria
W/O J.C. Stevens	Halifax W1180	06/08/42	Stalag 344 Lamsdorf
W/O G.J.U. Stevens	Halifax W7926	24/05/43	Stalag 357 Kopernikus
F/Sgt A.J. Stevenson	Halifax DT768	16/07/43	Stalag 357 Kopernikus
W/O J. Stewart	Halifax W1245	12/08/42	Stalag 344 Lamsdorf
F/Sgt J/R. Stewart	Halifax HX355	23/03/44	Stalag L1 Barth Vogelsang
Sgt A.E. Sturgeon	Halifax LW226	24/09/43	Stalag 357 Kopernikus
F/Sgt G.E. Swift	Halifax W1036	02/10/42	Stalag 344 Lamsdorf
Sgt J.E. Swindin	Halifax JD455	09/10/43	Stalag L3 Sagan/Belaria
F/O P.R. Terry	Halifax JD377	01/09/43	Stalag 4B Muhlberg-Elbe
Sgt H.E. Thompson	Halifax DT773	17/04/43	No Camp details known
F/Lt J.B. Thompson	Halifax JB973	04/05/43	Stalag L3 Sagan/Belaria
F/Sgt N.V. Thornton	Halifax W7937	04/04/43	Stalag L6 Heydekrug
W/O G.H. Tinniswood	Halifax JD160	24/05/43	Stalag 357 Kopernikus
F/Sgt H.F. Trowell	Halifax LW262	24/10/43	Stalag L3 Sagan/Belaria
F/Sgt H. Tyler	Halifax JB973	04/05/43	Stalag L6 Heydekrug

Sgt D. Wade	Halifax JD377	01/09/43	Stalag 4B Muhlberg-Elbe
F/Sgt G.J. Wallace	Halifax JD160	24/05/43	Stalag 357 Kopernikus
F/Sgt C.A. Walsh RAAF	Halifax JD455	09/10/43	Stalag 4B Muhlberg-Elbe
Sgt R. Wann	Halifax MZ577	08/06/44	No Camp details known
F/Sgt J.E. Ward	Halifax JD453	31/08/43	Stalag 4B Muhlberg-Elbe
Sgt S.A. Waterhouse	Halifax LW512	26/02/44	Stalag 357 Kopernikus
F/Sgt C. Wayte	Halifax W7937	04/04/43	Stalag 357 Kopernikus
F/Sgt F.W. Webb	Halifax JB873	14/05/43	Stalag L6 Heydekrug
F/Sgt R.C. Wellard	Halifax LW320	21/12/43	Stalag 4B Muhlberg-Elbe
F/O E.M. Wells	Halifax LV816	20/02/44	Stalag L3 Sagan/Belaria
Sgt P.A. Westcott	Halifax LW320	21/12/43	Stalag 4B Muhlberg-Elbe
F/Lt G.I. Whitehouse	Halifax JD329	31/07/43	Stalag L1 Barth Vogelsang
F/Sgt D.R. Wilcox	Halifax W7926	24/05/43	Stalag 357 Kopernikus
W/O J.W. Wilkinson	Whitley T4156	20/11/40	Stalag 357 Kopernikus
F/Sgt R.J. Williams	Halifax LW301	23/10/43	Stalag L3 Sagan/Belaria
Sgt T. Willis	Halifax LW507	25/03/44	Stalag 357 Kopernikus
W/O E.W. Willmore	Whitley P4950	29/12/40	Stalag 357 Kopernikus
W/O D. Willoughby	Halifax W1180	06/08/42	Stalag 344 Lamsdorf
F/O G.E. Wilson	Halifax LW320	21/12/43	Stalag L3 Sagan/Belaria
F/Sgt F.R. Wilson	Halifax LK762	31/03/44	Stalag 357 Kopernikus
Sgt K. Wisleman RCAF	Halifax LW509	25/02/44	No Camp details known
F/Sgt G.J. Woods RAAF	Halifax JN974	04/12/43	Stalag 4B Muhlberg-Elbe
Sgt A. Wright	Halifax DT780	04/04/43	No Camp details known
Sgt C.H. Wright	Halifax MX692	23/06/44	Stalag L7 Bankau-Kruelberg
W/O J.H. Wyatt	Halifax W1061	12/08/42	Stalag 344 Lamsdorf
Sgt W.G. Yeo	Halifax LW232	23/09/43	Stalag L6 Heydekrug

Roll of Honour

78 Squadron Aircrew Killed in Action

THE FOLLOWING LIST INCLUDES the names of the 910 airmen from 78 Squadron who died in the line of duty during the Second World War. Many of them have no known grave and are commemorated on the RAF Memorial at Runnymede in Surrey. Many of the others are buried in the countries where they fell to earth, Germany, France, Belgium and especially the Netherlands, where many lives were lost.

B/A F/Lt C.H. Abbot	22/10/1943
W/Op Sgt A.W. Adams	29/06/1941
A/G Sgt R.W. Airey	24/02/1944
B/A F/O E. Albon	12/06/1944
Nav F/O C.R.C.A. Allbery	03/04/1943
W/Op Sgt F.T. Allcock	13/12/1940
Pilot W/O B.E.E. Allden	22/10/1943
Nav Sgt F.G. Allen	23/10/1942
A/G Sgt G. Allenby	18/06/1944
B/A Sgt W.A. Anderson	22/06/1943
A/G Sgt W.D. Anderson RCAF	06/09/1943
B/A Sgt J.B. Anderton	05/10/1944
Pilot P/O N.H. Andrew	01/10/1940
Nav Sgt D. Angell	13/12/1940
B/A Sgt J.N. Angus	12/05/1943
W/O Sgt D.R. Armstrong	26/02/1941
B/A Sgt A.E. Arnold RNZAF	10/09/1942
Obs Sgt R.D. Ash	13/03/1942
A/G Sgt R. Askwith	23/08/1943
Nav P/O J.L. Asprey	16/08/1941
Pilot F/O J. Austin	23/08/1943
Nav Sgt L. Austin	11/10/1943
Nav Sgt R.F. Avis	23/08/1943
Obs Sgt G.A. Avory	02/07/1941
W/Op Sgt H.E. Bailey	08/05/1941
W/Op Sgt H. Bailey	16/06/1941
B/A F/Sgt R.C. Baille RCAF	29/07/1943

A/G Sgt F.J.R. Bain	22/06/1943
2/Plt F/Sgt V.R. Baker	05/09/1943
A/G Sgt W.G. Baker	24/03/1944
F/E Sgt D. Balmforth	07/06/1944
Pilot F/Sgt H.K. Barden	24/03/1944
A/G Sgt S.G.R. Barham	12/06/1944
A/G Sgt J.H. Barkwell RCAF	11/10/1943
F/E F/O R.J. Baron	21/11/1944
F/E Sgt W. Barry	24/06/1943
W/Op Sgt W.J. Batchouski	30/03/1944
A/G Sgt D. Baxter	13/05/1943
Pilot F/Sgt M. Baxter	12/05/1943
Nav F/O H.W. Bayliss	23/08/1943
F/E Sgt G. Beal	19/02/1944
W/Op Sgt P.F. Beard	22/03/1944
Nav Sgt J.C. Beardmore	16/08/1941
Pilot P/O A.J. Beazleigh	06/09/1943
Pilot P/O H.E. Bedford	05/06/1942
Pilot Sgt J.W. Bell	07/11/1941
Nav Sgt R.C. Bell	13/03/1942
A/G Sgt T.H. Bell	22/06/1943
Pilot Sgt G.G. Bell RNZAF	23/08/1943
F/E Sgt I. Bell	25/02/1944
Nav F/O A.A. Bell	26/04/1944
B/A Sgt D. Bell	27/05/1944
A/G Sgt G.E. Benson	11/03/1943
Nav Sgt H. Bentley	11/03/1943
Pilot F/Sgt A. Berry	11/10/1943
W/Op F/Sgt R.C. Berwick	18/06/1941
B/A Sgt J. Beveridge	23/10/1942
W/Op Sgt W.M. Biehl	12/06/1944
A/G F/Sgt G. Billing	07/06/1941
W/Op Sgt J.W. Bills	26/08/1941
B/A P/O J.B. Binns	11/05/1943
Nav Sgt H. Binns	09/08/1943
Pilot Sgt R.W. Bird	29/09/1941
F/E Sgt S.G. Bird	22/10/1943
2/Plt F/O A.J. Birtles RAAF	27/08/1943
W/Op F/Lt T.N.W. Bisset	07/06/1944
A/G Sgt G.A.R. Bissonette RCAF	26/06/1942
W/Op Sgt A.E. Blackwell	05/03/1943
B/A F/O B.A. Blackwell	22/10/1943
A/G Sgt J.M. Blake RCAF	20/12/1943

W/Op Sgt R.W. Bland	13/03/1942
F/E Sgt G.W. Bloomfield	31/08/1943
2/Plt Sgt J.H. Body	13/05/1943
Pilot W/O B. Bolsworth DFM	20/12/1943
B/A Sgt H. Bolton	30/05/1942
F/E Sgt B.J. Bond	30/07/1943
A/G F/Sgt E. Borkofsky RCAF	05/10/1944
A/G Sgt R. Boucher	07/11/1941
A/G Sgt T. Bourque RCAF	24/03/1944
Nav Sgt C.N. Boutle	08/10/1943
A/G Sgt M.J. Bovacanti RCAF	31/08/1943
A/G Sgt G. Bowden	13/07/1943
Nav Sgt F.R. Bowen	23/08/1943
B/A Sgt R. Boydell	04/05/1943
B/A F/O T.D.O. Boyle	30/08/1943
Pilot W/O J. Bradburn	05/10/1944
W/Op Sgt R. Bradbury	01/03/1941
Nav P/O A.G.T. Bradley	23/09/1942
Pilot F/Sgt R.E. Bragg	13/05/1943
A/G Sgt E.J. Bream	27/09/1943
A/G Sgt D.H.A. Brignell	24/03/1944
W/O Sgt W. Brookes	01/06/1942
B/A F/O K. Brookes RCAF	04/11/1944
A/G F/Sgt A. Brown	16/08/1941
B/A P/O J.B.F. Brown	29/03/1942
A/G Sgt R.A. Brown	25/06/1942
F/E Sgt D.N. Brown	04/05/1943
F/E Sgt W.J. Brown	09/08/1943
A/G Sgt D.R. Brown	18/06/1944
Nav F/O D.J. Bryant	07/06/1944
W/Op Sgt G.H.P. Buchanan RCAF	16/08/1941
Pilot P/O F. Buchanan	03/02/1943
Pilot F/Lt M.S. Buchanan,DFC RAAF	21/11/1944
2/Plt Sgt J.A. Buck	22/10/1943
W/Op Sgt E. Buckland	13/03/1944
Pilot Sqdn/Ldr P. Bunclark,DFC,DFM	23/08/1943
Nav P/O I.G. Bunn	19/02/1944
Pilot F/Sgt A. Burns	04/05/1943
B/A F/O C.E. Burns	29/07/1943
A/G P/O J.G. Burns	04/04/1945
A/G Sgt E.F. Burrell	11/08/1941
B/A F/Sgt H.J. Burridge	13/07/1943
Nav Sgt N.H. Burton	21/06/1940

Pilot P/O R.S. Bussey	03/10/1943
A/G Sgt G.H. Butler	24/05/1944
Obs Sgt H. Buttell	29/09/1941
A/G Sgt J.E. Byers RCAF	12/06/1944
A/G Sgt E.T.W. Byford	24/03/1944
A/G Sgt L. Byrne	08/07/1941
A/G Sgt A. Caie	30/05/1942
B/A F/O R.D. Caldecourt	22/06/1943
W/Op Sgt D. Cameron	07/11/1941
B/A F/O W.J. Cameron	06/09/1943
Obs F/Lt J.R. Campbell	01/11/1941
Obs F/Sgt D.R. Campbell RCAF	28/01/1942
A/G Sgt C.R. Campbell	29/03/1942
A/G Sgt T. Campbell	29/07/1943
W/Op Sgt A. Campbell	23/09/1944
F/E Sgt R.J. Campbell,MiD	12/06/1944
A/G Sgt A. Cantle-Jones	13/03/1944
A/G Sgt G.J.M. Cantwell	06/08/1942
Nav F/O J.H. Carrick RCAF	01/10/1942
Pilot F/Lt W.M. Carruthers	25/02/1944
F/E Sgt D.T. Cash	24/03/1944
A/G Sgt J.G. Castle RCAF	23/08/1943
F/E Sgt F.M. Chaffey	23/05/1943
W/Op Sgt G.J. Chambers	23/10/1942
W/Op Sgt J. Chaplin	13/07/1943
A/G Sgt R.J. Chaplin	19/02/1944
B/A Sgt S.W. Chapman	31/08/1943
A/G F/Sgt J.R. Charley RAAF	05/10/1944
Nav F/Sgt F. Christie	02/10/1942
Obs Sgt R. Clark	01/03/1941
W/Op Sgt H.M. Clark	02/10/1942
A/G Sgt C.F. Clark	05/11/1942
B/A Sgt W.L. Clark	23/08/1943
F/E Sgt K.E. Clark	15/02/1944
W/Op Sgt J.W. Clarke	05/08/1942
Nav F/O I.D.H. Clarson	18/06/1944
A/G Sgt P.D. Cleal RCAF	24/03/1944
Nav F/Sgt C. Clement	05/10/1944
W/Op Sgt D.J. Clow	08/07/1941
A/G Sgt A.J. Coburn	15/09/1944
B/A P/O A.B. Cocking	27/09/1943
A/G Sgt G.M. Coggans DFM	20/12/1943
Pilot W/O C.M. Colburn	13/07/1943

Nav Sgt W. Cole	06/08/1942
Pilot F/O J.A. Cole RCAF	07/06/1944
A/G Sgt E.W.J. Collingwood RNZAF	24/06/1943
Pilot Sgt R.G. Collins MiD	30/08/1943
W/Op F/Sgt K. Collins RCAF	04/11/1944
W/Op Sgt H.G. Colwell	12/06/1944
W/Op Sgt R.O. Connor	07/06/1944
Pilot F/Lt D.F. Constable,DFC RAAF	24/03/1944
Obs Sgt C.F. Cook	18/06/1941
Obs Sgt A. Cooke	28/05/1941
B/A F/O N.E. Cooper	14/06/1944
A/G P/O G.W. Copeland	03/05/1942
Pilot Sgt A.T. Copley	28/05/1941
B/A P/O A.G. Corby	29/09/1943
A/G Sgt L.J.V. Cotton	30/08/1943
A/G Sgt D.O. Cottrell	26/03/1944
Nav F/Sgt E.M. Coulter RCAF	19/02/1944
A/G Sgt M.W. Couper RCAF	12/06/1944
A/G Sgt F. Cowell	02/02/1945
B/A Sgt J.R. Cowen	11/10/1943
W/Op Sgt W. Cox	24/06/1943
W/Op Sgt G.N. Cox	11/10/1943
Pilot F/Lt R.E. Cox	04/04/1945
F/E Sgt P.J.S. Crawford	24/03/1944
Pilot F/O C.W. Crawford	05/10/1944
B/A Sgt D. Crerar	05/10/1944
Nav Sgt S.B. Cresswell	30/07/1943
B/A Sgt G.N. Cribbin	07/06/1944
B/A Sgt L. Croad	27/07/1943
Nav F/O W.L. Cruse	30/03/1944
Pilot F/Lt R.S. Cumming	14/02/1945
Pilot F/Sgt G.R.L. Cunningham	03/12/1943
W/Op Sgt D. Curnick	28/01/1942
F/E Sgt A. Currie	13/03/1944
F/E Sgt F. Curtis	24/03/1944
W/Op F/O S.A.C. Cutler	22/06/1943
Pilot F/O J.M.J.A. d'Ursel	06/08/1942
W/Op Sgt C.H.G. Daft	25/07/1943
W/Op Sgt T.I.L. Dagg	27/06/1943
B/A F/Lt A. Dalrymple	24/04/1944
B/A Sgt R.W. Dando	27/09/1943
Pilot Sgt G.H. Dane,MiD	13/05/1943
B/A Sgt W.K. Daniel	26/06/1942

A/G Sgt T.W.R. Daniel	11/05/1943
A/G Sgt L. Daniels	24/03/1944
Nav P/O M.J. David	01/03/1941
B/A F/Sgt N.S. Davidson RCAF	24/03/1944
Pilot P/O K.W. Davies	26/08/1941
W/Op Sgt J.I.E. Davies	13/03/1942
A/G Sgt T.P.W. Davies	03/05/1942
B/A P/O F.A. Davies	03/02/1943
W/Op Sgt T.A. Davies	11/05/1943
W/Op P/O M.H. Davies	30/08/1943
W/Op Sgt D.I. Davies RCAF	12/06/1944
A/G Sgt C.C. Davison	03/10/1943
Nav Sgt J. Dear	24/03/1944
Pilot F/Lt B. Denman	19/02/1944
A/G Sgt T.R. Derrington	20/12/1943
A/G Sgt E.E. Deverell RAAF	30/08/1943
A/G Sgt M.F. Dilkes	12/06/1944
W/Op Sgt J. Divens	05/10/1944
B/A P/O H.D. Dixon	10/04/1943
B/A Sgt K.T. Dixon	23/08/1943
A/G Sgt R.W. Dobson	28/01/1942
W/Op F/Sgt F.W. Doonan RAAF	20/12/1943
W/Op Sgt T.A.C. Dorn	27/09/1943
A/G Sgt B. Douglas	24/08/1941
B/A F/Sgt I.R.M. Douglas-Pulleyne	19/02/1944
A/G Sgt L.G. Dowling	26/06/1942
Pilot F/Lt A.P. Dowse DFC	10/04/1943
A/G Sgt D.T.F. Doyle	05/09/1943
F/E Sgt D.W. Drew	03/05/1942
F/E Sgt R.J. Drinkwater	27/09/1943
A/G Sgt H. Dronfield	25/06/1942
F/E Sgt L.J. Dugard	29/07/1943
Nav Sgt R.F. Duggan	01/11/1941
F/E Sgt W. Duncan	12/06/1944
F/E F/O R.H. Duncanson	18/06/1944
F/E Sgt R.O.M. Dunlop	03/04/1943
F/E Sgt C.G. Dyer	11/03/1943
A/G Sgt L.Y. Dyment RCAF	26/04/1944
A/G Sgt J.G. Earley	01/03/1941
Pilot P/O F.C. Ebeling RAAF	05/09/1943
W/Op Sgt W.D. Edge	24/08/1941
W/Op Sgt L.J. Edge	24/03/1944
Pilot Sgt F.J. Edser	05/09/1943

A/G Sgt G.M. Edwards	03/05/1942
A/G Sgt A.W. Edwards	20/12/1942
A/G Sgt W.E. Edwards RCAF	20/12/1943
B/A Sgt J.F. Egan	23/08/1943
2/Plt Sgt P.J. Elson	27/09/1943
W/Op Sgt M. Emmerson	06/09/1943
A/G Sgt P.M.R. Emmett	08/05/1941
A/G Sgt J. Enright	10/04/1943
A/G Sgt H. Entwhistle	23/09/1943
Nav Sgt W.H. Evans	30/08/1943
A/G Sgt E. Evans	03/12/1943
Nav Lt C.O. Evans USAAF	07/06/1944
Nav Sgt C.D. Evans	04/11/1944
Nav Sgt J.M. Farrell RCAF	13/05/1943
F/E Sgt J.C. Fell	26/04/1944
Pilot F/Lt A.E. Ferguson	05/09/1943
Pilot F/Sgt H. Ferme RAAF	27/09/1943
Pilot P/O C.F. Ferris	13/03/1942
A/G F/Sgt J.S. Ferris RCAF	22/10/1943
Nav Sgt E.C. Findon	24/08/1941
Pilot F/Sgt J. Fleetwood-May	11/08/1941
W/Op Sgt A.R. Fleming	05/09/1943
A/G Sgt R.B. Fletcher	23/08/1943
A/G Sgt E.H. Fletcher	02/02/1945
B/A P/O W.C.R. Foale	11/05/1943
Pilot F/Lt G.C. Foers	02/10/1942
W/Op Sgt J.R. Forder	15/02/1944
A/G Sgt W. Forster	08/07/1941
Pilot F/O T.N. Forster	03/04/1943
Nav Sgt G.A. Forsyth	26/02/1941
F/E Sgt P. Fowler	21/01/1944
Nav W/O1 J.B. Fowler RCAF	15/02/1944
Nav P/O A.L. Fox RCAF	20/12/1942
F/E Sgt P.R. Fox	27/09/1943
Pilot F/Sgt P.A. Fraser RAAF	29/07/1943
Nav F/O E. Freeman RCAF	25/08/1944
W/Op Sgt W.H. Freer	14/06/1944
Nav W/O2 T.W. Fry RCAF	08/04/1945
Nav F/O H.A. Fuhr RCAF	22/06/1944
Nav Sgt L.J. Furze	14/09/1940
A/G P/O A.E. Gale	25/07/1943
A/G Sgt H.M. Gall	05/08/1942
Obs Sgt N.T. Gander	13/03/1942

Obs F/Sgt R.J. Garlish	16/05/1941
W/Op Sgt G. Garman RNZAF	06/09/1941
Pilot P/O J.A.T. Garrould	16/05/1941
B/A P/O D.P. Garroway	26/04/1944
Obs P/O D.H. Gates	26/02/1941
Pilot F/Sgt J.M. Gavagan	11/05/1943
A/G Sgt P. Gennon RNZAF	26/08/1941
Nav F/Sgt H.R. George	18/06/1941
A/G Sgt W.V. Gerrard	13/07/1943
W/Op Sgt G.M. Gibb	29/07/1943
A/G P/O E.W.T. Gibbs	08/09/1942
F/E Sgt H. Gibbs	24/03/1944
A/G Sgt J.C. Gibney RAAF	05/09/1943
A/G Sgt J.C. Gibson	30/07/1943
A/G Sgt J.R. Gilbert	05/08/1942
2/Plt F/Sgt R.R. Gilbert	23/08/1943
Pilot P/O J.R. Gillespie	06/10/1944
A/G Sgt T. Gillicker	09/08/1943
B/A F/O G.M. Gillies RCAF	01/10/1942
A/G Sgt T. Gilmartin	12/06/1944
A/G F/O J.A. Glenn RCAF	25/08/1944
F/E Sgt E.H. Glibbery	19/02/1944
Nav F/O L. Gold RCAF	07/06/1944
A/G Sgt J. Goldflust	23/05/1943
W/Op Sgt W.E. Goodacre	29/07/1943
A/G Sgt T.I. Goodwin	30/08/1943
F/E Sgt R.E. Goodyear	23/05/1943
B/A Sgt W.H. Gosnell	11/03/1943
A/G Sgt R. Graham	10/04/1944
A/G Sgt L.J. Grange	22/09/1943
B/A Sgt W.M. Gray	20/12/1943
A/G Sgt R.W. Gray	20/02/1944
Pilot Sgt R.S. Green	29/06/1941
F/E P/O S. Greenlees	22/10/1943
A/G F/Sgt C. Greer	24/03/1944
W/Op Sgt A. Gregory	28/05/1941
Pilot Sgt J.K. Gregory	01/10/1942
Nav F/O W.V. Gregson	27/08/1943
A/G Sgt J.C. Greig	14/09/1940
A/G F/O W.T. Grew	23/09/1944
F/E F/Lt R. Grey	13/05/1943
W/Op Sgt I.B. Griffiths	11/08/1941
F/E Sgt A.N. Griffiths-Buchanan	08/10/1943

W/Op Sgt P. Groom	05/09/1943
W/O Sgt E.A.F. Grunsell, MiD	27/03/1941
Pilot F/O J.J. Gutzewitz RNZAF	02/02/1945
Nav Sgt G.W. Habgood	05/10/1944
Obs Sgt J. Hadfield	24/08/1941
F/E Sgt J.H. Hadwen	23/09/1942
Pilot Sgt D. Hadwin	30/07/1943
F/E Sgt W.R. Hales	20/02/1944
W/Op F/Sgt A.C. Hamilton	19/02/1944
A/G F/Sgt R. Hamilton RCAF	25/08/1944
Pilot Sgt S. Hampson	22/03/1944
W/Op Sgt G. Hampton	20/12/1943
A/G P/O J.W. Hardcastle	22/10/1943
B/A F/O W.T. Harding	18/06/1944
Pilot F/Lt N.M. Harding	15/09/1944
F/E Sgt G.F. Harding	04/11/1944
Obs Sgt G.T. Harper	26/08/1941
W/Op Sgt J.F. Harper	30/07/1943
F/E Sgt L. Harrett	08/10/1943
F/E Sgt W.H. Harries	13/07/1943
W/Op Sgt J.H. Harris	18/06/1941
W/Op Sgt E.H. Harris	25/08/1944
A/G Sgt J.O. Harrison	11/08/1941
A/G Sgt D.F. Hawkes	16/08/1941
Nav F/Sgt V.H. Hawkins	10/04/1944
F/E Sgt A.E. Hayes	11/05/1943
Nav F/O K.C.M. Hayman	12/06/1944
F/E Sgt A.G. Haywood	24/03/1944
B/A F/O B.D. Heading RAAF	20/12/1943
Nav P/O L.G. Heaney	08/10/1943
B/A P/O E.C.L. Hebblethwaite	03/05/1942
Pilot P/O A.W. Hedge RAAF	03/05/1942
Pilot W/O F. Hemmings	11/05/1943
A/G Sgt H. Hemmings	19/02/1944
B/A F/O F. Henderson	26/03/1944
W/Op F/Sgt J. Henderson	24/05/1944
Obs Sgt W.P. Herman	18/06/1941
Nav Sgt W.M.T. Hetherington RCAF	29/07/1943
A/G Sgt R. Heugh	05/10/1944
B/A Sgt J. Hewitson	03/05/1942
Obs Sgt R.M. Heyworth	14/09/1940
F/E P/O G.E. Hickling	27/09/1943
B/A F/Sgt G.H.D. Higgins RAAF	11/08/1941

A/G Sgt W.J. Higgs	03/02/1943
Obs Sgt C.G. Hill	21/06/1940
A/G Sgt F. Hill	27/06/1943
W/Op Sgt R. Hill	27/09/1943
Nav F/O F. Hill	06/10/1944
F/E Sgt H. Hillis	30/03/1944
Pilot F/O H.T. Hills	12/06/1944
W/Op Sgt C.H. Hilton	23/08/1943
W/Op Sgt P. Hinson	05/09/1943
Nav Sgt F.R. Hipwell	03/05/1942
A/G F/Sgt L. Hird	29/06/1941
A/G Sgt W.C.H. Hiscock	10/09/1942
A/G Sgt M.J. Hisley	11/08/1941
Obs Sqdn/Ldr(A) P.J. Hoad RN	27/03/1941
A/G Sgt J.G.A. Hoare	06/08/1942
Nav P/O D.R. Hockaday	13/03/1942
W/Op Sgt W. Hodgson	10/09/1942
Pilot F/Lt W.G. Hoffman RCAF	28/06/1944
Nav F/Sgt R.J. Holland	05/10/1944
W/Op Sgt J.F. Hollingworth	02/07/1941
A/G Sgt P. Hollyer RCAF	11/05/1943
A/G Sgt F.W. Holroyd	07/06/1944
F/E Sgt G.H.C. Horne	11/10/1943
Pilot W/O P. Horrocks	13/07/1943
Nav F/O C.D.A. Hosken RCAF	13/07/1943
Nav Sgt F.E.J. Hothersall RNZAF	20/12/1943
F/E Sgt L. Howarth	27/06/1943
Pilot F/Lt C.M. Howes RCAF	25/08/1944
B/A Sgt F.W. Hucker	27/09/1943
Pilot F/Lt H.M. Hudson RCAF	30/03/1944
A/G Sgt L.E. Hughes	27/09/1943
A/G P/O G.L. Hughes RCAF	08/10/1943
Nav F/O H.L. Humphries RCAF	05/11/1942
Pilot F/Sgt J.A. Hunter RCAF	20/12/1942
Pilot F/Lt R.T. Hunter	05/09/1943
A/G Sgt W.R. Huntley	05/09/1943
Nav P/O D.A. Hyne	20/12/1943
A/G Sgt W. Iddon	15/02/1944
Pilot Sgt W. Illingworth	10/04/1943
W/Op Sgt I. Illingworth	27/08/1943
Nav Sgt E.R. Ingram	29/06/1941
B/A Sgt G.H. Irons	30/07/1943
Pilot F/O D.L. Irwin RCAF	22/06/1944

Nav Sgt H.T. Ivory	16/06/1941
Pilot F/Sgt H. Jackson	24/03/1944
F/E Sgt L. Jakes	13/05/1943
Nav Sgt J.L. Jeal	11/05/1943
B/A Sgt A.S. Jelfs	13/07/1943
Pilot Sgt A. Jepson	02/07/1941
A/G F/Sgt M. Jodrell RCAF	04/11/1944
W/Op Sgt C.P. Johns	22/06/1943
Nav Sgt B.W. Johnson	01/10/1942
W/Op Sgt R.T. Johnson	08/10/1943
F/E Sgt J.S. Johnson	04/04/1945
B/A F/Sgt A.G. Johnstone	06/08/1942
Pilot Sgt A.D. Johnstone	30/08/1943
Obs Sgt K.I. Jones	29/06/1941
A/G Sgt A.W. Jones	23/09/1942
B/A Sgt H.R. Jones	23/08/1943
Obs F/Sgt R. Jopling	16/08/1941
Nav Sgt W.H. Jordan	12/05/1943
Nav F/O H.J. Kadwill	24/04/1944
B/A Sgt S.F.H. Kelley RCAF	07/06/1944
W/Op Sgt J. Kelly	14/09/1940
Nav Sgt L. Kelly	11/08/1941
A/G Sgt R.A. Kelly	23/09/1942
Pilot 1Lt L.M. Kelly USAAF	20/12/1943
B/A F/O R.S. Kelly RAAF	24/03/1944
A/G F/Sgt H.F. Kelter RCAF	19/02/1944
F/E Sgt G.E. Kemp	05/10/1944
Nav P/O G.M. Kennedy	02/07/1941
W/Op P/O J.R. Kennedy RCAF	03/05/1942
Nav Sgt P.A. Kennedy	24/06/1943
F/E Sgt S.W. Kent	23/08/1943
B/A Sgt R.J. Kernick	03/04/1943
A/G Sgt A.A. Kew	13/05/1943
Nav Sgt R.S.L. Keymer	16/05/1941
Pilot P/O C.J. Kierle	23/08/1943
A/G Sgt J.H.B. Killingbach	14/06/1944
Nav F/O F. King	25/07/1943
A/G F/Sgt J.L.R. Kingsley RCAF	20/12/1942
Pilot F/O D.A. Kingston	11/08/1941
B/A F/O P. Kinsella	20/02/1944
F/E Sgt B. Kirkham	29/09/1943
Pilot F/Lt L. Knight	22/06/1943
F/E Sgt E.P. Knight	06/10/1944

Pilot P/O D.S.W. Lake	16/06/1941
A/G Sgt T. Lanaghan	30/03/1944
B/A F/O G.J. Lancaster RCAF	12/06/1944
A/G Sgt N.L. Lane	26/02/1941
A/G Sgt C.R. Langley	29/07/1943
Pilot P/O J.S. Lawson,MiD RCAF	01/06/1942
A/G Sgt J.T.L. Leblanc RCAF	24/05/1944
W/Op Sgt E. Lee	23/08/1943
Nav F/O A. Lees	24/03/1944
F/E F/Sgt B. Legg	04/05/1943
F/E Sgt N. Legg	20/01/1944
Pilot Sgt A.C. Leppard	04/05/1943
F/E Sgt A.E. Lester	23/08/1943
Obs Sgt P.J. Lewis	08/05/1941
Nav F/Lt A.J. Lewsley	04/04/1945
A/G Sgt T.A. Liddy	22/03/1944
A/G Sgt C.W. Lillico	07/06/1944
A/G Sgt J.A. Lincoln	24/03/1944
A/G Sgt A. Line	24/03/1944
F/E Sgt L.D. Lingwood	22/06/1943
F/E Sgt W.A. Littlewood	30/03/1944
W/Op Sgt J.A. Lloyd	03/05/1942
A/G Sgt H. Lockett	05/10/1944
Obs Sgt D.V. Logan RAAF	06/09/1941
Pilot F/Sgt F. Lovatt	26/03/1944
Pilot F/O E.A. Love RCAF	04/11/1944
2/Plt F/Sgt G.T.A. Lovell	24/03/1944
Pilot W/O J.H. Lowery	23/08/1943
A/G Sgt C. Lowis	04/05/1943
F/E F/Sgt W.E.S. Luck	06/08/1942
Pilot W/O2 W.E. Lunan RCAF	11/08/1941
Nav W/O A.R. Lutes RCAF	13/07/1943
F/E Sgt J.E.R. Lyons	01/06/1942
Nav P/O G.W. Macallister	11/08/1941
Nav F/O W.R. Macgregor RCAF	20/01/1944
B/A P/O S. Macmanus RCAF	08/10/1943
B/A Sgt I. Macrae	24/06/1943
Nav Sgt F. Madden	08/10/1943
B/A F/O M.M. Maguire	15/09/1944
Pilot Sgt L.E. Maidment	27/07/1943
Pilot Sgt J.H. Malet-Warden	16/08/1941
A/G Sgt L.A. Mallory RCAF	23/08/1943
W/Op WO2 E.C. Malone RCAF	20/12/1942

Pilot Sgt F.A. Marean RCAF	11/03/1943
Pilot F/Sgt V.H. Marks	18/06/1941
Pilot F/Lt G.A. Marrows	07/06/1944
Pilot W/O O.P. Marshall	15/07/1943
Nav Sgt A.H. Marshall	30/07/1943
B/A F/O N.A. Marston,DFC	24/05/1944
Nav Sgt Mack Martin RCAF	08/07/1941
W/Op Sgt D.P. Martin	23/08/1943
W/Op Sgt H. Mason	30/04/1943
W/Op Sgt R.D. Matches	13/05/1943
Nav Sgt C.V. Matheson	06/09/1941
Obs Sgt G.E. Matson	01/10/1940
F/E F/Sgt E.F.C. Matthews	23/08/1943
A/G W/O2 E.F. McAneeley RCAF	19/02/1944
F/E Sgt P. McCann	11/08/1941
F/E F/O J. McCardle	25/08/1944
Nav Sgt I. McCarthy	29/09/1941
Pilot F/O J. McCartney	24/03/1944
B/A P/O C. McCartney RCAF	25/08/1944
Pilot Sgt O.W. McClean RAAF	08/07/1941
Pilot F/Sgt M. McClear RCAF	07/06/1944
W/Op Sgt W.J. McClelland	11/03/1943
A/G Sgt A. McCleod	13/03/1942
Pilot Sgt H.D. McColl	13/03/1942
Nav P/O G.M. McCombe	07/11/1941
A/G Sgt J. McCormick	03/04/1943
W/Op Sgt L. McCrurie	21/06/1940
F/E Sgt J.H. McDonald	29/03/1942
A/G Sgt A.F. McDonald RCAF	03/02/1943
F/E W/O J.S. McDonald	23/09/1943
A/G P/O J. McGannon	21/11/1944
A/G Sgt H. McGill	27/08/1943
F/E Sgt R. McGlen	01/06/1942
2/Plt F/O D. McGregor RCAF	05/10/1944
F/E Sgt A. McIlroy	14/06/1944
B/A Sgt J.A. McKillop	05/10/1944
Nav F/Sgt H.W. McLaughlan RCAF	03/02/1943
W/Op P/O B.M.E. McLeod RAAF	04/04/1945
A/G Sgt D.W. McMillan DFM	13/03/1944
A/G Sgt R.W. McNeil RCAF	24/03/1944
Pilot Sgt W.M. McQuitty RAAF	08/07/1941
Pilot F/Sgt J.C. McTait	26/03/1943
B/A P/O K.W. McTernaghan	27/08/1943

W/Op Sgt F.G. McVey	08/10/1943
A/G Sgt L.E. Mears	19/02/1944
A/G Sgt J.G. Mein	05/09/1943
W/Op Sgt P.E. Mellish	04/05/1943
F/E Sgt D. Menzies	05/10/1944
Pilot Sqdn/Ldr J. Mercer	01/11/1941
F/E Sgt A.E. Messer	23/10/1942
W/Op P/O R.G. Messer	19/02/1944
F/E Sgt A.D. Meynell	20/12/1943
F/E Sgt C. Milburn	03/02/1943
F/E Sgt R.E. Miles	12/06/1944
Obs Sgt A.J.R. Millard-Tucker	16/08/1941
F/E Sgt L. Millband	02/10/1942
W/Op Sgt C. Miller	06/10/1944
Nav Sgt H.W. Milligan	05/09/1943
Nav Sgt A.K. Mills	27/03/1941
Nav Sgt F.R. Mills	03/05/1942
Nav F/Sgt S.G. Mills	29/09/1943
B/A Sgt S.P. Mirams	20/12/1943
A/G Sgt J. Mitchell	27/03/1941
A/G Sgt J.A. Mitchell RCAF	11/08/1941
Pilot F/O C. Mitchener	26/06/1942
Pilot F/Sgt F.R. Moffat RCAF	20/01/1944
Pilot F/Sgt A. Molloy RAAF	20/12/1943
Pilot Sgt V.C. Monkhouse	21/06/1940
W/Op Sgt H. Monks	30/03/1944
A/G Sgt D. Montgomery	11/05/1943
Nav Sgt V.C.G. Moody	04/05/1943
A/G Sgt F. Moore	04/05/1943
F/E Sgt C.W. Moore	23/08/1943
Nav Sgt J.S. Moore	23/08/1943
A/G Sgt A.N. Moore RAAF	05/09/1943
W/Op F/O M.P. Moreton	18/06/1944
Nav P/O H.W. Morgan	01/10/1940
W/Op Sgt D. Morgan	26/06/1942
B/A Sgt C.A. Morris	27/06/1943
A/G Sgt T. Morris	25/07/1943
A/G Sgt J.W. Morris	30/03/1944
Pilot F/Sgt K.F. Morrison RNZAF	24/06/1943
Pilot F/Lt E.G. Mortenson	10/04/1943
W/Op Sgt A. Moss	05/10/1944
Obs P/O H.H. Mountain	08/07/1941
W/Op Sgt E. Moxen	21/01/1944

F/E Sgt J. Muir	11/05/1943
A/G Sgt M.G. Mulligan RCAF	21/01/1944
Pilot F/Lt W.J. Murray	14/06/1944
F/E Sgt V.G. Musselwhite	05/06/1942
W/Op P/O J.F. Myrick RCAF	11/08/1941
Nav Sgt T.J. Naish	29/03/1942
F/E Sgt H.J. Neal	24/03/1944
A/G Sgt G.A. Nelson	22/10/1943
A/G Sgt H.R. Nelson	24/03/1944
A/G F/Lt J.D. Nesbit	13/07/1943
Nav F/O K.J. Nethercott	15/09/1944
W/Op Sgt C.A. Newman	23/09/1942
A/G Sgt T. Newman	07/06/1944
F/E Sgt J.R. Nicholls	29/07/1943
W/Op Sgt F.R. Nicholls	24/03/1944
A/G Sgt L.W. Nichols	29/09/1943
A/G Sgt E.G. Nickels	29/07/1943
W/Op Sgt K. Noddle	08/07/1941
W/Op Sgt J. Norman	27/09/1943
Pilot P/O S. Norris	27/08/1943
A/G Sgt E.C. Nott	20/02/1944
F/E Sgt A. Nutbrown	23/09/1944
A/G Sgt F. O'Dwyer RAAF	05/09/1943
A/G Sgt R.G. O'Neill RAAF	19/02/1944
Nav Sgt J. O'Rourke	05/06/1942
W/Op Sgt E. Oakes	16/05/1941
F/E Sgt F. Oakley	13/07/1943
Pilot F/O M.H. Oddie	25/06/1943
A/G Sgt W. Oldroyd	30/04/1943
Nav Sgt D.C. Oliver	23/05/1943
Nav Sgt G.L. Olsen RCAF	16/08/1941
F/E Sgt W.G. Onion	30/08/1943
B/A F/O A.B. Orme	23/05/1943
Pilot F/O R.H. Orr RCAF	27/08/1943
A/G Sgt T.R. Owen	22/06/1944
F/E Sgt A.M. Parker	03/04/1943
A/G P/O V.H. Parry	02/10/1942
Nav Sgt H.E. Parsons	03/10/1943
W/Op Sgt H.D. Patchett	24/03/1944
Pilot F/Sgt C. Pattison	23/09/1942
A/G F/O M.H. Pattison	04/04/1945
A/G Sgt S.W. Patton	10/04/1943
Nav F/Lt G.G. Paul	27/09/1943

W/Op Sgt C.W. Payne	12/05/1943
A/G Sgt T.S. Payne	24/06/1943
A/G Sgt R.S. Payne	27/08/1943
B/A Sgt A.H. Peadon	30/08/1943
A/G Sgt J. Peart	11/08/1941
W/Op Sgt K. Perkins	20/12/1943
F/E Sgt G. Pesticcio	15/09/1944
Nav F/O S.C. Peterson RCAF	24/05/1944
Nav F/Sgt L.W.A. Pierce	14/06/1944
B/A Sgt R.J. Pike	30/04/1943
A/G Sgt D.A. Pitman	10/04/1943
Nav P/O E. Platt	23/08/1943
Nav P/O D.J. Polman	29/09/1943
B/A Sgt D.B. Polson	03/10/1943
Pilot W/O F.M. Poole RNZAF	23/09/1943
A/G Sgt H. Porter	06/10/1944
B/A F/Sgt J.M. Pougnet RCAF	08/04/1945
A/G Sgt H.J. Pratt	05/09/1943
2/Plt Sgt E. Pritchard	13/05/1943
F/E Sgt D.J. Purcell	27/08/1943
Nav F/Sgt B.L. Purvis	20/12/1943
W/Op Sgt C.S. Quelch	15/09/1944
Pilot Sgt J.W. Quincey	01/03/1941
F/E Sgt W. Quinn	08/10/1943
W/Op N.R. Jones RAAF	01/10/1942
A/G F/O W.K. Raby RCAF	26/04/1944
W/Op Sgt A.B. Radcliffe	30/07/1943
Obs Sgt R.C. Rae	16/06/1941
Pilot F/Sgt S.A. Rae RNZAF	12/06/1944
B/A Sgt T. Ratcliffe	24/03/1944
A/G Sgt W.S. Rausch RCAF	23/10/1942
A/G Sgt J.V. Reddington	21/11/1944
A/G Sgt J. Redman	23/05/1943
Pilot F/Sgt D.R.H. Rees	21/01/1944
Nav Sgt F.G. Rees	22/03/1944
W/Op Sgt A.E. Reeve	20/02/1944
F/E Sgt A.A. Reeves	30/08/1943
A/G Sgt P.J. Regan	03/12/1943
B/A F/O N.S.M. Reid	15/07/1943
F/E Sgt A. Reilly	05/10/1944
Pilot Sgt P.W.J. Rendle RAAF	27/06/1943
B/A Sgt R.A. Renwick	22/03/1944
W/Op Sgt G.F. Reynolds	19/02/1944

Pilot F/Lt H. Rhoden,DFC	23/10/1942
Pilot P/O G. Riach	03/04/1943
B/A P/O D.A. Riach RCAF	19/02/1944
W/Op F/O J.H. Rice	21/11/1944
F/E P/O J.S. Rice	14/02/1945
Pilot P/O T.C. Richards	18/06/1941
Pilot F/Lt T.H.O. Richardson	03/04/1943
W/O Sgt P.H. Richmond	01/10/1940
Nav F/O J.S. Ritchie RCAF	12/06/1944
A/G F/Sgt A. Roach RCAF	04/11/1944
Pilot Sgt W.G. Roberts	24/08/1941
A/G Sgt F. Roberts	23/08/1943
W/Op Sgt E.W. Roberts	26/03/1944
F/E Sgt W.J.R. Roberts	26/03/1944
W/Op Sgt C.W. Robertson	27/07/1943
Nav F/Lt W.J. Robertson RCAF	21/11/1944
A/G Sgt W. Robinson	13/07/1943
W/Op F/Sgt F.V. Robinson	02/02/1945
Pilot F/O C.S. Robson	14/09/1940
Nav F/Lt D.R. Rogers	22/10/1943
A/G Sgt A. Roscoe	01/10/1940
A/G F/Sgt G.A. Rourke RAAF	30/07/1943
A/G Sgt R.W. Rouse	13/07/1943
Nav Sgt S.E. Rowed RCAF	26/08/1941
F/E Sgt R.J. Roy	10/09/1942
A/G F/Sgt R.R. Rudd RAAF	10/04/1944
Pilot F/Sgt J.C. RuddDFM RAAF	30/04/1943
A/G Sgt H.W. Rudelhoff	20/01/1944
Nav F/O H. Sager RCAF	12/06/1944
W/Op F/Sgt F.R. Sampson RAAF	26/04/1944
Nav Sgt G.J. Samuel	27/06/1943
A/G P/O F.R. Sanderson	27/08/1943
Pilot Sgt E.J. Sargent	07/11/1941
A/G P/O G.A. Scarcliff	06/09/1943
A/G F/Sgt L. Schioler RCAF	24/03/1944
A/G Sgt G. Schofield	26/03/1944
Pilot Sgt G.E. Schubert	23/05/1943
A/G P/O M. Schwartz RCAF	14/02/1945
F/E Sgt E.B.F. Scorey	23/08/1943
Nav Sgt F.A. Scotland	11/08/1941
Nav P/O E.A. Scott	08/07/1941
W/Op Sgt W. Scott	06/08/1942
Pilot Sgt W.H. Scott	08/10/1943

B/A F/Sgt R. Scott	07/06/1944
Pilot P/O K.F. Seager	27/03/1941
Pilot Sqdn/Ldr G.A. Sells DFC	22/10/1943
B/A F/O R.G. Selman RCAF	20/01/1944
W/Op F/O L.R.C. Shadwell	03/04/1943
Pilot F/Lt R.N. Shard DFC,DFM	15/02/1944
B/A Sgt T.H. Sharpe	29/09/1943
A/G Sgt G. Sharrocks	06/10/1944
Pilot F/O R.M. Shattock	29/03/1942
W/Op Sgt A. Shaw	11/05/1943
A/G Sgt J.H. Sheehan	07/06/1944
F/E Sgt W. Sheffield	05/09/1943
Pilot Sgt R. Shelton	30/07/1943
W/Op F/O B. Shepstone	22/06/1944
Pilot Sgt T.A. Sherman RCAF	16/08/1941
Nav F/Sgt W.H. Shields	24/03/1944
Pilot F/Lt A.R. Short	30/08/1943
Pilot Sgt D.R. Simm	07/06/1941
W/Op P/O G. Simpson	22/10/1943
A/G Sgt G.A.M. Simpson	15/09/1944
Nav Sgt D.A. Sinclair RCAF	24/08/1941
A/G Sgt B.M. Singleton	11/03/1943
A/G F/Sgt C.W. Sisley RAAF	25/02/1944
A/G Sgt J. Skeat	24/03/1944
Pilot F/Sgt C.R. Skerrett RAAF	27/09/1943
W/Op Sgt A. Slack	13/07/1943
A/G F/Sgt A.P. Smith	16/05/1941
Nav Sgt W.B. Smith RCAF	28/05/1941
F/E Sgt E.C. Smith	03/05/1942
W/Op Sgt K.W. Smith	30/08/1943
Pilot F/Lt W.B. Smith RNZAF	27/09/1943
A/G Sgt R.A. Smith	27/09/1943
A/G Sgt S. Smith DFM	08/10/1943
A/G Sgt K.W. Smith MiD	20/12/1943
Pilot Sgt J. Smith	19/02/1944
Pilot P/O T.H. Smith	19/02/1944
Pilot Sgt B.T. Smith	24/03/1944
B/A Sgt J. Smith	24/03/1944
F/E Sgt W.N. Smith	10/04/1944
Pilot Sgt P.F. Snape	29/07/1943
Obs P/O A.V. Snelling	07/06/1941
Pilot Sqdn/Ldr A.J.D. Snow	03/05/1942
Pilot F/O T. Speller	24/04/1944

W/Op F/Sgt V.W. Spencer	24/03/1944
A/G Sgt W.R. Spiers	22/09/1943
A/G Sgt F.E. Spinks	12/06/1944
A/G Sgt S.K. Springham	29/03/1942
A/G Sgt H.E. St.H.Goom	29/09/1943
Pilot F/O R.L. Stanley	05/10/1944
Pilot P/O M.L. Stedman	13/12/1940
W/Op Sgt M.H. Steele	08/04/1945
A/G Sgt C.C. Stenning	31/08/1943
B/A F/Sgt T.A. Stephenson RCAF	02/10/1942
W/O Sgt J.B. Stevens	07/06/1941
Pilot P/O C.J. Stevenson	10/09/1942
A/G Sgt J.A. Stewart	20/01/1944
Nav Sgt J. Stone	11/05/1943
A/G Sgt C.J. Storer	06/09/1941
Pilot F/Sgt G.M. Storey	20/02/1944
Nav Sgt J.P. Strachan	27/09/1943
A/G Sgt J. Strang	01/06/1942
Pilot W/O G.H. Stratford	18/06/1944
Nav P/O F. Street	30/08/1943
A/G Sgt D.R. Strickland	28/05/1941
B/A Sgt G.H. Styler	08/10/1943
A/G Sgt J.A. Suffield	30/07/1943
A/G Sgt J. Sulter	21/06/1940
A/G Sgt E.C. Summerfield	29/06/1942
Nav F/Sgt J.S. Sutherland	20/02/1944
Pilot F/O J.S.R. Swanson	23/09/1944
Nav P/O T.H. Tabberer	27/08/1943
Pilot F/Sgt L. Tait	10/04/1944
F/E Sgt S.T. Tanser	07/06/1944
A/G Sgt H. Tattler	07/06/1944
Nav Sgt W.J. Taylor	26/06/1942
B/A Sgt A. Taylor	23/09/1942
A/G Sgt J.E. Taylor	11/10/1943
Nav F/O A.G. Taylor DFC	30/03/1944
B/A P/O A.K. Taylor	04/04/1945
2/Plt F/O D.F. Teague RCAF	23/10/1942
A/G Sgt R.M. Telfer	27/09/1943
W/Op Sgt A.C. Thewlis	23/08/1943
W/Op Sgt E.G. Thomas	10/04/1943
F/E F/Sgt F.N. Thomasson	11/08/1941
W/O Sgt W. Thompson	01/06/1942
Pilot P/O J.R. Thompson	05/03/1943

Pilot F/O P. Thompson	22/09/1943	
Nav P/O J.S. Thompson	14/02/1945	
A/G P/O A.G. Thorne	20/12/1943	
Pilot Sgt L. Thorpe	08/05/1941	
Pilot P/O F.B. Thorpe	06/09/1941	
A/G Sgt G.H. Tilburn	05/10/1944	
Pilot F/Sgt E.A. Tipler	22/06/1943	
Pilot F/Lt P.H. Tippets-Aylmer,DFC	08/09/1942	
W/Op Sgt J.P. Todd	08/10/1943	
A/G P/O A.C.L. Todd	05/10/1944	
Pilot Wg/Comm G.T. Toland	26/02/1941	
Nav Sgt J.S. Tomkinson	07/06/1941	
B/A Sgt F.G. Tomlinson	12/06/1944	
Pilot W/O K.A. Toon RNZAF	13/07/1943	
F/E Sgt S.L. Toon	22/03/1944	
Pilot W/O2 F.W. Topping RCAF	30/03/1944	
B/A F/Sgt G.D. Torbet RCAF	30/03/1944	
A/G F/Sgt W.R. Townsend RCAF	27/06/1943	
A/G Sgt J.R. Trace RCAF	05/09/1943	
B/A P/O S.A.W. Tressider	14/02/1945	
A/G Sgt D.E. Tuddenham	22/06/1943	
B/A F/O B.E. Turnbull	06/10/1944	
A/G F/Lt G.T. Turner	05/11/1942	
W/Op F/Sgt T.E. Turpin RCAF	01/10/1942	
F/E Sgt E.A. Tweedale	26/06/1942	
F/E Sgt E.H. Tytherleigh	01/10/1942	
B/A P/O W. Uyen RCAF	30/03/1944	
Nav Sgt W.A. Valley RCAF	19/10/1943	
A/G Sgt J.G. Vaughan RCAF	30/03/1944	
F/E Sgt W.H. Veale	20/12/1943	
A/G Sgt R.R. Vosper	29/09/1941	
A/G Sgt W. Voss	08/10/1943	
W/Op Sgt E.C. Wadsworth	03/10/1943	
B/A Sgt S.S. Waldman	01/10/1942	
Pilot W/O P.R. Waller	20/12/1943	
Nav P/O R.W. Wallis-Stokes	08/05/1941	
Nav P/O M.W.B. Walsh	05/09/1943	
W/Op Sgt J.E. Waltham	24/03/1944	
A/G Sgt E. Walton	23/10/1942	
A/G Sgt D.C.M. Walton RAAF	23/08/1943	
A/G Sgt N. Walton	15/02/1944	
W/Op Sgt B. Ward	29/09/1941	
W/Op P/O S.T. Wariner	29/09/1943	

Nav Sgt B.B. Warren	10/09/1942
A/G Sgt D.A. Watkins	10/04/1943
W/Op Sgt R.W. Watson	29/03/1942
Nav F/O C.B. Watt	21/01/1944
Obs Sgt G.T. Webb	07/11/1941
A/G Sgt E.T. Webb	03/05/1942
A/G Sgt T.H. Webb	03/04/1943
F/E F/Sgt W.J. Webb	19/02/1944
Nav P/O C.A. Weeks	26/03/1944
A/G Sgt N.E. Weighell	27/09/1943
B/A F/O L.A. Welsh RCAF	21/11/1944
B/A Sgt P.J. Wenmoth	27/08/1943
B/A Sgt D.E. West	01/06/1942
Nav Sgt R. West	10/04/1943
F/E Sgt B. West	22/09/1943
W/Op Sgt R. West	05/10/1944
A/G Sgt E.G. Westall	12/05/1943
B/A W/O2 C.L. Wetherby RCAF	10/04/1944
W/Op W/O J.P. Whelan RAAF	07/06/1944
Nav Sgt R.E.J. White	02/03/1943
A/G Sgt E.A. White	30/08/1943
F/E Sgt W.J. White	24/05/1944
Pilot F/O J.A. Whittingham	25/06/1942
A/G F/Sgt J.S. Wilkins RAAF	27/09/1943
Pilot F/Sgt J.H. Wilkinson	26/04/1944
Pilot Sgt A.N. Williams RAAF	28/01/1942
Nav P/O D.L. Williams	28/01/1942
A/G Sgt E.C.B. Williams	05/03/1943
F/E Sgt D. Williams	30/07/1943
A/G Sgt T.A.T. Williams RCAF	23/08/1943
F/E Sgt E.J. Williams	27/08/1943
Nav Sgt W.P. Williams	30/08/1943
Pilot F/Lt R.F. Williams	08/10/1943
A/G F/Sgt I. Williams	14/02/1945
W/Op Sgt A.D. Willis	16/08/1941
W/Op Sgt D.A. Wilson	16/08/1941
2/Plt Sgt J.A. Wilson RNZAF	26/03/1943
A/G Sgt A. Wilson	26/03/1943
Nav Sgt E.J. Wilson	30/04/1943
Nav P/O K. Wilson	29/07/1943
Pilot P/O G.W. Wilson	29/09/1943
B/A F/O G.S. Wilson	19/02/1944
Pilot P/O E.B. Wilson	24/05/1944

A/G Sgt C.G. Wilson	14/06/1944
Pilot F/O M.A. Wimberley	24/03/1944
B/A Sgt R.A. Winn	23/08/1943
W/Op P/O R.H. Winter	28/06/1944
Pilot W/O K.F. Withers RAAF	13/03/1944
W/Op F/Sgt V.R. Wood	03/02/1943
W/Op Sgt P.J. Wood	23/05/1943
A/G Sgt G.H. Woodcock RCAF	29/07/1943
F/E Sgt R. Woodhall	10/04/1943
W/Op Sgt T.P. Woodhouse	01/11/1941
A/G W/O2 E.D. Woods RCAF	07/06/1944
A/G F/Sgt J.H. Woodward RAAF	10/09/1942
Nav Sgt J.E. Woodward	22/06/1943
Nav Sgt J.G. Woolley	18/06/1941
A/G F/Sgt V.G. Wright	01/11/1941
A/G Sgt E. Wright	12/05/1943
B/A Sgt H.R. Wright RCAF	03/12/1943
Pilot F/O J.F. Wyllie RCAF	12/06/1944
W/Op F/Sgt E.P. Yates	14/02/1945
A/G F/Sgt G.R. Yeates	08/09/1942
F/E Sgt A.M. Young	12/05/1943
B/A W/O Z. Zonker RCAF	13/07/1943

To the fallen airmen of 78 Squadron RAF

We thank you all for your sacrifice

May your names never be forgotten.

SQUADRON MEMORIAL

ON SUNDAY 7TH SEPTEMBER 1986 a memorial to 78 Squadron was unveiled by Sir Guy Lawrence DSO, OBE, DFC in the Churchyard of All Saints Church, Bubwith. The metal plaque attached bears the inscription:

No.78 Squadron
4 Group Bomber Command
Yorkshire
To All Who Served

Beneath the inscription the outline of a Halifax bomber can be seen. It brings back poignant memories of all the men and women who served at nearby RAF Breighton.